M000084721

Reference Guide to
Anti-Money Laundering and
Combating the Financing of Terrorism

Second Edition
and Supplement on
Special Recommendation IX

Reference Guide to Anti-Money Laundering and Combating the Financing of Terrorism

*Second Edition
and Supplement on
Special Recommendation IX*

www.amlcft.org

Contents

Part B: The Elements of an Effective AML/CFT Framework

Part C: The Role of the World Bank and International Monetary Fund

Reference Guide to Anti-Money Laundering and Combating the Financing of Terrorism

Annexes

Diagrams

Foreword

Efforts to launder money and finance terrorism have been evolving rapidly in recent years in response to heightened countermeasures. The international community has witnessed the use of increasingly sophisticated methods to move illicit funds through financial systems across the globe and has acknowledged the need for improved multilateral cooperation to fight these criminal activities.

The World Bank and International Monetary Fund developed this second edition of the *Reference Guide to Anti-Money Laundering and Combating the Financing of Terrorism* to help countries understand the new international standards. The Reference Guide will hopefully serve as a single, comprehensive source of practical information for countries to fight money laundering and terrorist financing. It discusses the problems caused by these crimes, the specific actions countries need to take to address them and the role international organizations, such as the Bank and the Fund, play in the process.

We offer this new version as a tool for countries to establish and improve their legal and institutional frameworks and their preventive measures according to the new international standards and best practices. This Second Edition of the Reference Guide and Supplement on Special Recommendation IX will also be translated into Arabic, Chinese, French, Portuguese, Russian, and Spanish in order to better serve a broader audience.

We intend to keep the Reference Guide under review as money laundering and terrorist financing trends and techniques, as well as the international response, evolve and to update it as necessary. We welcome your feedback and recommendations on how this resource can be more useful.

Margery Waxman	**R. Barry Johnston**	**Jean-François Thony**
Program Director and	Assistant Director	Assistant General Counsel
Senior Adviser	Monetary and Financial	Legal Department
Financial Market Integrity	Systems Department	International Monetary Fund
World Bank	International Monetary Fund	

Acknowledgments

This publication was written by Paul Allan Schott, consultant with the Financial Market Integrity Unit of the Financial Sector of The World Bank. The author is especially grateful to Margery Waxman, Director, Financial Market Integrity, World Bank, for her support, encouragement and patience in producing the first and second edition of this Reference Guide.

The author is grateful to his Bank and Fund colleagues for their willingness to read multiple drafts of the first edition and provide advice and insights based on their work in the development and implementation of the joint Bank/Fund program to combat money laundering and terrorist financing: John Abbott, Maud Julie Bokkerink, Pierre-Laurent Chatain, Alain Damais, Ross Delston, Gabriella Ferencz, Ted Greenberg, Raul Hernandez Coss, Barry Johnston, Nadim Kyriakos-Saad, Samuel Maimbo, John McDowell, Bess Michael, Michael Moore, Pramita Moni Sengupta, Takashi Miyahara, Thomas Rose, Heba Shams, Jean-François Thony, and Cari Votava.

Most importantly, the author wishes to thank Joseph Halligan for his work in updating the Reference Guide to reflect the revision of the FATF 40 Recommendations and the methodology. Finally, the author could not have produced this comprehensive second edition without the work of Bank staff members who helped organize the material carefully, checked all references and made this publication a reality: Oriana Bolvaran, Nicolas de la Riva, Martín Joseffson, Amanda Larson, Annika Lindgren, Maria Orellano, James Quigley, Dafna Tapiero, Emiko Todoroki, and Tracy Tucker.

Abbreviations and Acronyms

AML	anti-money laundering
APG	Asia/Pacific Group on Money Laundering
Bank	World Bank Group
Basel Committee	Basel Committee on Bank Supervision
BCCI	Bank of Credit and Commerce International
CAS	Country Assistance Strategy
CFATF	Caribbean Financial Action Task Force
CFT	combating the financing of terrorism
CTC	United Nations Security Council Counter Terrorism Committee
Egmont Group	The Egmont Group of Financial Intelligence Units
ESAAMLG	Eastern and Southern Africa Anti-Money Laundering Group
FATF	Financial Action Task Force on Money Laundering, Group d'action Financière sur le blanchiment de capital (GAFI)
FSRB	FATF Style Regional Bodies
FIU	Financial Intelligence Unit
The Forty Recommendations	The Forty Recommendations on Money Laundering issued by FATF
Fund	International Monetary Fund
GAFI	Group d'action Financière sue le blanchiment de capital (FATF)
GAFISUD	Financial Action Task Force on Money Laundering in South America

IAIS	International Association of Insurance Supervisors
IFTs	informal funds transfer systems
IMF	International Monetary Fund
IOSCO	International Organization of Securities Commissions
KYC	"know-your-customer"
MONEYVAL	Council of Europe the Select Committee of Experts on the Evaluation of Anti-Money Laundering Measures
MOU	memorandum of understanding
NCCT	Non-Cooperative Countries and Territories
OAS	Organization of American States
OFC	Offshore Financial Center
Palermo Convention	United Nations Convention Against Transnational Organized Crime (2000)
PC-R-EV	Now known as MONEYVAL
ROSC	Report on Observance of Standards and Codes
Special Recommendations	Nine Special Recommendations on Terrorist Financing issued by FATF
Strasbourg Convention	Convention on Laundering, Search, Seizure and Confiscation of the Proceeds of Crime (1990)
STR	suspicious transaction reports
TA	Technical Assistance
UN	United Nations
UNSCCTC	United Nations Security Council Counter Terrorism Committee
Vienna Convention	United Nations Convention Against Illicit Traffic in Narcotic Drugs and Psychotropic Substances (1988)
Wolfsberg Group	Wolfsberg Group of Banks

Introduction:
How to Use this Reference Guide

This Second Edition of the Reference Guide is intended to serve as a single, comprehensive source of information for countries that wish to establish or improve their legal and institutional frameworks for anti-money laundering (AML) and combating the financing of terrorism (CFT). These issues have become increasingly important in a global economy where funds can be easily and immediately transferred from one financial institution to another, including transfers to institutions in different countries. The international community is relying upon all countries to establish effective AML/CFT regimes that are capable of successfully preventing, detecting and prosecuting money laundering and terrorist financing in order to fight the devastating economic and social consequences of these criminal activities.

Part A of this Reference Guide describes the problem of money laundering and terrorist financing, their adverse consequences, and the benefits of an effective regime. It also identifies the relevant international standard-setting organizations and discusses their specific efforts and instruments that fight these activities.

Part B describes the various elements that are part of a comprehensive legal and institutional AML and CFT framework for any country. Each of these components has been established by the Financial Action Task on Money Laundering (FATF) and the other international standard setters and each element is essential to a comprehensive and effective regime. This part of the Reference Guide is a step-by-step approach to achieve compliance with international standards, although it does not dictate the specific methods or actions to be adopted. Rather, it raises the issues that must be addressed and discusses the options that a country has to resolve these issues.

Part C describes the role of the World Bank and International Monetary Fund (IMF) in the global effort and the coordination of technical assistance available to countries in order to help them achieve compliance with international standards.

Each chapter is a self-contained discussion of the topics covered in that chapter (although references are made to related discussions in other chapters) with detailed references to background and original source materials. Annexes I, II and III provide complete citations to reference materials that are used in the Reference Guide or that are otherwise useful to a country in dealing with the many difficult issues associated with AML and CFT. For convenience, Annexes IV and V restate the international standards set by FATF, The Forty Recommendations on Money Laundering (revised in 2003), Glossary and Interpretative Notes and the nine Special Recommendations on Terrorist Financing, respectively. Annex VI is FATF's Interpretative Notes and Guidance Notes for the Special Recommendations on Terrorist Financing and Self-Assessment Questionnaire for countries on terrorist financing. Finally, Annexes VII and VIII are cross references for the FATF recommendations to discussions in the Reference Guide.

As a country reviews its AML and CFT legal and institutional frameworks, it may wish to use the Comprehensive Methodology on AML/CFT referred to in Chapter X as its own checklist and self-assessment mechanism. This is the same Methodology used by FATF, the FATF-style regional bodies, the Bank and IMF in making assessments of either their own members or of other countries.

Chapter I

Money Laundering and Terrorist Financing: Definitions and Explanations

A. What Is Money Laundering?

B. What is Terrorist Financing?

C. The Link Between Money Laundering and Terrorist Financing

D. The Magnitude of the Problem

E. The Processes
1. Placements
2. Layering
3. Integration

F. Where Do Money Laundering and Terrorist Financing Occur?

G. Methods and Typologies

For most countries, money laundering and terrorist financing raise significant issues with regard to prevention, detection and prosecution. Sophisticated techniques used to launder money and finance terrorism add to the complexity of these issues. Such sophisticated techniques may involve different types of financial institutions; multiple financial transactions; the use of intermediaries, such as financial advisers, accountants, shell corporations and other service providers; transfers to, through, and from different countries; and the use of different financial instruments and other kinds of value-storing assets. Money laundering is, however, a fundamentally simple concept. It is the process by which *proceeds* from a criminal activity are disguised to conceal their illicit origins. Basically, money laundering involves the proceeds of criminally derived property rather than the property itself.

The financing of terrorism is also a fundamentally simple concept. It is the financial support, in any form, of terrorism or of those who encourage, plan, or engage in terrorism. Less simple, however, is defining terrorism itself, because the term may have significant political, religious, and national implications from country to country. Money laundering and terrorist financing often display similar transactional features, mostly having to do with concealment.

Money launderers send illicit funds through legal channels in order to conceal their criminal origins, while those who finance terrorism transfer funds that may be legal or illicit in origin in such a way as to conceal their source and ultimate use, which is the support of terrorism. But the result is the same—reward. When money is laundered, criminals profit from their actions; they are rewarded by concealing the criminal act that generates the illicit proceeds and by disguising the origins of what appears to be legitimate proceeds. Similarly, those who finance terrorism are rewarded by concealing the origins of their funding and disguising the financial support to carry out their terrorist stratagems and attacks.

A. What Is Money Laundering?

Money laundering can be defined in a number of ways. Most countries subscribe to the definition adopted by the United Nations Convention Against Illicit Traffic in Narcotic Drugs and Psychotropic Substances (1988) (*Vienna Convention*)[1] and the United Nations Convention Against Transnational Organized Crime (2000) (*Palermo Convention*):[2]

- The conversion or transfer of property, knowing that such property is derived from any [drug trafficking] offense or offenses or from an act of participation in such offense or offenses, for the purpose of concealing or disguising the illicit origin of the property or of assisting any person who is involved in the commission of such an offense or offenses to evade the legal consequences of his actions;
- The concealment or disguise of the true nature, source, location, disposition, movement, rights with respect to, or ownership of property, knowing that such property is derived from an offense or offenses or from an act of participation in such an offense or offenses, and;

1. http://www.incb.org/e/conv/1988/.
2. http://www.undcp.org/adhoc/palermo/convmain.html.

- The acquisition, possession or use of property, knowing at the time of receipt that such property was derived from an offense or offenses or from an act of participation in such offense...or offenses.[3]

The Financial Action Task Force on Money Laundering (FATF), which is recognized as the international standard setter for anti-money laundering (AML) efforts,[4] defines the term "money laundering" succinctly as "the processing of...criminal proceeds to disguise their illegal origin" in order to "legitimize" the ill-gotten gains of crime.[5]

A money laundering predicate offense is the underlying criminal activity that generated proceeds, which when laundered, results in the offense of money laundering. By its terms, the *Vienna Convention* limits predicate offenses to drug trafficking offenses. As a consequence, crimes unrelated to drug trafficking, such as, fraud, kidnapping and theft, for example, do not constitute money laundering offenses under the *Vienna Convention*. Over the years, however, the international community has developed the view that predicate offenses for money laundering should go well beyond drug trafficking. Thus, FATF and other international instruments have expanded the *Vienna Convention*'s definition of predicate offenses to include other serious crimes.[6] For example, the *Palermo Convention* requires all participant countries to apply that convention's money laundering offenses to "the widest range of predicate offenses."[7]

In its 40 recommendations for fighting money laundering (*The Forty Recommendations*), FATF specifically incorporates the technical and legal definitions of money laundering set out in the Vienna and Palermo Conventions and lists 20 designated categories of offences that must be included as predicate offences for money laundering.[8]

---

3. See *Vienna Convention*, articles 3(b) and (c)(i); and Palermo Convention, article 6(i).
4. See Chapter III, B., FATF.
5. FATF, *What is money laundering?*, *Basic Facts About Money Laundering*, http://www.fatf-gafi.org/MLaundering_en.htm.
6. See discussion at Chapter V, A.,2., The Scope of the Predicate Offenses.
7. The *Palermo Convention*, Article 2 (2), http://www.undcp.org/adhoc/palermo/convmain.html.
8. *The Forty Recommendations*, Rec. 1; http://www.fatf-gafi.org/pdf/40Recs-2003_en.pdf. See also Chapter V, Criminalization of Money Laundering, of this Reference Guide.

B. What Is Terrorist Financing?

The United Nations (UN) has made numerous efforts, largely in the form of international treaties, to fight terrorism and the mechanisms used to finance it. Even before the September 11th attack on the United States, the UN had in place the International Convention for the Suppression of the Financing of Terrorism (1999), which provides:

1. Any person commits an offense within the meaning of this Convention if that person by any means, directly or indirectly, unlawfully and willingly, provides or collects funds with the intention that they should be used or in the knowledge that they are to be used, in full or in part, in order to carry out:

   a. An act which constitutes an offence within the scope of and as defined in one of the treaties listed in the annex; or

   b. Any other act intended to cause death or serious bodily injury to a civilian, or to any other person not taking any active part in the hostilities in a situation of armed conflict, when the purpose of such act, by its nature or context, is to intimidate a population, or to compel a government or an international organization to do or to abstain from doing an act.

2. ...

3. For an act to constitute an offense set forth in paragraph 1, it shall not be necessary that the funds were actually used to carry out an offense referred to in paragraph 1, subparagraph (a) or (b).[9]

The difficult issue for some countries is defining terrorism. Not all of the countries that have adopted the convention agree on specifically what actions constitute terrorism. The meaning of terrorism is not universally accepted due to significant political, religious and national implications that differ from country to country.

---

9. International Convention for the Suppression of the Financing of Terrorism (1999), Article 2, http://www.un.org/law/cod/finterr.htm. The conventions referred to in the annex in sub-paragraph 1(a) are listed in Annex III of this Reference Guide.

FATF, which is also recognized as the international standard setter for efforts to combat the financing of terrorism (CFT),[10] does not specifically define the term financing of terrorism in its nine *Special Recommendations on Terrorist Financing (Special Recommendations)*[11] developed following the events of September 11, 2001. Nonetheless, FATF urges countries to ratify and implement the 1999 United Nations International Convention for Suppression of the Financing of Terrorism.[12] Thus, the above definition is the one most countries have adopted for purposes of defining terrorist financing.

C. The Link Between Money Laundering and Terrorist Financing

The techniques used to launder money are essentially the same as those used to conceal the sources of, and uses for, terrorist financing. Funds used to support terrorism may originate from legitimate sources, criminal activities, or both. Nonetheless, disguising the source of terrorist financing, regardless of whether the source is of legitimate or illicit origin, is important. If the source can be concealed, it remains available for future terrorist financing activities. Similarly, it is important for terrorists to conceal the use of the funds so that the financing activity goes undetected.

For these reasons, FATF has recommended that each country criminalize the financing of terrorism, terrorist acts and terrorist organizations,[13] and designate such offenses as money laundering predicate offenses.[14] Finally, FATF has stated that the nine *Special Recommendations* combined with *The Forty Recommendations* on money laundering[15] constitute the basic framework for preventing, detecting and suppressing both money laundering and terrorist financing.

Efforts to combat the financing of terrorism also require countries to consider expanding the scope of their AML framework to include non-profit organizations, particularly charities, to make sure such organizations are not

---

10. See Chapter III, B., FATF.
11. *The Special Recommendations* are reprinted in Annex V of this Reference Guide.
12. *Id.*, at Spec. Rec. I.
13. *Id.*, at Spec. Rec. II.
14. *Id.*
15. *Id.*, at introductory paragraph.

used, directly or indirectly, to finance or support terrorism.[16] CFT efforts also require examination of alternative money transmission or remittance systems, such as *hawalas*. This effort includes consideration of what measures should be taken to preclude the use of such entities by money launderers and terrorists.[17]

As noted above, a significant difference between money laundering and terrorist financing is that the funds involved may originate from legitimate sources as well as criminal activities. Such legitimate sources may include donations or gifts of cash or other assets to organizations, such as foundations or charities that, in turn, are utilized to support terrorist activities or terrorist organizations. Consequently, this difference requires special laws to deal with terrorist financing. However, to the extent that funds for financing terrorism are derived from illegal sources, such funds may already be covered by a country's AML framework, depending upon the scope of predicate offenses for money laundering.

D. The Magnitude of the Problem

By their very nature, money laundering and terrorist financing are geared towards secrecy and do not lend themselves to statistical analysis. Launderers do not document the extent of their operations or publicize the amount of their profits, nor do those who finance terrorism. Moreover, because these activities take place on a global basis, estimates are even more difficult to produce. Launderers use various countries to conceal their ill-gotten proceeds, taking advantage of differences among countries with regard to AML regimes, enforcement efforts and international cooperation. Thus, reliable estimates on the size of the money laundering and terrorist financing problems on a global basis are not available.

With regard to money laundering only, the International Monetary Fund has estimated that the aggregate amount of funds laundered in the world could range between two and five per cent of the world's gross domestic product. Using 1996 statistics, these percentages would approximate between

---

16. *Special Recommendations*, Spec. Rec. VIII.
17. *Special Recommendations*, Spec. Rec. VI.

US $590 billion and US $1.5 trillion.[18] Thus, by any estimate, the size of the problem is very substantial and merits the complete attention of every country.

E. The Processes

The initial concern over money laundering began with its early connection to illegal trafficking in narcotic drugs. The objective of drug traffickers was to convert typically small denominations of currency into legal bank accounts, financial instruments, or other assets. Today, ill-gotten gains are produced by a vast range of criminal activities—among them political corruption, illegal sales of weapons, and illicit trafficking in and exploitation of human beings. Regardless of the crime, money launderers resort to placement, layering, and integration in the process of turning illicit proceeds into apparently legal monies or goods.

1. Placement

The initial stage of the process involves placement of illegally derived funds into the financial system, usually through a financial institution. This can be accomplished by depositing cash into a bank account. Large amounts of cash are broken into smaller, less conspicuous amounts and deposited over time in different offices of a single financial institution or in multiple financial institutions. The exchange of one currency into another, as well as the conversion of smaller notes into larger denominations, may occur at this stage. Furthermore, illegal funds may be converted into financial instruments, such as money orders or checks, and commingled with legitimate funds to divert suspicion. Furthermore, placement may be accomplished by the cash purchase of a security or a form of an insurance contract.

---

18. Vito Tanzi, "Money Laundering and the International Finance System," IMF Working Paper No. 96/55 (May 1996), at 3 and 4.

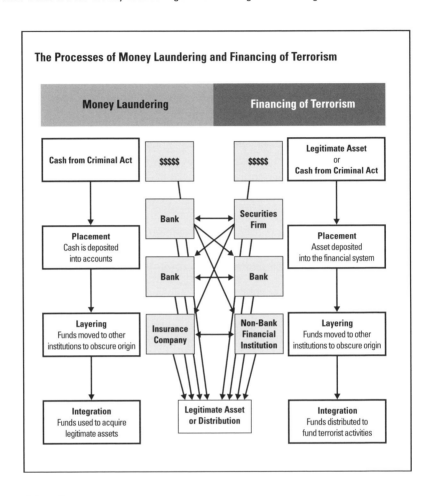

The Processes of Money Laundering and Financing of Terrorism

2. Layering

The second money laundering stage occurs after the ill-gotten gains have entered the financial system, at which point the funds, securities or insurance contracts are converted or moved to other institutions, further separating them from their criminal source. Such funds could then be used to purchase other securities, insurance contracts or other easily transferable investment instruments and then sold through yet another institution. The funds could also be transferred by any form of negotiable instrument such as check, money order or bearer bond, or the may be transferred electronically to other accounts in various jurisdictions. The launderer may also disguise the transfer as a payment for goods or services or transfer the funds to a shell corporation.

3. Integration

The third stage involves the integration of funds into the legitimate economy. This is accomplished through the purchase of assets, such as real estate, securities or other financial assets, or luxury goods.

These three stages are also seen in terrorist financing schemes, except that stage three integration involves the distribution of funds to terrorists and their supporting organizations, while money laundering, as discussed previously, goes in the opposite direction—integrating criminal funds into the legitimate economy.

F. Where Do Money Laundering and Terrorist Financing Occur?

Money laundering and the financing of terrorism can, and do, occur in any country in the world, especially those with complex financial systems. Countries with lax, ineffective, or corrupt AML and CFT infrastructures are also likely targets for such activities. No country is exempt.

Because complex international financial transactions can be abused to facilitate the laundering of money and terrorist financing, the different stages of money laundering and terrorist financing occur within a host of different countries. For example, placement, layering, and integration may each occur in three separate countries; one or all of the stages may also be removed from the original scene of the crime.

G. Methods and Typologies

Money can be laundered in a number of ways, ranging from small cash deposits in unremarkable bank accounts (for subsequent transfer) to the purchase and resale of luxury items such as automobiles, antiques, and jewelry.

Illicit funds can also be transferred through a series of complex international financial transactions. Launderers are very creative—when overseers detect one method, the criminals soon find another.

The various techniques used to launder money or finance terrorism are generally referred to as *methods* or *typologies*. The terms, methods or typologies, may be referred to interchangeably, without any distinction between the two. At any point in time, it is impossible to describe accurately the universe of the different methods criminals use to launder money or finance terrorism. Moreover, their methods are likely to differ from country to country because of a number of characteristics or factors unique to each country, including its economy, complexity of financial markets, AML regime, enforcement effort and international cooperation. In addition, the methods are constantly changing.

Nevertheless, various international organizations have produced excellent reference works on money laundering methods and techniques. FATF has produced reference materials on methods in its annual reports and annual typologies report.[19] The various FATF-style regional bodies also provide information on the various typologies seen in their regions. For the most up to-date information on money laundering methods and typologies, please consult the websites for these entities.[20] In addition, the Egmont Group has produced a compilation of one hundred sanitized cases about the fight against money laundering from its member financial intelligence units.[21]

---

19. See, for example, 2003–04 FATF Report on Money Laundering Typologies, http://www.fatf-gafi.org/pdf/TY2004_en.pdf, and prior reports, http://www.fatf-gafi.org/FATDocs_en.htm.
20. See Chapter IV for a discussion of the FATF-style regional bodies.
21. http://www.fincen.gov/fiuinaction.pdf. See Chapter III, The Egmont Group.

Chapter II

Money Laundering Impacts Development

A. The Adverse Implications for Developing Countries
1. Increased Crime and Corruption
2. International Consequences and Foreign Investment
3. Weakened Financial Institutions
4. Compromised Economy and Private Sector
5. Damaged Privatization Efforts

B. The Benefits of an Effective AML/CFT Framework
1. Fighting Crime and Corruption
2. Enhancing Stability of Financial Institutions
3. Encouraging Economic Development

Criminal enterprises and terrorist financing operations succeed largely to the extent that they are able to conceal the origins or sources of their funds and sanitize the proceeds by moving them through national and international financial systems. The absence of, or a lax or corrupt, anti-money laundering regime in a particular country permits criminals and those who finance terrorism to operate, using their financial gains to expand their criminal pursuits and fostering illegal activities such as corruption, drug trafficking, illicit trafficking and exploitation of human beings, arms trafficking, smuggling, and terrorism.

While money laundering and the financing of terrorism can occur in any country, they have particularly significant economic and social consequences for developing countries, because those markets tend to be small and, therefore, more susceptible to disruption from criminal or terrorist influences.

Money laundering and terrorist financing also have significant economic and social consequences for countries with fragile financial systems because they too are susceptible to disruption from such influences. Ultimately, the economy, society, and security of countries used as money-laundering or terrorist financing platforms are all imperiled.[1] The magnitude of these adverse consequences is difficult to establish, however, since such adverse impacts cannot be quantified with precision, either in general for the international community, or specifically for an individual country.

On the other hand, an effective framework for anti-money laundering (AML) and combating the financing of terrorism (CFT) have important benefits, both domestically and internationally, for a country. These benefits include lower levels of crime and corruption, enhanced stability of financial institutions and markets, positive impacts on economic development and reputation in the world community, enhanced risk management techniques for the country's financial institutions, and increased market integrity.

A. The Adverse Implications for Developing Countries

1. Increased Crime and Corruption

Successful money laundering helps make criminal activities profitable; it rewards criminals. Thus, to the extent that a country is viewed as a haven for money laundering, it is likely to attract criminals and promote corruption. Havens for money laundering and terrorist financing have:

- A weak AML/CFT regime;
- Some or many types of financial institutions that are not covered by an AML/CFT framework;
- Little, weak or selective enforcement of AML/CFT provisions;
- Ineffective penalties, including difficult confiscation provisions; and
- A limited number of predicate crimes for money laundering.

---

1. For a detailed discussion of negative economic effects of money laundering see Brent L. Bartlett, "Negative Effects of Money Laundering on Economic Development" (an Economic Research Report prepared for the Asian Development Bank, June 2002). See also John McDowell and Gary Novis, "Economic Perspectives," United States, State Department (May 2001).

If money laundering is prevalent in a country, it generates more crime and corruption. It also enhances the use of bribery in critical gateways to make money laundering efforts successful, such as:

- Employees and management of financial institutions,
- Lawyers and accountants,
- Legislatures,
- Enforcement agencies,
- Supervisory authorities,
- Police authorities,
- Prosecutors, and
- Courts.

A comprehensive and effective AML/CFT framework, together with timely implementation and effective enforcement, on the other hand, significantly reduce the profitable aspects of this criminal activity and, in fact, discourage criminals and terrorists from utilizing a country. This is especially true when the proceeds from criminal activities are aggressively confiscated and forfeited as part of a country's overall AML/CFT legal framework.

2. International Consequences and Foreign Investment

A reputation as a money laundering or terrorist financing haven, alone, could cause significant adverse consequences for development in a country. Foreign financial institutions may decide to limit their transactions with institutions from money laundering havens; subject these transactions to extra scrutiny, making them more expensive; or terminate correspondent or lending relationships altogether. Even legitimate businesses and enterprises from money laundering havens may suffer from reduced access to world markets or access at a higher cost due to extra scrutiny of their ownership, organization and control systems.

Any country known for lax enforcement of AML/CFT is less likely to receive foreign private investment. For developing nations, eligibility for foreign governmental assistance is also likely to be severely limited.

Finally, the Financial Action Task Force on Money Laundering (FATF) maintains a list of countries that do not comply with AML requirements or that do not cooperate sufficiently in the fight against money laundering. Being placed on this list, known as the "non-cooperating countries and territories" (NCCT) list,[2] gives public notice that the listed country does not have in place even minimum standards. Beyond the negative impacts referred to here, individual FATF member countries could also impose specific counter-measures against a country that does not take action to remedy its AML/CFT deficiencies.[3]

3. Weakened Financial Institutions

Money laundering and terrorist financing can harm the soundness of a country's financial sector, as well as the stability of individual financial institutions in multiple ways. The following discussion focuses on banking institutions, but the same consequences, or similar ones, are also applicable to other types of financial institutions, such as securities firms, insurance companies, and investment management firms. The adverse consequences generally described as reputational, operational, legal and concentration risks are interrelated. Each has specific costs:

- Loss of profitable business,
- Liquidity problems through withdrawal of funds,
- Termination of correspondent banking facilities,
- Investigation costs and fines,
- Asset seizures,
- Loan losses and
- Declines in the stock value of financial institutions.[4]

Reputational risk is the potential that adverse publicity regarding a bank's business practices and associations, whether accurate or not, will

---

2. See Chapter III, FATF, The NCCT List.
3. *Id.*
4. Basel Committee on Bank Supervision, *Customer due diligence for banks*, (October 2001), paragraphs 8–17, http://www.bis.org/publ/bcbs85.pdf.

cause a loss of confidence in the integrity of the institution.[5] Customers, both borrowers and depositors, as well as investors cease doing business with an institution whose reputation has been damaged by suspicions or allegations of money laundering or terrorist financing.[6] The loss of high quality borrowers reduces profitable loans and increases the risk of the overall loan portfolio. Depositors may also withdraw their funds, thereby reducing an inexpensive source of funding for the bank.

Moreover, funds placed on deposit with a bank by money launderers cannot be relied upon as a stable source of funding. Large amounts of laundered funds are often subject to unanticipated withdrawals from a financial institution through wire transfers or other transfers, causing potential liquidity problems.

Operational risk is the potential for loss resulting from inadequate or failed internal processes, people and systems, or external events.[7] As noted above, such losses occur when institutions incur reduced, terminated, or increased costs for inter-bank or correspondent banking services. Increased borrowing or funding costs can also be included in such losses.

Legal risk is the potential for law suits, adverse judgments, unenforceable contracts, fines and penalties generating losses, increased expenses for an institution, or even closure of such an institution.[8] Money laundering involves criminals in almost every aspect of the money laundering process. As a consequence, legitimate customers may also be victims of a financial crime, lose money and sue the institution for reimbursement. There may be investigations, by banking or other law enforcement authorities resulting in increased costs, as well as fines and other penalties involved. Also, certain contracts may be unenforceable due to fraud on the part of the criminal customer.

Concentration risk is the potential for loss resulting from too much credit or loan exposure to one borrower.[9] Statutory provisions or regulations usually restrict a bank's exposure to a single borrower or group of related borrowers. Lack of knowledge about a particular customer, the customer's

---

5. *Id.*, paragraph 11.
6. *Id.*
7. *Id.*, paragraph 12.
8. Id., paragraph 13.
9. Id., paragraph 14.

business, or what the customer's relationship is to other borrowers, can place a bank at risk in this regard. This is particularly a concern where there are related counter-parties, connected borrowers, and a common source of income or assets for repayment. Loan losses also result, of course, from unenforceable contracts and contracts made with fictitious persons.

Banks and their account holders are protected when effective due diligence regimes are in place.[10] Identification of the beneficial owners of an account is critical to an effective AML/CFT regime. Such identification procedures protect against business relationships with fictitious persons or corporate entities without substantial assets, such as shell corporations, as well as known criminals or terrorists. Due diligence procedures also help the financial institution to understand the nature of the customer's business interests and underlying financial issues.

4. Compromised Economy and Private Sector

Money launderers are known to use "front companies," i.e., business enterprises that appear legitimate and engage in legitimate business but are, in fact, controlled by criminals.

These front companies co-mingle the illicit funds with legitimate funds in order to hide the ill-gotten proceeds. Front companies' access to illicit funds, allows them to subsidize the front company's products and services, even at below-market prices. As a consequence, legitimate enterprises find it difficult to compete with such front companies, the sole purpose of which is to preserve and protect the illicit funds, not to produce a profit.

By using front companies and other investments in legitimate companies money laundering proceeds can be utilized to control whole industries or sectors of the economy of certain countries. This increases the potential for monetary and economic instability due to the misallocation of resources from artificial distortions in asset and commodity prices.[11] It also provides a vehicle for evading taxation, thus depriving the country of revenue.

---

10. See Chapter VI, Customer Identification and Due Diligence.
11. John McDowell and Gary Novis, *Economic Perspectives*, U.S. State Department, May 2001.

5. Damaged Privatization Efforts

Money launderers threaten the efforts of many countries to reform their economies through privatization.[12] These criminal organizations are capable of outbidding legitimate purchasers of former state-owned enterprises. When illicit proceeds are invested in this manner, criminals increase their potential for more criminal activities and corruption, as well as deprive the country of what should be a legitimate, market-based, tax paying enterprise.

B. The Benefits of an Effective AML/CFT Framework

1. Fighting Crime and Corruption

A strong AML/CFT institutional framework that includes a broad scope of predicate offenses for money laundering helps to fight crime and corruption in general.[13] When money laundering itself is made a crime, it provides another avenue to prosecute criminals, both those who commit the underlying criminal acts and those who assist them through laundering illegally obtained funds. Similarly, an AML/CFT framework that includes bribery as a predicate offense and is enforced effectively provides fewer opportunities for criminals to bribe or otherwise corrupt public officials.

An effective AML regime is a deterrent to criminal activities in and of itself. Such a regime makes it more difficult for criminals to benefit from their acts. In this regard, confiscation and forfeiture of money laundering proceeds are crucial to the success of any AML program. Forfeiture of money laundering proceeds eliminates those profits altogether, thereby reducing the incentive to commit criminal acts. Thus, it should go without saying that the broader the scope of predicate offenses for money laundering, the greater the potential benefit.

---

12. *Id.*
13. See Chapter I, What is Money Laundering; see also Chapter V, Scope of the Predicate Offense.

2. Enhancing Stability of Financial Institutions

Public confidence in financial institutions, and hence their stability, is enhanced by sound banking practices that reduce financial risks to their operations. These risks include the potential that either individuals or financial institutions will experience loss as a result of fraud from direct criminal activity, lax internal controls, or violations of laws and regulations.

Customer identification and due diligence procedures, also known as "know your customer" (KYC) rules, are part of an effective AML/CFT regime. These rules are not only consistent with, but also enhance, the safe and sound operation of banks and other types of financial institutions. These policies and procedures are an effective risk management tool. For example, in situations where a given individual or corporation may own several businesses that are seemingly separate entities and an institution has comprehensive knowledge of that particular customer's operations by performing KYC procedures, that institution can limit its exposure to that borrower and, thereby, its lending risk. Because of the risk management benefits of KYC procedures, the Basel Committee on Banking Supervision incorporates a KYC policy as part of its Core Principles for Effective Banking Supervision, aside from the AML reasons.[14]

In addition to the public confidence benefits, an effective AML/CFT regime reduces the potential that the institution could experience losses from fraud. Proper customer identification procedures and determination of beneficial ownership provide specific due diligence for higher risk accounts and permit monitoring for suspicious activities. Such prudential internal controls are consistent with the safe and sound operation of a financial institution.

3. Encouraging Economic Development

Money laundering has a direct negative effect on economic growth by diverting resources to less productive activities. Laundered illegal funds follow a different path through the economy than legal funds. Rather than being

---

14. See Core Principles for Effective Banking Supervision, Principle 15, Basel Committee on Bank Supervision, www.bis.org/publ/bcbs30.pdf.

placed in productive channels for further investment, laundered funds are often placed into "sterile" investments to preserve their value or make them more easily transferable. Such investments include real estate, art, jewelry, antiques or high-value consumption assets such as luxury automobiles. Such investments do not generate additional productivity for the broader economy.

Even worse, criminal organizations may transform productive enterprises into sterile investments by operating them for the primary purpose of laundering illegal proceeds, rather than as profit-generating enterprises. Such an enterprise does not respond to consumer demand or to other legitimate and productive uses for capital. Having a country's resources dedicated to sterile investments, as opposed to investments that drive other productive purposes, ultimately reduces the productivity of the overall economy.

Strong AML/CFT regimes provide a disincentive for the criminal involvement in the economy. This permits investments to be put into productive purposes that respond to consumer needs and help the productivity of the overall economy.

Chapter III

International Standard Setters

In response to the growing concern about money laundering and terrorist activities, the international community has acted on many fronts. The international response is, in large part, recognition of the fact that money laundering and terrorist financing take advantage of high speed international transfer mechanisms, such as wire transfers, to accomplish their goals. Therefore, concerted cross-border cooperation and coordination are needed to thwart the efforts of criminals and terrorists.

The international effort began with the recognition that drug trafficking was an international problem and could only be addressed effectively on a multilateral basis. Thus, the first international convention concerning money laundering had drug trafficking offenses as the only predicate offenses. (A predicate offense is the underlying crime that produces the proceeds that are the subject of money laundering.) Because many more types of crimes are now international concerns, most countries now include a wide range of serious offenses as money laundering predicate offenses.

This chapter discusses the various international organizations that are viewed as the international standard setters. It further describes the documents and instrumentalities that have been developed for anti-money laundering (AML) and combating the financing of terrorism (CFT) purposes.

A. The United Nations

The United Nations (UN) was the first international organization to undertake significant action to fight money laundering on a truly world-wide basis.[1] The UN is important in this regard for several reasons. First, it is the international organization with the broadest range of membership. Founded in October of 1945, there are currently 191 member states of the UN from throughout the world.[2] Second, the UN actively operates a program to fight money laundering; the Global Programme Against Money Laundering (GPML),[3] which is headquartered in Vienna, Austria, is part of the UN Office of Drugs and Crime (ODC).[4] Third, and perhaps most importantly, the UN has the ability to adopt international treaties or conventions that have the effect of law in a country once that country has signed, ratified and implemented the convention, depending upon the country's constitution and legal structure. In certain cases, the UN Security Council has the authority to bind all member countries through a Security Council Resolution, regardless of other action on the part of an individual country.

1. The *Vienna Convention*

Due to growing concern about increased international drug trafficking and the tremendous amounts of related money entering the banking system, the UN, through the United Nations Drug Control Program (UNDCP) initiated

---

1. There were other international efforts, e.g., "Measures Against the Transfer and Safekeeping of Funds of Criminal Origin," adopted by the Committee of the Council of Europe on June 27, 1980. It is beyond the purpose of this Reference Guide, however, to discuss in detail the history of the international effort to fight money laundering.
2. "List of Member States," www.un.org/Overview/unmember.html.
3. See http://www.imolin.org/imolin/gpml.html.
4. The UNDCP was renamed the Office of Drug Control and Crime Prevention (ODCCP) in 1997, and renamed the Office of Drugs and Crime (ODC) in October of 2002.

an international agreement to combat drug trafficking and money laundering. In 1988, this effort resulted in the adoption of the *United Nations
Convention Against Illicit Traffic in Narcotic Drugs and Psychotropic
Substances* (1988) (*Vienna Convention*).[5] The *Vienna Convention*, which
was named for the city in which it was signed, deals primarily with provisions to fight the illicit drug trade and related law enforcement issues; 169
countries are party to the convention.[6] Although it does not use the term
money laundering, the convention defines the concept and calls upon countries to criminalize the activity.[7] The *Vienna Convention* is limited, however,
to drug trafficking offenses as predicate offenses and does not address the
preventive aspects of money laundering. The convention came into force on
November 11, 1990.

2. The *Palermo Convention*

In order to expand the effort to fight international organized crime, the UN
adopted *The International Convention Against Transnational Organized
Crime* (2000) (*Palermo Convention*).[8] This convention, also named for the
city in which it was signed, contains a broad range of provisions to fight organized crime and commits countries that ratify this convention to implement its
provisions through passage of domestic laws. With respect to money laundering, the *Palermo Convention* specifically obligates each ratifying country to:

- Criminalize money laundering and include all serious crimes as predicate offenses of money laundering, whether committed in or outside of
  the country, and permit the required criminal knowledge or intent to
  be inferred from objective facts;[9]
- Establish regulatory regimes to deter and detect all forms of money
  laundering, including customer identification, record-keeping and
  reporting of suspicious transactions;[10]

---

5. http://www.incb.org/e/conv/1988/.
6. As of August 1, 2004. See, http://www.unodc.org/unodc/treaty_adherence.html.
7. The *Vienna Convention*, Article 3 (b) and (c) (i).
8. http://www.undcp.org/adhoc/palermo/convmain.html.
9. The Palermo Convention, Article 6.
10. Id., Article 7 (1) (a).

- Authorize the cooperation and exchange of information among administrative, regulatory, law enforcement and other authorities, both domestically and internationally, and consider the establishment of a financial intelligence unit to collect, analyze and disseminate information;[11] and
- Promote international cooperation.[12]

This convention went into force on the 29th of September 2003, having been signed by 147 countries and ratified by 82 countries.[13] The *Palermo Convention* is important because its AML provisions adopt the same approach previously adopted by the Financial Action Task Force on Money Laundering (FATF) in its *Forty Recommendations on Money Laundering.*[14]

3. International Convention for the Suppression of the Financing of Terrorism

The financing of terrorism was an international concern prior to the attacks on the United States of September 11, 2001. In response to this concern, the UN adopted the *International Convention for the Suppression of the Financing of Terrorism* (1999).[15] This convention came into force on April 10, 2002, with 132 countries signing the convention and 112 countries ratifying it.[16] (See Annex III of this Reference Guide for a listing of specified conventions.)

This convention requires ratifying states to criminalize terrorism, terrorist organizations and terrorist acts. Under the convention, it is unlawful for any person to provide or collect funds with the (1) intent that the funds be used for, or (2) knowledge that the funds be used to, carry out any of the acts of terrorism defined in the other specified conventions that are annexed to this convention.

---

11. *Id.*, Article 7 (1) (b).
12. *Id.*, Article 7 (3) and (4).
13. As of August 1, 2004. See, http://www.unodc.org/unodc/crime_cicp_signatures_convention. html.
14. See Discussion in this Chapter, FATF.
15. http://www.un.org/law/cod/finterr.htm.
16. As of March 2004. See, http://www.unausa.org/newindex.asp?place=http://www.unausa.org/ policy/newsactionalerts/advocacy/fin_terr.asp.

4. Security Council Resolution 1373

Unlike an international convention, which requires signing, ratification, and implementation by the UN member country to have the effect of law within that country, a Security Council Resolution passed in response to a threat to international peace and security under Chapter VII of the UN Charter, is binding upon all UN member countries.[17] On September 28, 2001, the UN Security Council adopted Resolution 1373,[18] which obligates countries to criminalize actions to finance terrorism. It further obligates countries to:

- deny all forms of support for terrorist groups;
- suppress the provision of safe haven or support for terrorists, including freezing funds or assets of persons, organizations or entities involved in terrorist acts;
- prohibit active or passive assistance to terrorists; and
- cooperate with other countries in criminal investigations and sharing information about planned terrorist acts.

5. Security Council Resolution 1267 and Successors

The UN Security Council has also acted under Chapter VII of the UN Charter to require member States to freeze the assets of the Taliban, Osama Bin Laden and Al-Qaeda and entities owned or controlled by them, as designated by the "Sanctions Committee" (now called the 1267 Committee). The initial Resolution 1267 of October 15, 1999,[19] dealt with the Taliban and was followed by 1333 of December 19, 2000,[20] on Osama Bin Laden and Al-Qaeda. Later Resolutions established monitoring arrangements (1363 of July 30, 2001[21]), merged the earlier lists (1390 of January 16, 2002[22]),

---

17. http://www.un.org/aboutun/charter/index.html.
18. http://www.state.gov/p/io/rls/othr/2001/5108.htm.
19. http://www.un.org/Docs/scres/1999/sc99.htm.
20. http://www.un.org/Docs/scres/2000/sc2000.htm.
21. http://www.un.org/Docs/scres/2001/sc2001.htm.
22. http://www.un.org/Docs/scres/2002/sc2002.htm.

provided some exclusions (1452 of December 20, 2002[23]), and measures to improve implementation (1455 of January 17, 2003[24]).

The 1267 Committee issues the list of individuals and entities whose assets are to be frozen and has procedures in place to make additions or deletions to the list on the basis of representations by member States. The most recent list is available on the website of the 1267 Committee.[25]

6. Global Programme against Money Laundering

The UN Global Programme against Money Laundering (GPML) is within the UN Office of Drugs and Crime (ODC).[26] The GPML is a research and assistance project with the goal of increasing the effectiveness of international action against money laundering by offering technical expertise, training and advice to member countries upon request. It focuses its efforts in the following areas:

- Raise the awareness level among key persons in UN member states;
- Help create legal frameworks with the support of model legislation for both common and civil law countries;
- Develop institutional capacity, in particular with the creation of financial intelligence units;
- Provide training for legal, judicial, law enforcement regulators and the private financial sectors;
- Promote a regional approach to addressing problems; develop and maintain strategic relationships with other organizations; and
- Maintain a database of information and undertake analysis of relevant information.

Thus, the GPML is a resource for information, expertise and technical assistance in establishing or improving a country's AML infrastructure.

---

23. http://www.un.org/Docs/scres/2002/sc2002.htm.
24. http://www.un.org/Docs/sc/unsc_resolutions03.html.
25. http://ods-dds-ny.un.org/doc/UNDOC/GEN/N99/300/44/PDF/N9930044.pdf?OpenElement.
26. "Global Programme against Money Laundering," http://www.imolin.org/imolin/gpml.html.

7. The Counter-Terrorism Committee

As noted above, on September 28, 2001, the UN Security Council adopted a resolution (Resolution 1373) in direct response to the events of September 11, 2001.[27] That resolution obligated all member countries to take specific actions to combat terrorism. The resolution, which is binding upon all member countries, also established the Counter Terrorism Committee (CTC) to monitor the performance of the member countries in building a global capacity against terrorism. The CTC, which is comprised of the 15 members of the Security Council, is not a law enforcement agency; it does not issue sanctions, nor does it prosecute or condemn individual countries.[28] Rather, the Committee seeks to establish a dialogue between the Security Council and member countries on how to achieve the objectives of Resolution 1373.

Resolution 1373 calls upon all countries to submit a report to the CTC on the steps taken to implement the resolution's measures and report regularly on progress. In this regard, the CTC has asked each country to perform a self-assessment of its existing legislation and mechanism to combat terrorism in relation to the requirements of Resolution 1373. The CTC identifies the areas where a country needs to strengthen its statutory base and infrastructure, and facilitate assistance for countries, although the CTC does not, itself, provide direct assistance.

The CTC maintains a website with a directory for countries seeking help in improving their counter-terrorism infrastructures.[29] It contains copies of model legislation and other helpful information.

B. The Financial Action Task Force on Money Laundering

Formed in 1989 by the G-7 countries,[30] the Financial Action Task Force on Money Laundering (FATF) is an intergovernmental body whose purpose is to develop and promote an international response to combat money launder-

---

27. UN Security Council Resolution 1373.
28. See http://www.un.org/sc/ctc.
29. *Id.*
30. *Id.* The G-7 countries are Canada, France, Germany, Italy, Japan, United Kingdom, and United States.

ing.[31] In October of 2001, FATF expanded its mission to include combating the financing of terrorism.[32]

FATF is a policy-making body, which brings together legal, financial and law enforcement experts to achieve national legislation and regulatory AML and CFT reforms. Currently, its membership consists of 31 countries and territories and two regional organizations.[33] In addition, FATF works in collaboration with a number of international bodies[34] and organizations.[35] These entities have observer status with FATF, which does not entitle them to vote, but otherwise permits full participation in plenary sessions and working groups.

FATF's three primary functions with regard to money laundering are:

1. monitoring members' progress in implementing anti-money laundering measures;

2. reviewing and reporting on laundering trends, techniques and counter-measures; and

3. promoting the adoption and implementation of FATF anti-money laundering standards globally.

---

31. About FATF, and Terrorist Financing at http://www.fatf-gafi.org/.
32. *Id.* at Terrorist Financing.
33. The 31 member countries and territories are: Argentina, Australia, Austria, Belgium, Brazil, Canada, Denmark, Finland, France, Germany, Greece, Hong Kong-China, Iceland, Ireland, Italy, Japan, Luxemburg, Mexico, Kingdom of the Netherlands, New Zealand, Norway, Portugal, Russia, Singapore, South Africa, Spain, Sweden, Switzerland, Turkey, United Kingdom, and United States. The two regional organizations are the European Commission and the Gulf Co-operation Council.
34. The international bodies are regional FATF-style regional bodies (FSRBs) that have similar form and functions to those of FATF. Some FATF members also participate in the FSRBs. These bodies are: Asia/Pacific Group on Money Laundering (APG), Caribbean Financial Action Task Force (CFATF), Council of Europe MONEYVAL (previously PC-R-EV) Committee, Eastern and Southern Africa Anti-Money Laundering Group (ESAAMLG) and Financial Action Task Force on Money Laundering in South America (GAFISUD). For a discussion of these organizations, See Chapter IV, Regional Bodies and Relevant Groups, FATF-Style Regional Bodies. FATF also works with the Egmont Group.
35. Each of the international organizations, which have, among other functions, a specific anti-money laundering mission or function, are: African Development Bank, Asia Development Bank, The Commonwealth Secretariat, European Bank for Reconstruction and Development, European Central Bank (ECB), Europol, Inter-American Development Bank (IDB), Intergovernmental Action Group Against Money-Laundering in Africa (GIABA), International Association of Insurance Supervisors (IAIS), International Monetary Fund (IMF), Interpol, International Organization of Securities Commissions (IOSCO), Organization of American States/Inter-American Committee Against Terrorism (OAS/CICTE), Organization of American States/Inter-American Drug Abuse Control Commission (OAS/CICAD), Organization for Economic Co-operation and Development (OECD), Offshore Group of Banking Supervisors (OGBS), United Nations Office on Drugs and Crime (UNODC), World Bank and World Customs Organization (WCO).

1. The Forty Recommendations

FATF has adopted a set of 40 recommendations, *The Forty Recommendations on Money Laundering (The Forty Recommendations)*, which constitute a comprehensive framework for AML and are designed for universal application by countries throughout the world.[36] *The Forty Recommendations* set out principles for action; they permit a country flexibility in implementing the principles according to the country's own particular circumstances and constitutional requirements. Although not binding as law upon a country, *The Forty Recommendations* have been widely endorsed by the international community and relevant organizations as the international standard for AML.

The Forty Recommendations are actually mandates for action by a country if that country wants to be viewed by the international community as meeting international standards. The individual recommendations are discussed in detail throughout this Reference Guide and, particularly in Chapters V, VI, VII, and VIII.

The Forty Recommendations were initially issued in 1990 and have been revised in 1996 and 2003 to take account of new developments in money laundering and to reflect developing best practices internationally.

2. Monitoring Members Progress

Monitoring the progress of members to comply with the requirements of *The Forty Recommendations* is facilitated by a two-stage process: self assessments and mutual evaluations. In the self-assessment stage, each member responds to a standard questionnaire, on an annual basis, regarding its implementation of *The Forty Recommendations*. In the mutual evaluation stage, each member is examined and assessed by experts from other member countries.

In the event that a country is unwilling to take appropriate steps to achieve compliance with *The Forty Recommendations*, FATF recommends that all financial institutions give special attention to business relations and transactions with persons, including companies and financial institutions, from such non-compliant countries and, where appropriate, report questionable transactions, i.e., those that have no apparent economic or visible lawful

---

36. *The Forty Recommendations*, http://www.fatf-gafi.org/pdf/40Recs-2003_en.pdf.

purpose, to competent authorities.[37] Ultimately, if a member country does not take steps to achieve compliance, membership in the organization can be suspended. There is, however, the process of peer pressure before these sanctions are enforced.

3. Reporting on Money Laundering Trends and Techniques

One of FATF's functions is to review and report on money laundering trends, techniques and methods (also referred to as typologies). To accomplish this aspect of its mission, FATF issues annual reports on developments in money laundering through its Typologies Report.[38] These reports are very useful for all countries, not just FATF members, to keep current with new techniques or trends to launder money and for other developments in this area.

4. The NCCT List

One of FATF's objectives is to promote the adoption of international AML/ CFT standards for all countries. Thus, its mission extends beyond its own membership, although FATF can only sanction its member countries and territories. Thus, in order to encourage all countries to adopt measures to prevent, detect and prosecute money launderers, i.e., to implement *The Forty Recommendations*, FATF has adopted a process of identifying those jurisdictions that serve as obstacles to international cooperation in this area. The process uses 25 criteria, which are consistent with *The Forty Recommendations*, to identify such non-cooperative countries and territories (NCCT's) and place them on a publicly available list.[39]

An NCCT country is encouraged to make rapid progress in remedying its deficiencies. In the event an NCCT country does not make sufficient progress, counter-measures may be imposed. Counter measures consist of specific actions by FATF member countries taken against an NCCT-listed country.

---

37. *Id.*, Rec. 21.
38. See FATF Documents, Money Laundering Trends and Techniques at http://www.fatf-gafi.org/ pdf/TY2004_en.PDF.
39. NCCT Initiative, http://www.fatf-gafi.org/NCCT_en.htm.

In addition to the application of applying special attention to business relationships and transactions from such countries,[40] the FATF can also impose further counter-measures, which are to be applied in a gradual, proportionate and flexible manner; these include:

- Stringent requirements for identifying clients and enhancement of advisories, including jurisdiction-specific financial advisories, to financial institutions for identification of the beneficial owners before business relationships are established with individuals or companies from these countries;
- Enhanced relevant reporting mechanisms or systematic reporting of financial transactions on the basis that financial transactions with such countries are more likely to be suspicious;
- In considering requests for approving the establishment in FATF member countries of subsidiaries or branches or representative offices of banks, taking into account the fact that the relevant bank is from an NCCT;
- Warning non-financial sector businesses that transactions with entities within the NCCTs might run the risk of money laundering.[41]

Finally, these counter measures may include FATF-member countries terminating transactions with financial institutions from such a country.

Most countries make a concerted effort to be taken off the NCCT list because it causes significant problems for their financial institutions and businesses with respect to international transactions, as well as their reputation internationally.

5. Terrorist Financing

FATF also focuses its expertise on the world-wide effort to combat terrorist financing. To accomplish this expanded mission FATF has adopted nine *Special Recommendations on Terrorist Financing (Special*

---

40. *The Forty Recommendations*, Rec. 21.
41. FATF, FATF statements and documents on NCCT. See, for example, Press Release, December 20, 2002, http://www.fatf-gafi.org/pdf/PR-20021220_en.pdf.

Recommendations).[42] As part of this effort, FATF members use a self-assessment questionnaire[43] of their country's actions to come into compliance with the *Special Recommendations*. FATF is continuing to develop guidance on techniques and mechanisms used in the financing of terrorism. Chapter IX of this *Reference Guide* contains a more detailed discussion of the *Special Recommendations* and the Questionnaire.

6. Methodology for AML/CFT Assessments

In 2002, following lengthy consultations, the FATF, International Monetary Fund (IMF), and World Bank adopted a single assessment methodology to be used both by FATF in its mutual evaluations and by the IMF and World Bank in their assessments under their financial sector assessment and offshore financial center programs. The FATF-style regional bodies (FSRBs), geographical sector organizations, which had been involved in the development of the methodology, subsequently agreed to use it for their mutual evaluations.

The methodology was revised in 2004, following the 2003 revision of *The Forty Recommendations*. The methodology sets out over 200 "essential criteria" that assessors should examine when carrying out assessments of an AML and CFT regime. It covers the legal and institutional AML/CFT framework for a country, including financial intelligence units. The methodology also includes relevant elements from United Nations Security Council resolutions and international conventions, as well as supervisory and regulatory standards for the banking, insurance and securities sectors. Those essential criteria describe the mandatory elements that need to be present to comply fully with each of *The Forty Recommendations* and *Special Recommendations*. The methodology includes guidance on how to rate compliance and is based on performance against the essential criteria.

The methodology also includes a number of "additional elements," which are options for further strengthening AML/CFT systems. Although performance against these elements is reviewed as part of the overall assessment, they are not mandatory and are not assessed for compliance purposes.

---

42. See *Special Recommendations*. These Special Recommendations are set out in Annex V, http://www.fatf-gafi.org/pdf/SRecTF_en.pdf.
43. http://www.fatf-gafi.org/SAQTF_en.htm.

The adoption of this single, comprehensive assessment methodology by the FATF, IMF, World Bank, and the FSRBs means a more uniform approach worldwide to the conduct of assessments and the ratings of country performance. A country undergoing an assessment will be required, at the first stage of the assessment, to prepare a self-assessment of its AML/CFT system according to the methodology document. The document is also a useful detailed guide to a country on measures that need to be in place to comply with the international standards.[44]

C. The Basel Committee on Banking Supervision

Fed represents US

The Basel Committee on Banking Supervision (Basel Committee)[45] was formed in 1974 by the central bank governors of the Group of 10 countries.[46] Individual countries are represented by their central bank, or by the relevant authority with formal responsibility for prudential supervision of banking where that authority is not the central bank. The committee has no formal international supervisory authority or force of law. Rather, it formulates broad supervisory standards and guidelines and recommends statements of best practices on a wide range of bank supervisory issues. These standards and guidelines are adopted with the expectation that the appropriate authorities within each country will take all necessary steps to implement them through detailed measures, statutory, regulatory or otherwise, that best suit that country's national system. Three of the Basel Committee's supervisory standards and guidelines concern money laundering issues.

---

44. The methdology may be found at Methodology on AML/CFT, http://www.fatf-gafi.org/pdf/Meth_2002_en.pdf. See also Chapter X, Development of a Universal AML/CFT Assessment Methodology, for a more detailed discussion of the methodology and its use by the World Bank and the IMF.
45. http://www.bis.org/index.htm.
46. The Group of 10 countries is a misnomer, since there are actually 13 member countries. The Basel Committee members, (as well as the Group of 10) are: Belgium, Canada, France, Germany, Italy, Japan, Luxemburg, the Netherlands, Spain, Sweden, Switzerland, United Kingdom and United States.

1. Statement of Principles on Money Laundering

In 1988, the Basel Committee issued its *Statement on Prevention of Criminal Use of the Banking System for the Purpose of Money Laundering (Statement on Prevention)*.[47] The *Statement on Prevention* outlines basic policies and procedures that bank managements should ensure are in place within their institutions to assist in suppressing money laundering through the banking system, both domestically and internationally. The statement notes that banks can be used "unwittingly" as intermediaries by criminals. Thus, the committee considers the first and most important safeguard against money laundering to be "the integrity of banks own managements and their vigilant determination to prevent their institutions from becoming associated with criminals or being used as a channel for money laundering."[48]

There are essentially four principles contained in the *Statement on Prevention*:

- Proper customer identification; 326
- High ethical standards and compliance with laws;
- Cooperation with law enforcement authorities; and
- Policies and procedures to adhere to the statement.

First, banks should make reasonable efforts to determine the true identity of all customers requesting the institution's services.[49] It should be a bank's explicit policy that significant business transactions are not conducted with customers who fail to provide evidence of their identity.

Second, banks should ensure that business is conducted in conformity with high ethical standards and that banks should adhere to laws and regulations pertaining to financial transactions.[50] Here, banks should not offer services or provide active assistance in transactions where the bank has good reason to believe they are associated with money laundering.

Third, banks should cooperate fully with national law enforcement authorities to the extent permitted by local laws or regulations relating to

---

47. http://www.bis.org/publ/bcbsc137.pdf.
48. *Id.*, at Preamble paragraph 6.
49. *Id.*, at Customers identification.
50. *Id.*, at Compliance with laws.

customer confidentiality.[51] No support or assistance should be provided to customers seeking to deceive law enforcement authorities through altered, incomplete or misleading information. Where a bank has a reasonable presumption that funds on deposit are from criminal activity or that transactions entered into are for a criminal purpose, the bank should take appropriate measures, including denial of assistance, severing of the customer relationship, and closing or freezing the account.

Fourth, banks should adopt formal policies consistent with the *Statement on Prevention*.[52] Furthermore, banks should assure that all staff members are aware of the bank's policies and given proper training in matters covered by the bank's policies. As part of a bank's policies, specific procedures for customer identification should be adopted. Finally, the internal audit function within the institution should establish an effective means of testing for compliance.

2. Core Principles for Banking

In 1997, the Basel Committee issued its *Core Principles for Effective Banking Supervision (Core Principles)*,[53] which provides a comprehensive blueprint for an effective bank supervisory system and covers a wide range of topics. Of the total 25 Core Principles, one of them, Core Principle 15, deals with money laundering; it provides:

> Banking supervisors must determine that banks have adequate policies, practices and procedures in place, including strict "know your customer" rules, that promote high ethical and professional standards in the financial sector and prevent the bank from being used; intentionally or unintentionally, by criminal elements.[54]

These "know your customer" or "KYC" policies and procedures are a crucial part of an effective AML/CFT institutional framework for every country.

---

51. *Id.*, at Cooperation with law enforcement authorities.
52. *Id.*, at Adherence to the Statement.
53. http://www.bis.org/publ/bcbs30.pdf.
54. *Id.* Core Principle 15.

In addition to the *Core Principles*, the Basel Committee issued a "Core Principles Methodology" in 1999, which contains 11 specific criteria and five additional criteria to help assess the adequacy of KYC policies and procedures.[55] These, additional criteria include specific reference to compliance with *The Forty Recommendations*.[56]

3. Customer Due Diligence

In October of 2001, the Basel Committee issued an extensive paper on KYC principles entitled, *Customer due diligence for banks* (*Customer Due Diligence*).[57] This paper was issued in response to noted deficiencies in KYC procedures on a world-wide basis. These KYC standards build upon and provide more specific information on the Statement on Prevention and Core Principle 15. The essential elements of KYC standards are set out in detail in this document.

It is worth noting that these KYC standards set out in *Customer Due Diligence* are intended to benefit banks beyond the fight against money laundering by protecting the safety and soundness of banks and the integrity of banking systems. In addition, the Basel Committee, in this document, strongly supports the "adoption and implementation of the FATF recommendations, particularly those relating to banks," and intends that the standards of *Customer Due Diligence* "be consistent with the FATF recommendations."[58]

D. International Association of Insurance Supervisors

The International Association of Insurance Supervisors (IAIS), established in 1994, is an organization of insurance supervisors from more than 100 different countries and jurisdictions.[59]

---

55. Core Principles Methodology at http://www.bis.org/publ/bcbs61.pdf.
56. *Id.*, Annex 2, Excerpts from FATF recommendations.
57. *Id.*
58. *Id.*, at paragraph 3.
59. For a list of member countries and jurisdictions, see Members at http://www.iaisweb.org/132_176_ENU_HTML.asp. The listing of members contains hyperlinks to individual member websites.

Its primary objectives are to:

• Promote cooperation among insurance regulators,
• Set international standards for insurance supervision,
• Provide training to members, and
• Coordinate work with regulators in the other financial sectors and international financial institutions.[60]

In addition to member regulators, the IAIS has more than 60 observer members, representing industry associations, professional associations, insurance and reinsurance companies, consultants and international financial institutions.[61]

While the IAIS covers a wide range of topics including virtually all areas of insurance supervision, it specifically deals with money laundering in one of its papers. In January 2002,[62] the association issued Guidance Paper No. 5, *Anti-Money Laundering Guidance Notes for Insurance Supervisors and Insurance Entities (AML Guidance Notes)*. It is a comprehensive discussion on money laundering in the context of the insurance industry. Like other international documents of its type, the *AML Guidance Notes* are intended to be implemented by individual countries taking into account the particular insurance companies involved, the products offered within the country, and the country's own financial system, economy, constitution and legal system.

The *AML Guidance Notes* contain four principles for insurance entities:

• Comply with anti-money laundering laws,
• Have "know your customer" procedures,
• Cooperate with all law enforcement authorities, and
• Have internal AML policies, procedures and training programs for employees.

These four principles parallel the four principles in the Basel Committee's *Statement on Prevention*. The *AML Guidance Notes* are entirely consistent

---

60. *Id.*, at Home page.
61. *Id.*, at Observers, for a listing of observer organizations.
62. *Id.*, at Guidance Paper No.5, Anti-Money Laundering Guidance Notes for Insurance Supervisors & Insurance Entities, January 2002.

with *The Forty Recommendations*, including suspicious activity reporting and other requirements. In fact, *The Forty Recommendations* are included in an appendix to the IAIS's *AML Guidance Notes*.

E. International Organization of Securities Commissioners

The International Organization of Securities Commissioners (IOSCO)[63] is an organization of securities commissioners and administrators that have day-to-day responsibilities for securities regulation and the administration of securities laws in their respective countries. The current membership of IOSCO is comprised of regulatory bodies from 105 countries.[64] In the event that there is no governmental authority charged with administration of securities laws in a given country, a self-regulatory body, such as a stock exchange, from that country is eligible for voting membership. There are also associate members, which are international organizations, and affiliate members, which are self regulatory organizations; neither of these two types of membership has voting privileges.

IOSCO has three core objectives for securities regulation:

- The protection of investors;
- Ensuring that markets are fair, efficient and transparent; and
- The reduction of systematic risk.[65]

With regard to money laundering, IOSCO passed a "Resolution on Money Laundering" in 1992. Like other international organizations of this type, IOSCO does not have law-making authority. Similar to the Basel Committee and IAIS, it relies on its members to implement its recommendations within their respective countries. The resolution provides as follows:

Each IOSCO member should consider:

1. The extent to which customer identifying information is gathered and recorded by financial institutions under its supervision, with a view to

---

63. http://www.iosco.org/iosco.html.
64. See Membership Lists, http://www.iosco.org/iosco.html.
65. http://www.iosco.org/pubdocs/pdf/IOSCOPD125.pdf.

enhancing the ability of relevant authorities to identify and prosecute money launderers;

2. The extent and adequacy of record-keeping requirements, from the perspective of providing tools to reconstruct financial transactions in the securities and future markets;

3. Together with their national regulators charged with prosecuting money laundering offenses, the appropriate manner in which to address the identification and reporting of suspicious transactions;

4. The procedures in place to prevent criminals from obtaining control of securities and futures businesses, with a view to working together with foreign counterparts to share such information as needed;

5. The appropriate means to ensure that securities and futures firms maintain monitoring and compliance procedures designed to deter and detect money laundering;

6. The use of cash and cash equivalents in securities and futures transactions, including the adequacy of documentation and the ability to reconstruct any such transactions;

7. The most appropriate means, given their particular national authorities and powers, to share information in order to combat money laundering.[66]

F. The Egmont Group of Financial Intelligence Units

As part of the effort to fight money laundering, governments have created agencies to analyze information submitted by covered entities and persons pursuant to money laundering reporting requirements. Such agencies are commonly referred to as financial intelligent units (FIUs). These units serve as the focal point for national AML programs, because they provide for the exchange of information between financial institutions and law enforcement. Because money laundering is practiced on a worldwide scale, there has also been the need to share information on a cross-border basis.[67]

In 1995, a number of governmental units known today as FIUs began working together and formed the Egmont Group of Financial Intelligence

---

66. http://www.iosco.org/library/index.cfm?whereami=resolutions.
67. See discussion in Chapter VII of this Reference Guide.

Units (Egmont Group) (named for the location of its first meeting at the Egmont-Arenberg Palace in Brussels).[68] The purpose of the group is to provide a forum for FIUs to improve support for each of their national AML programs and to coordinate AML initiatives. This support includes expanding and systematizing the exchange of financial intelligence information, improving expertise and capabilities of personnel, and fostering better communication among FIUs through technology, and helping to develop FIUs worldwide.[69]

The mission of the Egmont Group was expanded in 2004 to include specifically financial intelligence on terrorist financing.[70] To be a member of the Egmont Group,[71] a country's FIU must first meet the Egmont FIU definition, which is "a central, national agency responsible for receiving (and, as permitted, requesting), analyzing and disseminating to the competent authorities, disclosures of financial information: (i) concerning suspected proceeds of crime and potential financing of terrorism, or (ii) required by national regulation, in order to counter money laundering and terrorist financing."[72] A member must also commit to act in accordance with the Egmont Group's Principles for Information Exchange Between Financial Intelligence Units for Money Laundering Cases.[73] These principles include conditions for the exchange of information, limitation on permitted uses of information, and confidentiality.

Membership of the Egmont Group is currently comprised of 94 jurisdictions.[74] Members of the Egmont Group have access to a secure website, which is not available to the public, to exchange information.

The Egmont Group is an informal body without a secretariat or a permanent location. The Egmont Group meets in a plenary session once a year, and in working group sessions three times a year. Within the Egmont Group, the FIU heads make all the policy decisions, including membership. The group

---

68. http://www.egmontgroup.org/.
69. See Statement of Purpose, Egmont Group. http://www.egmontgroup.org/statement_of_purpose.pdf.
70. Id.
71. For discussion on membership, see Egmont paper on its website with the procedures for joining the Egmont Group, http://www.egmontgroup.org/procedure_for_being_recognised.pdf.
72. http://www.egmontgroup.org/info_paper_final_092003.pdf.
73. See Statement of Purpose, Egmont Group. http://www.egmontgroup.org/statement_of_purpose.pdf.
74. As of June 2, 2004. See http://www.egmontgroup.org/list_of_fius_062304.pdf.

established the Egmont Committee to help coordinate with the Working Groups and the FIU heads in between the annual plenary sessions.

Finally, the Egmont Group has produced training material with access for the public. The group compiled sanitized cases about the fight against money laundering from its member FIUs.[75] It has also produced a video and Egmont-related documents that are available on its website.

---

75. http://www.fincen.gov/fiuinaction.pdf.

Chapter IV

Regional Bodies and Relevant Groups

A. FATF-Style Regional Bodies
1. Asia/Pacific Groups on Money Laundering
2. Caribbean Financial Action Task Force
3. Council on Europe—MONEYVAL
4. Eastern and Southern Africa Anti-Money Laundering Group
5. Financial Action Task Force on Money Laundering in South America

B. Wolfsberg Group of Banks
1. Anti-Money Laundering Principles for Private Banking
2. Statement on the Suppression of the Financing of Terrorism
3. Anti-Money Laundering Principles for Correspondent Banking

C. The Commonwealth Secretariat

D. Organization of American States–CICAD

In addition to the International Standard Setters discussed in Chapter III, there are other international organizations that play crucial roles in the fight against money laundering and terrorist financing. These groups tend to be organized according to geographic region or by the special purpose of the organization.

A. FATF-Style Regional Bodies

Financial Action Task Force on Money Laundering (FATF) regional groups or FATF-Style Regional Bodies (FSRBs) are very important in the promotion and implementation of anti-money laundering (AML) and combating the financing of terrorism (CFT) standards within their respective regions. FSRBs are to their regions what FATF is to the world.

They are modeled after FATF and, like FATF, have AML and CFT efforts as their sole objectives. They encourage implementation and enforcement of FATF's *The Forty Recommendations on Money Laundering* (*The Forty Recommendations*) and the nine *Special Recommendations on Terrorist Financing* (*Special Recommendations*).[1] They also administer mutual evaluations of their members, which are intended to identify weaknesses so that the member may take remedial action. Finally, the FSRBs provide information to their members about trends, techniques and other developments for money laundering in their Typology Reports, which are usually produced on an annual basis.

The FSRBs are voluntary and cooperative organizations. Membership is open to any country or jurisdiction within the given geographic region that is willing to abide by the rules and objectives of the organization. Some members of FATF are also members of the FSRBs. In addition to voting members, non-voting observer status is available to jurisdictions and organizations that wish to participate in the activities of the organization.

The FSRBs that are currently recognized by FATF are:

1. Asia/Pacific Group on Money Laundering (APG)[2]
2. Caribbean Financial Action Task Force (CFATF)[3]

---

1. *The Forty Recommendations*, http://www.fatf-gafi.org/pdf/40Recs-2003_en.pdf , reprinted in Annex IV of this Reference Guide; and Special Recommendations, http://www.fatf-gafi.org/pdf/SRecTF_en.pdf. reprinted in Annex V of this Reference Guide.
2. Member jurisdictions are: Australia, Bangladesh, Brunei Darussalam, Cambodia, Chinese Taipei, Cook Islands, Fiji, Hong Kong-China, India, Indonesia, Japan, Macau-China, Malaysia, Marshall Islands, Mongolia, Nepal, New Zealand, Niue, Pakistan, Republic of Korea, Palau, Philippines, Samoa, Singapore, Sri Lanka, Thailand, United States and Vanuatu. Observer jurisdictions are: Canada, France, Lao People's Democratic Republic, Papua New Guinea, Republic of Kiribati, Republic of the Maldives, Republic of Nauru, Tonga, Union of Myanmar, United Kingdom and Vietnam. Observer organizations are: Asian Development Bank (ADB), Asia Pacific Economic Cooperation (APEC), Association of South East Asian nations (ASEAN), Caribbean Financial Action Task Force (CFATF), Commonwealth Secretariat, Egmont Group, FATF, International Monetary Fund (IMF), INTERPOL, Offshore Group of Banking Supervisors (OGBS), Pacific Financial Technical Assistance Centre (PFTAC), Pacific Islands Forum Secretariat (PIFS), The World Bank, World Customs Organization (WCO) and United Nations (UN) International Drug Control Programme (UNDCP) and United Nations Office on Drugs and Crime (ODC). http://www.apgml.org.
3. Member countries are: Anguilla, Antigua and Barbuda, Aruba, Bahamas, Barbados, Belize, Bermuda, British Virgin Islands, Cayman Islands, Costa Rica, Dominica, Dominican Republic, El Salvador, Grenada, Guatemala, Guyana, Haiti. Honduras, Jamaica, Montserrat, Netherland Antilles, Nicaragua, Panama, St. Kitts and Nevis, St. Lucia, St. Vincent and the Grenadines, Suriname, Trinidad and Tobago, Turks and Caicos Islands and Venezuela. Co-operating and Supporting Nations are: Canada, France, Mexico, Netherlands, Spain, United Kingdom and United States. Observers are: Asia/Pacific Group Secretariat, Caribbean Customs and Law Enforcement Council (CCLEC), Caribbean Development Bank (CDB), CARICOM, Commonwealth Secretariat, European Commission, FATF Secretariat, UN Global Programme on Money Laundering (GPML), Inter-American Development Bank (IADB), Interpol, Offshore

3. Council of Europe–MONEYVAL[4]
4. Eastern and Southern Africa Anti-Money Laundering Group (ESAAMLG)[5]
5. Financial Action Task Force on Money Laundering in South America (GAFISUD).[6]

Certain FSRBs have issued their own conventions or instruments on AML. For example, in 1990, CFATF issued its "Aruba Recommendations," which are 19 recommendations that address money laundering from the Caribbean regional perspective and which complement *The Forty Recommendations*.[7] Further, in 1992, a Ministerial meeting produced the "Kingston Declaration," which affirmed the CFATF respective governments' commitment to implementing international AML standards.[8] Similarly, the Council of Europe, in 1990, adopted its "Convention on Laundering, Search, Seizure and Confiscation of the Proceeds of Crime" (the Strasbourg Convention).[9] These are important instruments in the implementation of AML standards for their respective regions.

Group of Banking Supervisors (OGBS), Organization of American States/Inter-American Drug Abuse Control Commission (OAS/CICAD) and United Nations Office on Drugs and Crime (UNODC). http://www.cfatf.org.

4. Members are: Albania, Andorra, Armenia, Azerbaijan, Bosnia and Herzegovina, Bulgaria, Croatia, Cyprus, Czech Republic, Estonia, Georgia, Hungary, Latvia, Liechtenstein, Lithuania, Malta, Moldova, Poland, Romania, Russian Federation, San Marino, Serbia and Montenegro, Slovakia, Slovenia, 'Former Yugoslav Republic of Macedonia' and Ukraine. Observer jurisdictions are: Canada, Holy See, Japan, Mexico, United States. Observers are: Commission of the European Communities, Commonwealth Secretariat, European Bank for Reconstruction and Development (EBRD), FATF (Secretariat and Member Countries), International Monetary Fund (IMF), Interpol, Offshore Group of Banking Supervisors (OGBS), Secretariat General of the Council of the European Union, United Nations Crime Prevention and Criminal Justice Division, United Nations Office on Drugs and Crime (UNODC), World Bank and World Customs Organisation (WCO). http://www1.oecd.org/fatf/Ctry-orgpages/org-pcrev_en.htm.

5. Members who have signed the ESAAMLG memorandum of understanding are: Botswana, Kenya, Malawi, Mauritius, Mozambique, Namibia, Seychelles, South Africa, Swaziland, Tanzania, Uganda. Members who have not signed the ESAAMLG MOU are: Lesotho, Zambia, and Zimbabwe Observers are: Commonwealth Secretariat, FATF Secretariat, the UN Global Programme Against Money Laundering, Interpol, The World Custom Organization (WCO), African Development Bank (ADB), SADC Secretariat, the COMESA Secretariat, EAC Secretariat, East African Development Bank, Eastern and Southern Africa Development Bank, United Kingdom, United States, the IMF and World Bank. http://www.esaamlg.org.

6. Members are: Argentina, Bolivia, Brazil, Chile, Colombia, Ecuador, Paraguay, Perú and Uruguay. Observers are: France, IDB, World Bank, Egmont, Germany, IMF, the United Nations, Mexico, Portugal, Spain, and United States. http://www.gafisud.org/english/index.html.

7. http://www.cfatf.org/eng/recommendations/cfatf/.

8. http://www.cfatf.org/eng/kingdecl/.

9. http://conventions.coe.int/Treaty/en/Treaties/Html/141.htm.

In addition, the establishment of three other FSRBs is either under consideration or actively underway.[10] The three new geographic areas would be for:

- The Middle East and North Africa[11] (MENA);
- Central and Western Africa (GIABA); and
- Eurasia

Membership and other organizational issues need to be resolved, as well as mutual; evaluation procedures, before any of these organizations will be recognized by FATF.

B. Wolfsberg Group of Banks

The Wolfsberg Group is an association of 12 global banks, representing primarily international private banking concerns.[12] The group, which was named after the Château Wolfsberg in north-eastern Switzerland where the group was formed, has established four sets of principles for private banking.

1. Anti-Money Laundering Principles for Private Banking

These principles represent the group's view of appropriate AML guidelines when dealing with the high net worth individuals and the private banking departments of financial institutions. They deal with customer identification, including establishing beneficial ownership for all accounts, and situations involving extra due diligence, such as unusual or suspicious transactions.

---

10. FATF, Annual Report 2003-2004, p. 15, http://www1.oecd.org/fatf/pdf/AR2004_en.PDF.
11. *Id.*; Preparatory meetings involved representations from the following countries: Algeria, Bahrain, Egypt, Jordan, Kuwait, Lebanon, Morocoo, Oman, Qatar, Saudi Arabia, Syria, Tunisia, United Arab Emirates and Yemen.
12. The Wolfsberg Group consists of the following international banks: ABN Amro N.V., Santander Central Hispano S.A., Bank of Tokyo-Mitsubishi Ltd., Barclays Bank, Citigroup, Credit Suisse Group, Deutsche Bank A.G., Goldman Sachs, HSBC, J.P. Morgan Chase, Société Générale, UBS AG. http://www.wolfsberg-principles.com/index.html.

The eleven principles involve:

1. Client acceptance: general guidelines
2. Client acceptance: situations requiring additional diligence/attention
3. Updating client files
4. Practices when identifying unusual or suspicious activities
5. Monitoring
6. Control responsibilities
7. Reporting
8. Education, training and information
9. Record retention requirements
10. Exceptions and deviations
11. Anti-money-laundering organization.[13]

2. Statement on the Suppression of the Financing of Terrorism

The Wolfsberg Statement on the Suppression of the Financing of Terrorism describes the role that financial institutions should play in combating terrorist financing, with a view toward enhancing the contribution financial institutions can make toward this international problem.[14] The statement emphasizes that financial institutions need to assist competent authorities in fighting terrorist financing through prevention, detection and information sharing.

This statement provides that "know your customer" (KYC) policies and procedures should be enhanced with searches of lists of known or suspected terrorists. In addition, banks should play an active role in helping governments by applying extra due diligence whenever they see suspicious or irregular activities. Extra due diligence is especially important when customers are engaged in sectors or activities that have been identified by competent authorities as being used for the financing of terrorism.[15] The statement goes on to endorse the need for enhanced global cooperation and adoption of the FATF *Special Recommendations.*[16]

---

13. http://www.wolfsberg-principles.com/privat-banking.html.
14. http://www.wolfsberg-principles.com/financing-terrorism.html.
15. *Id.*, principles 4 and 5.
16. *Id.*, principle 7.

3. Anti-Money Laundering Principles for Correspondent Banking

The Wolfsberg Group has adopted a set of 14 principles to govern the establishment and maintenance of correspondent banking relationships on a global basis.[17] The principles prohibit international banks from doing business with "shell banks."[18] In addition, the principles use a risk-based approach to correspondent banking that is designed to ascertain the appropriate level of due diligence that a bank should adopt with regard to its correspondent banking clients.

In evaluating prospective risks, the Wolfsberg principles require a correspondent bank to consider the client bank's:

- Domicile;
- Ownership and management structure;
- Business portfolio, and
- Client base.[19]

This risk profile is intended to assist the banks in the application of KYC procedures when providing correspondent banking services. The principles also specify the identification and follow-up of unusual or suspicious transactions or activities.

The principles for correspondent banking cover the following topics:

1. Preamble
2. Correspondent Banking
3. Responsibility and Oversight
4. Risk-Based Due Diligence
5. Due Diligence Standards
6. Enhanced Due Diligence
7. Shell Banks
8. Central Banks and Supra-National Organizations
9. Branches, Subsidiaries and Affiliates

---

17. http://www.wolfsberg-principles.com/corresp-banking.html.
18. *Id.*, principle 7.
19. *Id.*, principle 5.

10. Application to Client Base

11. Updating Client Files

12. Monitoring and Reporting of Suspicious Activities

13. Integration with Anti-Money Laundering Programme

14. Recommendation for an International Registry.[20]

4. Monitoring Screening and Searching

This set of principles identifies issues that should be addressed in order for financial institutions to develop suitable monitoring, screening and searching processes,[21] using a risk-based profile approach. The principles recognize that the risk profile may be different for a financial institution, as a whole, than for its individual units, depending on the business conducted in a particular unit (e.g., retail, private banking, correspondent banking, broker-dealer). The principles further recognize that any process for monitoring, screening or searching is limited to detecting those clients and transactions that have identifiable characteristics that are distinguishable from apparently legitimate behavior.

Under these principles, financial institutions should have appropriate processes in place that provide for the identification of unusual activity and unusual patterns of activity or transactions. Since unusual transactions, patterns or activity need not be suspicious in all cases, financial institutions must have the ability to analyze and determine if particular activity, patterns and transactions are suspicious in nature with regard to, among other things, potential money laundering.[22]

The principles encourage the use of a risk-based approach to monitoring activities.[23] Further, the principles encourage the use of real-time screening or filtering, which involves the examination of the transaction prior to actual execution, whenever there is an embargo or sanction in place.[24]

---

20. *Id.*, Introduction Index.
21. http://www.wolfsberg-principles.com/monitoring.html.
22. *Id.*, principle 3.
23. *Id.*, principle 4.
24. *Id.*, principle 4.1.

Retroactive searches are encouraged based upon the institution's risk-based approach.

The majority of ongoing monitoring for unusual and potentially suspicious activity should be accomplished by transaction monitoring.[25] Risk-based transaction monitoring for potential money laundering requires the development of risk models that identify the potential risks to money laundering and provide a means of ranking the risks in order to compare the risks to completed transactions. An appropriate transaction monitoring process should compare the transaction information against the identified risks (such as geographic location of transaction, the type of products and services being offered and the type of client engaging in the transaction) with the different typologies for money laundering and other illicit activities to determine if transaction is unusual or suspicious.

C. The Commonwealth Secretariat

The Commonwealth Secretariat is a voluntary association of 53 sovereign states that consult and cooperate in the common interest of their peoples on a broad range of topics, including the promotion of international understanding and world peace.[26] All of the member states, except for Mozambique, have experienced direct or indirect British rule or have been linked administratively to another Commonwealth country.

With regard to AML and CFT, the Commonwealth Secretariat provides assistance to countries to implement *The Forty Recommendations* and *Special Recommendations*. It works with national and international organizations and assists governments in the implementation of the FATF recommendations. It is an observer of FATF, CFATF, APG and ESAAMLG.

---

25. *Id.*, principle 5.
26. Commonwealth countries are: Antigua and Barbuda, Australia, Bangladesh, Barbados, Belize, Botswana, Brunei Darussalam, Cameron, Canada, Cyprus, Dominica, Fiji Islands, Ghana, Grenada, Guyana, India, Jamaica, Kenya, Kiribati, Lesotho, Malawi, Malaysia, Maldives, Malta, Mauritius, Mozambique, Namibia, Nauru, New Zealand, Nigeria, Pakistan, Papua New Guinea, Samoa, Seychelles, Sierra Leone, Singapore, Solomon Islands, South Africa, Sri Lanka, St. Kitts and Nevis, St. Lucia, St. Vincent and the Grenadines, Swaziland, The Bahamas, The Gambia, Tonga, Trinidad and Tobago, Tuvalu, Uganda, United Kingdom, United Republic of Tanzania, Vanuatu and Zambia. http://www.thecommonwealth.org/.

The Commonwealth Secretariat has published "A Manual of Best Practices for Combating Money Laundering in the Financial Sector."[27] The manual is for government policy-makers, regulators and financial institutions.

D. Organization of American States–CICAD

The Organization of American States (OAS) is the regional body for security and diplomacy in the Western Hemisphere. All 35 countries of the Americas have ratified the OAS charter.[28] In 1986, the OAS created the Inter-American Drug Abuse Control Commission (known by its Spanish acronym CICAD) to confront the growing problem of drug-trafficking in the hemisphere. By 1994, the Heads of State and Government of the Western Hemisphere endorsed the role of CICAD to include regional AML efforts. CICAD has developed comprehensive regional strategies and model regulations to combat drug trafficking and use, the proliferation of precursor chemicals and arms trafficking, as well as money laundering.[29]

---

27. The manual is only available directly from the Commonwealth Secretariat; it is not currently available online.
28. OAS nations are: Argentina, Bolivia, Brazil, Chile, Colombia, Costa Rica, Cuba, Dominican Republic, Ecuador, El Salvador, Guatemala, Haiti, Honduras, Mexico, Nicaragua, Panama, Paraguay, Peru, United States, Uruguay, Venezuela, Barbados, Trinidad and Tobago, Jamaica, Grenada, Suriname, Dominica, Saint Lucia, Antigua and Barbuda, Saint Vincent and the Grenadines, The Bahamas, St. Kitts and Nevis, Canada, Belize and Guyana. http://www.oas.org/main/english/.
29. http://www.cicad.oas.org/Desarrollo_Juridico/eng/legal-regulations-money.htm.

Chapter V

Legal System Requirements

There are a number of steps that each country needs to take to assure that its anti-money laundering (AML) institutional framework meets international standards. International standard setters recognize that countries have diverse legal systems and, therefore, no country is in a position to adopt specific laws that are identical to those of another country. Specific requirements for combating the financing of terrorism (CFT) are discussed in Chapter IX. Consequently, this chapter discusses eight legal system requirements that concern primarily AML.

These eight requirements are categorized as legal system requirements for purposes of convenient discussion within the context of this Reference Guide. Some of the requirements could, however, just as easily be discussed under different categories. For example, "Supervision and Regulation—Integrity Standards" could be discussed in Chapter VI, "Preventative Measures." Regardless of how they are categorized, each of these eight legal system requirements is necessary for a country's legal framework against money laundering. Under these principles, each country is permitted to adopt laws that are consistent with its own cultural circumstances, legal precepts and constitution, as well as international standards. They are:

- Criminalization of money laundering in accordance with the *Vienna* and *Palermo Conventions*;
- Criminalization of terrorism and terrorist financing;
- Laws for seizure, confiscation and forfeiture and illegal proceeds;
- The types of entities and persons to be covered by AML laws;
- Integrity standards for financial institutions; and
- Consistent laws for implementation of FATF recommendations.
- Cooperation among competent authorities
- Investigations

The legal system requirements for AML, and the other international standards in this Reference Guide, are based upon *The Forty Recommendations on Money Laundering* (*The Forty Recommendations*) issued by the Financial Action Task Force on Money Laundering (FATF); countries may also wish to consult the Methodology for AML/CFT for further explanations of these requirements and how they are evaluated.[1] *The Forty Recommendations* are phrased as recommendations, but are much more than mere suggestions or recommendations. They are mandates for action by every country, not just FATF members, if that country is to be viewed as compliant with international standards. Thus, each FATF recommendation should be considered very carefully by a country in crafting the language of its laws.

A. Criminalization of Money Laundering

The starting place for a country to establish or improve its AML framework is by making money laundering a crime within that country. Criminalization serves three principal objectives. First, it compels compliance with AML preven-

---

1. *The Forty Recommendations*, http://www.fatf-gafi.org/pdf/40Recs-2003_en.pdf are reprinted in Annex IV of this Reference Guide, together with the Glossary and Interpretive Notes. Methodology on AML/CFT, http://www.fatf-gafi.org/pdf/Meth-2004_en.pdf.

tive measures. Second, it ties acts that may appear innocent to outright criminal activity, i.e., the actions of the party processing illegal proceeds are made a criminal act. Third, criminalization establishes a specific basis for greater international cooperation in this critical law enforcement function. Because of the criminal nature and the international aspects of money laundering offenses, competent authorities within a country have recourse to powerful international tools, especially mutual legal assistance mechanisms and, thereby, can more effectively track, enforce, and prosecute international money laundering.

1. Defining the Crime

The criminalization of money laundering should be done in accordance with the *United Nations Convention against Illicit Traffic in Narcotic Drugs and Psychotropic Substances* (1988) (*Vienna Convention*)[2] and the *United Nations Convention against Transnational Organized Crime* (2000) (*Palermo Convention*).[3] The relevant provisions of these conventions are Articles 3 (1) (b) and (c) of the *Vienna Convention* and Article (6) (1) of the *Palermo Convention*. Criminalization of money laundering according to those articles is the first recommendation of FATF.[4] Many countries have signed and ratified these conventions, but this is not sufficient to comply with Recommendation 1. Countries must implement domestically the requirements of the relevant Articles.

Although the *Vienna Convention* is limited in scope to drug trafficking and does not use the term "money laundering," the three categories of offenses specified in the *Vienna Convention* form the basis of the money laundering offense. The categories are:

i. the conversion or transfer of property with the knowledge that such property is derived from a drug-trafficking offense for the purpose of concealing and disguising its illicit origin or assisting any person

---

2. *Vienna Convention*, http://www.incb.org/e/conv/1988/.
3. *Palermo Convention*, http://www.undcp.org/adhoc/palermo/convmain.html.
4. *The Forty Recommendations*, Rec. 1.

involved in a drug-trafficking offense to evade the legal consequences
of his or her actions;[5]

ii. the concealment or disguise of the true nature, source, location, disposition, movement, rights with respect to, or ownership of property
with the knowledge that the property was derived from a drug-trafficking offense;[6]

iii. the acquisition, possession, or use of property with the knowledge that
the property is derived from a drug-trafficking offense.[7]

According to the *Vienna Convention*, the first two categories must be
incorporated into domestic law; the third offense is not mandatory, but
subject to each country's "constitutional principles and basic concepts of its
legal system."[8]

The *Vienna Convention*'s definition of money laundering offenses is the
most widely accepted and is used in all current international legal instruments on this topic.[9] Using the *Vienna Convention*'s definition, the *Palermo
Convention* expands the money laundering definition to:

a. when committed intentionally:

i. the conversion or transfer of property, knowing that such property
is the proceeds of crime, for the purpose of concealing or disguising the illicit origin of the property or of helping any person who
is involved in the commission of the predicate offense to evade the
legal consequences of his or her action;

ii. the concealment or disguise of the true nature, source, location,
disposition, movement or ownership of or rights with respect to
property, knowing that such property is the proceeds of crime;

b. subject to the basic concepts of its legal system:

i. the acquisition, possession or use of property, knowing, at the time
of receipt, that such property is the proceeds of crime;

---

5. *Vienna Convention*, article 3(1)(b)(i).
6. *Id.*, article 3(1)(b)(ii).
7. *Id.*, article (3)(c)(i).
8. *Id.*
9. See also Chapter III, the United Nations, the *Vienna Convention*.

ii. Participation in, association with or conspiracy to commit, attempts to commit and aiding, abetting, facilitating and counseling the commission of any of the offenses established in accordance with this article.[10]

The United Nations (UN) has adopted model legislation using these concepts as set out in the United Nations model legislation on laundering, confiscation and international cooperation in relation to the proceeds of crime (1999)[11] and the United Nations model Money Laundering and Proceeds of Crime Bill (2000).[12]

The Council of Europe adopted elements of the *Vienna Convention* in drafting its Convention on Laundering, Search, Seizure, and Confiscation of the Proceeds from Crime (1990).[13] Other international organizations followed suit: the Organization of American States, with its Model Regulations Concerning Laundering Offenses Connected to Illicit Drug Trafficking and Other Serious Crime (1999) (OAS-Model Regulations),[14] the United Nations Model Legislation on Laundering, Confiscation, and International Cooperation in Relation to the Proceeds of Crime (1999) (UN Model Legislation),[15] and United Nations Model Money Laundering and Proceeds of Crime Bill (2000) (UN Model Crime Bill).[16]

2. Scope of the Predicate Offense

a. Widest Possible Range of Offenses to be Included as Predicate Offenses

A predicate offense for money laundering is the underlying criminal activity that generates proceeds, which when laundered, leads to the offense of money

---

10. *Palermo Convention*, article 6 (1).
11. Article 1.1.1, http://www.imolin.org/imolin/en/ml99eng.html.
12. Section 17, http://www.unodc.org/pdf/lap_money-laundering-proceeds_2000.pdf.
13. Council of Europe, Convention on Laundering, Search, Seizure, and Confiscation of the Proceeds from Crime (1990), article 6(1)., http://conventions.coe.int/treaty/en/Treaties/Html/141.htm.
14. Organization of American States, *Model Regulations Concerning Laundering Offenses Connected to Illicit Drug and other Serious Offenses* (1999), article 2(1), (1) & (3)., http://www.cicad.oas.org/Desarrollo_Juridico/ebg/legal-regulations-money.htm.
15. Article 1.1.1, http://www.imolin.org/imolin/en/ml99eng.html.
16. Section 17, http://www.unodc.org/pdf/lap_money-laundering-proceeds_2000.pdf.

laundering.[17] Designating certain criminal activities as predicate offenses for money laundering is necessary to comply with international standards. The designation of an increasingly wider range of criminal offenses as money laundering predicates has occurred as international standards have developed.

The first international effort against money laundering was contained in the *Vienna Convention*. However, the *Vienna Convention* is an international drug control instrument and the predicate offenses for money laundering relate only to drug trafficking offenses.[18] The *Palermo Convention* imposes an obligation on all State parties to apply the Convention's money laundering offenses to "the widest range of predicate offenses."[19] Recommendation 4 of the 1996 version of the FATF 40 Recommendations specified that predicate offenses should be "based on serious offenses." However, neither the *Palermo Convention* nor the 1996 version of the 40 Recommendations defined in any detail what constituted the "widest range" of predicate offenses or "serious offenses." Thus, the scope of the predicate offense was left to the judgment of each country, subject only to the *Vienna Convention*'s requirement that drug trafficking should be a predicate offense.

The scope of predicate offenses used in the current version of *The Forty Recommendations* is much more widely based.[20] Recommendation 1, which is quite lengthy, begins by repeating the previous language of the *Palermo Convention* and the 1996 version of the 40 Recommendations that countries should apply the crime of money laundering to all serious offenses, with a view to including the widest range of offenses as money laundering predicate offenses.[21] After setting out the various methods of describing predicate offenses (see below) the recommendation states that, (as a minimum), countries must include "a range of offenses within each of the designated categories of offenses."[22] There are 20 designated categories of offenses:

- Participation in an organized criminal group and racketeering;
- Terrorism, including terrorism financing;

17. See *Palermo Convention*, article 2(h); Council of Europe, Convention on Laundering, Search, Seizure and Confiscation of the Proceeds from Crime (1990), article 1(e).
18. *Vienna Convention*, article 3.
19. *Palermo Convention*, article 2(a).
20. *The Forty Recommendations*, Rec. 1.
21 *Id.*
22 *Id.*, Rec. 1.

- Trafficking in human beings and migrant smuggling;
- Sexual exploitation, including sexual exploitation of children;
- Illicit trafficking in narcotic drugs and psychotropic substances;
- Illicit arms trafficking;
- Illicit trafficking in stolen and other goods;
- Corruption and bribery;
- Fraud;
- Counterfeiting currency;
- Counterfeiting and piracy of products;
- Environmental crime;
- Murder, grievous bodily injury;
- Kidnapping, illegal restraint and hostage taking;
- Robbery or theft;
- Smuggling;
- Extortion;
- Forgery;
- Piracy; and
- Insider trading and market manipulation.[23]

There are two further important points concerning the description of predicate offenses. First, the requirement is to include "a range of offenses" within each of the designated categories of offenses. For example, a country would not comply with this recommendation if under "robbery or theft" it designated only the proceeds of "vehicle theft" as a money laundering predicate offense and excluded the proceeds of thefts of other goods. Second, countries are provided with discretion on how to define the offenses in the above list and the nature of any particular elements of those offenses that make them money laundering predicate offenses.

The essential requirement is to criminalize the proceeds from the type of conduct described in the above list. Furthermore, it is not necessary to have an offense in the penal code described in exactly the terms that are used in the above list. For example, some countries do not have a specific offense designated as "fraud," but criminalize fraudulent behavior under some other

---

23. See the definition of "designated category of offences" in the Glossary of *The Forty Recommendations*.

offense, such as "theft." Provided that it is possible to obtain a conviction for laundering the proceeds of fraudulent behavior, the country has discretion in terms of how to describe or categorize the conduct of that behavior.

The one exception to this discretion is terrorist financing. Under the nine *Special Recommendations on Terrorist Financing (Special Recommendations)* FATF specifically requires that the financing of terrorism, terrorist acts and terrorist organizations should be designated as money laundering predicate offenses.[24] It is not acceptable to criminalize these activities solely on the basis of legislation against aiding and abetting, attempting or conspiracy.

b. Methods of Describing Predicate Offenses

FATF describes the types or categories of criminal conduct that should be money laundering predicate offenses, but each individual country has the discretion to determine the specific legal method of criminalization. This can be accomplished by reference to:

- All offenses;
- A threshold linked either to a category of serious offenses or to the penalty of imprisonment applicable to the predicate offense (threshold approach);
- A list of predicate offenses; or
- A combination of these approaches.

Where countries apply a threshold approach, predicate offenses must, at a minimum, cover all offenses that are designated "serious offenses" under national law or offenses punishable by a maximum penalty of more than one year's imprisonment (for countries with minimum penalties, more than six months). Examples of categories of serious offenses, include "indictable offenses" (as opposed to summary offenses), "felonies" (as opposed to misdemeanors), and "crimes" (as opposed to delits). It should be noted that

---

24. *Special Recommendations*, Spec. Rec. II. http://www.fatf-gafi.org/pdf/SRecTF_en.pdf. The crime of terrorist financing is defined in article 2(1) of the United Nations International Convention for the Suppression of the Financing of Terrorism (1999).

countries using the threshold approach for designated predicate offenses are subject to two additional minimum requirements, which are not alternatives:

- The threshold must cover all 20 designated categories of offenses (see above); and
- All serious offenses or all offenses with a maximum period of imprisonment exceeding one year (six months for countries applying minimum thresholds)

This means that any offense that is not on the designated categories of offenses list, but that is defined by the country as a "serious offense" or punished by a maximum prison term exceeding one year would also have to be designated as a money laundering predicate offense by that country.

3. Cross Border Considerations for International Cooperation

As noted above, the FATF recommendations establish a minimum category of offenses that must be predicate offenses for money laundering, but encourage countries to go beyond this.[25] How far beyond the minimum and the method of criminalization is left to the discretion of each country. The extent to which a country does so, however, has implications for that country's ability to cooperate internationally and exchange information with other national authorities.

Recommendation 1 provides that predicate offenses should extend to conduct that occurred in another country, which constitutes an offense in that country, and which would have constituted an offense if it had occurred domestically.[26] This is the so-called "dual criminality" test, under which the conduct committed in the other country must be a predicate offense both in the other country and domestically. This is, however, the minimum standard. This recommendation also states that countries may provide that the only condition for prosecuting money laundering is that the conduct committed in the other country would have constituted a predicate offense had it occurred

---

25. *The Forty Recommendations*, Rec. 1.
26. *Id.*

domestically.[27] This approach would allow for prosecution where the proceeds were generated by conduct that was not a predicate offense in the country where the conduct was committed, but was an offense in the country where the proceeds were laundered.

While FATF does not necessarily encourage countries to adopt this latter approach, FATF does encourage countries to provide mutual legal assistance even if dual criminality is absent.[28]

FATF also provides that where dual criminality is required for mutual legal assistance or extradition, that requirement should be regarded as satisfied regardless of whether the offenses are described under the same category in the different countries, provided both countries criminalize the underlying conduct. For example, if country A requests assistance from country B with respect to laundering the proceeds of fraud and country B has no specific offense of fraud, country B should provide assistance if it criminalizes fraudulent conduct under some other offense (e.g., theft).

4. State of Mind—Knowledge and Intent

According to the *Vienna Convention*, the perpetrator's state of mind—his or her intent or purpose in committing the money laundering offense—means "knowing" that the proceeds are the product of the predicate offense.[29] Countries may extend the scope of liability, however, to "negligent money laundering," where the perpetrator should have known that the property was, or was obtained with, the proceeds of a criminal act.

Countries have various options in determining the "state of mind" connected with a money-laundering offense.[30] The legislature of a country may decide that actual knowledge about the illicit origin of property, or that mere suspicion about that illicit origin, constitutes the requisite state of mind or mental element for obtaining convictions for money laundering. The legislature may also accept a "should have known" standard of culpability. This latter definition constitutes a form of negligent money

---

27. *The Forty Recommendations*, Rec. 1.
28. *Id.*, Rec. 37.
29. *Vienna Convention*, article 3(b)(i).
30. UN Model Legislation, http://www.imolin.org/imolin/en/ml99eng.html.

laundering.[31] In addition to this general intent requirement, the law might provide for a specific intent to "conceal or disguise the illicit origin" of the property, or the intent to help another "evade the legal consequences of his or her actions."[32]

According to the UN Model Legislation, actual knowledge, or "having reason to believe," that property is derived from criminal acts, constitutes the so-called mental element of money laundering.[33] The Model Bill envisages, however, that specific intent may apply to certain money-laundering offenses, such as concealing or disguising the origin, nature, location, disposition, movement, or ownership of the property. Also, certain money-laundering offenses could require proving the specific intent of an individual to assist another, for example, in evading the legal consequences of his or her actions.[34]

A broad definition of the "state of mind" was adopted in the OAS Model Regulations.[35] These model regulations address three different states of mind: (i) the accused had knowledge that the property constitutes proceeds of a criminal activity as defined in the convention; (ii) the accused should have known that the property was obtained with the proceeds of criminal activity; and (iii) the accused was intentionally ignorant of the nature of the proceeds.[36] Under this third category of state of mind, the accused neither "did not know" nor "should have known" the source of the proceeds, but nevertheless suspected its criminal provenance and chose not to conduct further investigation to verify or dispel this suspicion. In that sense, the accused intended to remain ignorant of the nature of proceeds or was "willfully blind" when he or she "could have known" of the criminal offense by investigation or inquiry. In terms of culpability, this state of mind standard falls between the negligence and specific knowledge standard of intent. The OAS Model Regulations further provide that these three culpable states of mind can be inferred from objective and factual circumstances.[37]

---

31. *Id.*, Article 1.1.1.
32. *Id.*, at subparagraph (a).
33. UN Model Crime Bill, at Section 17(a).
34. *Id.*, at subparagraph (b).
35. OAS Model Regulations.
36. OAS Model Regulations, Article 2.
37. *Id.*, at subparagraph (5).

Finally, it may be very difficult to prove the state of mind of a person engaging in an activity that otherwise appears to be ordinary on its face. Thus, the *Vienna Convention*, the *Palermo Convention*, the *Forty Recommendations* and many of the other legal instruments provide that the law should permit the inference of the required state of mind from objective factual circumstances.[38] If the objective factual circumstances fit the situation, the state of mind requirement is satisfied.

5. Corporate Liability

Money laundering often takes place through corporate entities. The concept of corporate criminal liability, however, varies greatly among different countries. Some countries, mainly those with a common law tradition, subject corporations to criminal liability laws. In countries with a tradition of civil law, corporations may not be covered by criminal laws. Thus, consideration should be given to modifying such a country's laws to provide for corporate criminal liability where permissible.

FATF recommends that corporations, not only their employees, be subject to criminal liability whenever possible under the general principles of a country's legal system.[39] Significant civil or administrative sanctions could be a sufficient substitute in cases where the legal or constitutional framework does not subject corporations to criminal liability.

The UN Model Legislation does not provide for criminal liability for corporations. It does provide, however, for applying other sanctions to corporate entities,[40] and for applying them whenever money laundering offenses are committed on behalf of, or for the benefit of, a corporation by one of the corporation's agents or representatives. The sanctions envisioned by the UN Model Legislation include fines, bans on carrying out certain business activities, closure or winding up, and the publication of rulings.[41] The UN Model Legislation does not categorize these as criminal sanctions and it specifically

---

38. *Vienna Convention*, article 3(3); *Palermo Convention*, article 6(2)(f); *The Forty Recommendations*, Rec. 2; Council of Europe Convention on Laundering, Search, Seizure and Confiscation of the Proceeds from Crime (1990), article 6(2)(c).
39. *The Forty Recommendations*, Rec. 2; OAS-Model Regulations, article 15.
40. UN Model Legislation, Article 4.2.3.
41. *Id.*

provides that these should not derogate from the personal liability of the agent or the employee of the corporation for the acts.[42]

Criminal liability is extended to corporate entities on the same basis as natural persons in the OAS Model Regulations. In fact, one provision specifically defines a "person" for the purposes of the regulation as meaning "any entity, natural or juridical, including among others a corporation, partnership, trust or estate, joint stock company, association, syndicate, joint venture, or other unincorporated organization or group, capable of acquiring rights or entering into obligations."[43] In the UN Model Crime Bill, the term, "person" is defined to include both natural and legal persons.[44] While this language defines "person" more narrowly that that of the OAS, it still acknowledges the principle of criminal liability for corporations.

6. Predicate Offense Perpetrator Liability for Laundering

An important question is whether money laundering liability extends to the person who committed the predicate offense, as well as to the person who has laundered the ill-gotten proceeds. Some countries do not hold the perpetrator of the predicate offense liable for laundering the proceeds of his or her criminal actions, if he or she is not involved in the laundering activity. The basic rationale for this approach is that punishing the perpetrator for evading the legal consequences of his or her criminal activity could amount to double jeopardy, i.e., multiple punishments for a single criminal offense.

Other countries hold the perpetrator of the predicate offense liable for laundering the ill-gotten proceeds on the basis that the conduct and the harm of evasion are distinct from the predicate offense. There are also practical reasons for this approach. Exempting perpetrators of predicate offenses from money-laundering liability could severely penalize third parties for their conduct in handling criminal proceeds, while perpetrators remain immune from liability. This could occur when the predicate offense has been committed extraterritorially, placing it beyond the jurisdiction of the state prosecuting third parties for their laundering activities.

---

42. *Id.*
43. OAS Model Regulations, Article 1(6).
44. Section 2(l).

Overall, the general international standard in this area provides for a broad laundering offense that permits the perpetrator to be liable for laundering the proceeds of his or her own criminal activities regardless of active participation in laundering activities.[45] This standard, however, also permits national variations to be employed in this regard.

7. Lawyers' Fees

Lawyers are now included in the list of designated non-financial businesses and professions that must be considered as covered by AML/CFT regimes.[46] This deserves special attention in the drafting of predicate offenses.

Predicate offenses for money laundering can be defined in legislation so broadly that, in their totality, they include any transaction involving the use of the proceeds derived from a criminal activity. Given such a broad interpretive construction, these laws could have the effect of criminalizing the mere receipt of a fee by a lawyer for the purpose of providing criminal defense. This poses unique problems of due process.

Considering that the right of the accused to adequate defense in criminal trials is now established as one aspect of the right to a fair trial, countries should be careful in drafting the scope of the money laundering offenses.

Countries may also wish to consider an effective provision excluding lawyers from such potential criminal liability for merely rendering their services, provided that the services were limited to, or were rendered only in connection with, defending the accused at trial.[47]

Notwithstanding the right of an accused to a fair trial, lawyers also have a duty regarding the integrity of the financial system and integrity of their profession. If a lawyer has knowledge that his or her fees were derived from a criminal activity, the attorney should observe these integrity standards and

---

45. United Nations Convention against Transnational Organized Crime (2000), article 6(2)(f); Council of Europe, Convention on Laundering, Search, Seizure and Confiscation of the Proceeds from Crime (1990), article 6(2)(b), UN Model Legislation, Article 1.1.1; UN Model Crime Bill, Sec. 17; OAS-Model Regulations, Article 2.
46. See this Chapter, Designated Non-Financial Businesses and Professions.
47. Council of Europe, Convention on Laundering, Search, Seizure and Confiscation of the Proceeds from Crime: Explanatory Report, para. 33. The model laws and regulations in this area are silent on this point. See UN Model Legislation; UN Model Crime Bill; OAS Model Regulations.

not blindly accept laundered money, especially if he or she is also rendering other services to the client besides defending the accused in a trial.

B. Criminalization of Terrorism and the Financing of Terrorism

Those who finance terrorism, like other criminals, may use the national and international financial systems to hide the funds they need to support their activities, even if these funds have legitimate sources. Criminalizing all aspects of terrorism and terrorist financing is a practical way to undermine the capacity of terrorist organizations by preventing their funds from entering the financial system. In addition, a country needs legislation to help detect when terrorist funds are within its borders so that the funds can be confiscated and forfeited. This further helps thwart terrorist efforts.

In its nine *Special Recommendations on Terrorist Financing* (*Special Recommendations*), FATF urges countries to criminalize the financing of terrorism, terrorist acts and terrorist organizations and to designate these as predicate offenses of money laundering.[48]

As noted above in "Scope of the Predicate Offense," FATF provides that one of the designated categories of offenses is terrorism, including terrorist financing.[49] Thus, taking *The Forty Recommendations* and the *Special Recommendations* together, terrorism, terrorist acts, terrorist organizations and terrorist financing each should be deemed a predicate offense for a country's money laundering laws.

C. Seizure, Confiscation, and Forfeiture

The current approaches to international crime and terrorist financing are designed to make criminal activities unprofitable and keep terrorists from accessing funds. These goals cannot be achieved without effective confiscation

---

48. *Special Recommendations*, Spec. Rec. II.
49. *The Forty Recommendations*, Glossary, Designated categories of offenses; and *Special Recommendations*, Spec. Rec. II.

laws, whereby authorities may permanently deprive criminals and terrorists of their ill-gotten proceeds.[50]

1. Confiscation of Direct and Indirect Proceeds of Crime

FATF encourages countries to adopt laws permitting a broad interpretation of the confiscation of proceeds of crime, in accordance with the *Vienna* and *Palermo Conventions*.[51] In the past under most legal systems, confiscation has largely been confined to the instruments used in the commission of the crime, such as the murder weapon, or the subjects of the crime, such as drugs in drug trafficking, as opposed to the proceeds derived from the crime. The *Vienna Convention* and the *Palermo Convention* define the term, "proceeds of crime," as "any property derived from or obtained, directly or indirectly, through the commission of an offense."[52] Many countries have now adopted this broader understanding of forfeitable property in response to the profits generated by certain criminal activities, particularly in light of the fungibility of these profits and the ease with which funds can be moved into, and out of, the international financial system.

FATF encourages countries to adopt laws that permit the confiscation of the laundered property, the proceeds of laundering and predicate offenses, the instrumentalities used, or intended for use in, laundering, and property of corresponding value.[53] This broad definition is useful since criminals are likely to convert property to some other form if only specifically-named property is subject to confiscation prior to the issuance of the confiscation order or its enforcement. Criminals are also likely to transfer the property beyond the reach of authorities or to commingle it with property legitimately derived. In order to address these various situations, which under a traditional understanding of confiscation could render confiscation orders useless, governments should consider adopting the "value confiscation" approach, which gives

---

50. *Vienna Convention*, article 1(f), Council of Europe Convention, Convention on Laundering, Search, Seizure and Confiscation of the Proceeds from Crime (1990), article 1(d).
51. *The Forty Recommendations*, Rec.3.
52. *Vienna Convention*, article 1(p); *Palermo Convention*, article 2(e).
53. *The Forty Recommendations*, Rec. 3.

the government the power to confiscate any property of the perpetrator of a value equivalent to the value of the ill-gotten proceeds.[54]

2. Enforcement of Confiscated Property

The effective enforcement of confiscation orders requires that the relevant authorities possess the powers necessary to identify, trace and evaluate property that could be subject to confiscation.[55] This in turn requires that such authorities have the power to require disclosure or to seize commercial and financial records.[56] FATF specifically recommends that banking secrecy laws, or other privacy protection statutes, for example, should be designed so that they do not create barriers to such disclosure or seizure for these purposes.[57]

Today, funds can now be transferred out of a national jurisdiction with a keystroke on a computer. Thus, authorities should also be granted the power to take preventive measures. For example, they should be able to freeze and seize assets that might be subject to confiscation. This power is a necessary condition for an effective law enforcement framework for preventing the laundering of money.[58] (See Chapter IX, Freezing and Confiscating Terrorist Assets for a detailed discussion of freezing, seizing and confiscating assets. That discussion is equally applicable to AML-related assets.)

3. Third Party Liability

While international law on confiscation does not preclude the confiscation of assets in the hands of third parties, FATF and various international agreements qualify the permissibility of such action by requiring countries to take

---

54. *Vienna Convention*, article 5; Council of Europe, Convention on Laundering, Search, Seizure and Confiscation of the Proceeds from Crime (1990), article 2.
55. *The Forty Recommendations*, Rec. 3.
56. *Vienna Convention*, article 5(3); Council of Europe, Convention on Laundering, Search, Seizure and Confiscation of the Proceeds from Crime (1990), article 4(1).
57. *The Forty Recommendations*, Rec. 4, *The Vienna Convention*, article 5(3); Council of Europe, Convention on Laundering, Search, Seizure and Confiscation of the Proceeds from Crime (1990), article 4(1).
58. *The Forty Recommendations*, Rec. 3, *Vienna Convention*, article 5(2); Council of Europe, Convention on Laundering, Search, Seizure and Confiscation of the Proceeds from Crime (1990), article 3.

measures to protect the rights of *bona fide* third parties.[59] Third parties that enter into an agreement, and either know or should know that the contract would prejudice the capacity of the state to enforce its confiscation are not *bona fide*. A country's laws should address specially the issue of validity of such agreements under such circumstances.[60]

According to the OAS Model Regulations, the relevant authority is required to give notification of the proceedings.[61] The notification must allow potential third parties to make claims to the property subject to confiscation. According to the model regulations, the court or other competent authority should return the property to the claimant, if it is satisfied that the claimant: (1) has proper legal title to the property; (2) did not participate in, collude with, or was not in any other way involved in the predicate offense; (3) did not have knowledge of the use of property for illegal purposes and did not consent freely to this use; (4) did not acquire rights that were specifically designed to evade the confiscation proceedings; and (5) did whatever could reasonably be expected to prevent the illegal use of the property.

In addressing the question of *bona fide* third parties, the UN Model Crime Bill provides that the court can deny the third-party claim to the property in cases where the court finds that the person (1) was involved in the commission of the predicate offense; (2) acquired the property for insufficient consideration; or (3) acquired the property knowing its illicit origin.[62] By comparison, the UN Model Legislation uses a more strict standard, which does not require involvement in the predicate offense as a basis for denying the claim to the property.[63]

4. International Aspects of Confiscation

Establishing an effective confiscation regime for domestic purposes is only the first step toward eliminating the profitability at the heart of so many interna-

---

59. *The Forty Recommendations*, Rec. 3; The Vienna Convention, article 5(8); Council of Europe, Convention on Laundering, Search, Seizure and Confiscation of the Proceeds from Crime (1990), article 5; The *Palermo Convention*, article 12(8).
60. *The Forty Recommendations*, Rec. 3.
61. OAS Model Regulations, Article 6.4.
62. UN Model Crime Bill, Section 36. This is a model law designed for common law jurisdictions.
63. See UN Model Legislation , Article 4.2.9 This is a model Law designed for civil law jurisdictions.

tional money laundering activities. The second necessary step, and one vital to the overall success of this effort, is creating cooperative mechanisms for enforcing cross-border confiscation orders. Countries may enable the relevant authorities to implement confiscation requests from other countries, employing such measures as tracing, identification, freezing, and seizure.

As an incentive for international cooperation, countries may consider establishing asset-sharing arrangements. The general principle in the disposal of confiscated assets is that such disposal be subject to the domestic laws and regulations of the country that executed the confiscation order.[64] The international legal instruments, however, encourage countries to enter into mutual arrangements that provide for the sharing of the confiscated property among all the countries that cooperated in the investigation and confiscation process.[65] The legal instruments also encourage allocating some of the confiscated funds to the intergovernmental agencies that are dedicated to the fight against crime.[66]

D. Types of Covered Entities and Persons

FATF recommendations impose numerous requirements upon financial institutions and non-financial businesses and professions to prevent money laundering and terrorist financing.[67] Moreover, the recommendations provide exceptions in applying these preventative measures. Thus, a crucial decision for a country is to determine which entities and persons should be covered by which requirements. In this regard, all of the preventative measures apply to "financial institutions,"[68] while certain of the preventive measures apply to certain "designated non-financial businesses and professions" on a more limited basis.

---

64. *Vienna Convention*, article 5(a); Council of Europe, Convention on Laundering, Search, Seizure and Confiscation of the Proceeds from Crime (1990), article 15; The Palermo Convention, article 14(1).
65. *Vienna Convention*, article 5(b); The *Palermo Convention*, article 14(3)(b); OAS-Model Regulations, article 7(d).
66. *Vienna Convention*, article 5(b)(i); The *Palermo Convention* (2000), article 14(3)(a); OAS Model Regulations, article 7(e).
67. *The Forty Recommendations*, see generally Recs. 5–25.
68. *Id.*

1. Financial Institutions

It is axiomatic that money launderers and those who finance terrorism must have access to financial institutions. These institutions provide the means for such individuals to transfer funds among other financial institutions, both domestically and internationally. These institutions also provide the means to convert currencies and pay for the assets used in the money laundering and terrorist financing process. The types of financial institutions and their capabilities vary greatly among different countries. Under FATF recommendations, the term, "financial institutions," is defined as "any person or entity who conducts as a business one or more of the following activities, or operations on behalf of a customer":

- Acceptance of deposits and other repayable funds from the public (including private banking);
- Lending (including consumer credit; mortgage credit; factoring, with or without
  recourse; and finance of commercial transactions (including forfeiting);
- Financial leasing (but excluding financial leasing for consumer products);
- The transfer of money or value[69] (including formal and informal sectors, such as alternative remittance activity);
- Issuing and managing means of payment (e.g. credit and debit cards, cheques, traveler's cheques, money orders and banker's drafts, electronic money);
- Financial guarantees and commitments;
- Trading in:
  a. money market instruments (cheques, bills, CDs derivatives, etc);
  b. foreign exchange;
  c. exchange, interest rate and index instruments;
  d. transferable securities;
  e. commodity futures trading;
- Participation in securities issues and the provision of financial services related to such issues;
- Individual and collective portfolio management;

---

69. See also interpretive note to *The Special Recommendations*, Spec. Rec. VI and VII.

- Safekeeping and administration of cash or liquid securities on behalf of other persons;
- Otherwise investing, administering or managing funds or money on behalf of other persons;
- Underwriting and placement of life insurance and other investment related insurance (this applies to both insurance undertakings and intermediaries, such as agents and brokers); and
- Money and currency changing.[70]

This is a functional definition rather than an institutional or designation one. The test is whether an entity or individual carries out any of the above functions or activities for customers, not what the business is called or how the business is designated. For example, any person or business that accepts deposits and/or makes loans to the public is covered, regardless of whether the person or business is called a bank. In many cases, law or regulation will limit the conduct of such activities to licensed financial institutions and, in those situations, countries that apply AML/CFT controls to licensed financial institutions would satisfy the standard. On the other hand, if such activities can be carried out legally by unlicensed entities, the AML/CFT controls should apply to these entities as well.

There are two qualifications to this requirement. First, if a financial activity, described above, is carried out occasionally or on a very limited basis, such that there is little money laundering risk, a country may decide not to apply all, or indeed any, money laundering requirements.[71] A possible example of such a case might be a hotel, which offers very limited foreign currency exchange facilities to its guests on an occasional basis or a travel agency which can wire money to clients overseas in emergencies.

A second qualification is that in "strictly limited and justified circumstances" and when there is "a proven low risk of money laundering" a country may decide not to apply some or all of *The Forty Recommendations* to the above list of financial activities.[72] The FATF does not offer clear guidance as to what those circumstances might be. However, countries are encouraged to adopt a risk-based approach, which may lead to increased measures

---

70. *The Forty Recommendations*, Glossary, Financial Institutions.
71. *Id.*
72. *Id.*

in high-risk areas, or in strictly limited and justified circumstances, may lead to lesser measures based on a proven low AML/CFT risk. Financial activity should only be excluded or subject to limited controls generally after a proper study has established that the money laundering risk is low. The starting presumption should be that all of the above financial activities should be subject to all of the AML requirements.

2. Designated Non-Financial Business and Professions

The FATF recommendations were revised in 2003 to include certain designated non-financial businesses and professions within coverage of *The Forty Recommendations* for the first time. The requirements applicable to these entities and professionals are more limited and apply in more limited circumstances than financial institutions. Details of what requirements apply to which non-financial businesses and professions are described in Chapter VI, but countries are required to bring the following entities and persons within coverage of certain AML/CFT provisions:

- Casinos (which also includes internet casinos);
- Real estate agents;
- Dealers in precious metals;
- Dealers in precious stones;
- Lawyers, notaries, other independent legal professionals, and accountants which refers to sole practitioners, partners or employed professionals within professional firms. It is not meant to refer to 'internal' professionals that are employees of other types of businesses, nor to professionals working for government agencies, who may already be subject to measures that would combat money laundering;
- Trust and company service providers, which refers to all persons or businesses that are not covered elsewhere under these recommendations, and which as a business, provide any of the following services to third parties:

a. Acting as a formation agent of legal persons;

b. Acting as (or arranging for another person to act as) a director or secretary of a company, a partner of a partnership, or a similar position in relation to other legal persons;

c. Providing a registered office; business address or accommodation, correspondence or administrative address for a company, a partnership or any other legal person or arrangement;

d. Acting as (or arranging for another person to act as) a trustee of an express trust; or

e. Acting as (or arranging for another person to act as) a nominee shareholder for another person.[73]

3. Other Potential Covered Entities and Persons

Finally, in a separate, and all-embracing recommendation, FATF states that countries should consider applying the recommendations to businesses and professions, other than those listed above, that pose a money laundering or terrorist financing risk.[74] It is a matter for each country to consider which businesses or professions would be included and to determine what is the appropriate response to the risk. Examples could include dealers in high value and luxury goods (antiques, automobiles, boats, etc.), pawnshops, auction houses and investment advisers. There is no requirement to cover any or all of this list of any other but there is a requirement to consider the risks and appropriate response to such risks.

E. Supervision and Regulation—Integrity Standards

Money cannot be laundered, nor terrorism financed, without the involvement of financial institutions, certain business entities and certain persons. When criminals control financial institutions or hold senior management positions in financial institutions, countries find it exceedingly difficult to prevent and

---

73. *The Forty Recommendations*, Glossary, Designated Non-Financial Businesses and Professions.
74. *Id.*, Rec. 20.

detect money laundering. Similarly, when certain persons are involved with money laundering actions, countries find prevention and detection more difficult. Integrity and licensing requirements help prevent such entities and individuals from participation in money laundering and terrorist financing efforts.

1. Financial Institutions

a. Core Principles Institutions

These institutions, i.e., banks, insurance companies, securities industry, are subject to comprehensive supervisory regimes as set out in the standards issued by the Basle Committee on Banking Supervision, International Association of Insurance Supervisors, and International Organization of Securities Commissions, respectively.[75] The provisions include requirements for:

- Licensing and authorization to engage in business;
- Evaluation (fit and proper determination) of directors and senior managers, with regard to integrity, expertise and experience;
- Prohibitions against participation by directors and managers with criminal records or adverse regulatory findings; and
- Prohibitions against ownership or control by those with criminal records.

These requirements should apply both for prudential purposes and for purposes of AML/CFT controls, and supervision includes the authority to compel the production of records and information for determining compliance.[76]

b. Other Financial Institutions

These institutions are not normally subject to the same stringent requirements as Core Principles Institutions (largely because the same prudential issues do not arise). For example, directors and senior management are not evaluated

---

75. See Chapter IV.
76. *The Forty Recommendations*, Rec. 23.

as to their "fit and proper" standing in relation to their integrity, expertise and experience. For AML/CFT purposes, the minimum requirements for these other financial institutions are as follows:

- Such institutions should be licensed or registered;
- They should be subject to supervision or oversight for AML purposes according to the risk of money laundering and terrorist financing in the that sector.[77]

This imposes a licensing or registration requirement with respect to all of those "other financial institutions," but allows each country discretion over the extent to which there should be oversight of their implementation of AML/CFT measures. In some cases, the oversight could be limited to law enforcement action against institutions that do not comply with applicable regulations, but no proactive inspection or oversight of compliance.

However, for money transfer and exchange businesses, the FATF requires that, as well, as licensing or registration, there should be "effective systems" for monitoring and ensuring compliance.[78] What constitutes an effective system in practice is not described further in the recommendation, but the implication is that the requirement goes beyond law enforcement action against non-compliant institutions.

2. Designated Non-Financial Businesses and Professions

Non-financial businesses and professions fall into two categories: casinos and all other non-financial businesses and professions (other NFBPs).

For casinos, there are strict requirements involving:

- Licensing;
- Measures to prevent casinos being owned, controlled or operated by criminals; and
- Supervision of their compliance with AML/CFT requirements.

---

77. *Id.*
78. *Id.*

For all other NFBPs, the requirement is that effective systems for monitoring and ensuring compliance on a risk-sensitive basis are in place. The monitoring may be carried out either by a government agency or a self-regulatory organization. Unlike other financial institutions (see above), there is no licensing or registration system.

F. Laws Consistent with Implementation of FATF Recommendations

A crucial aspect of any legal system is to have laws and regulations that are internally consistent and work in coordination with each other. Thus, it is important that one law not conflict with another law, unless there is a basis in policy for making an exception, and that the two laws can be read as working together without contradiction.

One area where there is potential for conflict is with secrecy laws. Often, countries have general laws protecting the privacy of financial information from disclosure. Such laws may conflict with the specific requirement, for example, that financial institutions report suspicious transactions.[79]

In order to effectuate AML/CFT requirements, FATF provides that each country should make sure that its financial institution secrecy laws do not inhibit implementation of the FATF recommendations.[80]

G. Cooperation Among Competent Authorities

Each country needs to provide that there are effective mechanisms in place to enable its policy makers, FIU, law enforcement authorities (including customs where appropriate), financial institution supervisors and other relevant authorities to cooperate with each other.[81] If appropriate under the country's laws and enforcement system, this requirement extends to coordinating the development and implementation of policies and activities to combat money laundering and terrorist financing.

---

79. See *The Forty Recommendations*, Rec. 13.
80. *Id.*, Rec. 4.
81. *Id.*, Rec. 31.

Ideally, this recommendations means that a country's laws and mechanisms should be viewed as facilitating cooperation among the various competent authorities, as well as facilitating coordination among such authorities, involved in AML and CFT efforts. Most importantly, a country's laws and mechanisms should not be viewed as prohibiting or restricting such cooperative efforts.

H. Investigations

Each country should assure that designated law enforcement authorities are responsible for money laundering and terrorist financing investigations.[82] In the effort to utilize investigations to the fullest extent in the fight against money laundering and terrorist financing, FATF encourages countries to authorize, support and develop special investigative techniques and mechanisms, such as undercover operations, specialized asset investigations and cooperative investigations with other countries.[83]

Investigative endeavors, as with all competent authorities involved in the fight against money laundering and terrorist financing in a country, should receive adequate financial, staffing and technical resources, including staff that meet high integrity standards.[84]

Finally, the effectiveness of a country's AML/CFT regime depends upon useful information. Thus, each country should maintain statistics on the effectiveness and efficiency of its investigations and other aspects of its regime.[85]

---

82. *Id.*, Rec. 27.
83. *Id.*
84. *Id.*, Rec. 30.
85. *Id.*, Rec. 32.

Chapter VI

Preventive Measures

Money launderers and those who finance terrorism use various types of financial institutions and certain non-financial businesses and professionals to help in their criminal activities. In fact, access to such entities and persons is crucial if criminals are to succeed because financial institutions, and other, provide the means to transfer funds to other financial institutions, both domestically and internationally; to exchange currencies, and to convert proceeds of crime into different financial instruments and other assets.

In *The Forty Recommendations on Money Laundering* (*The Forty Recommendations*),[1] the Financial Action Task Force on Money Laundering (FATF) has established a number of preventative measures that a country should adopt in the anti-money laundering (AML) area. These preventative

---

1. http://www.fatf-gafi.org/pdf/40Recs-2003_en.pdf.

measures are applicable to all financial institutions and, on a more limited basis, to designated non-financial businesses and professions. Furthermore, these preventative AML measures are equally applicable in combating the financing of terrorism (CFT) under FATF's *Special Recommendations on Terrorist Financing* (*Special Recommendations*).[2]

Like all of *The Forty Recommendations*, the preventative measures, generally recommendations 5–25, are not recommendations, but mandates for action by a country if that country wishes to be viewed as compliant with international standards in AML and CFT. These mandates for action are also flexible, however, to permit a country to adopt requirements that are consistent with its own economic circumstances, legal system and constitution. Countries may also wish to examine the Methodology for Assessing Compliance with *The Forty* and *Special Recommendations* for further explanation of the requirements.[3]

A. Customer Identification and Due Diligence

In accordance with international standards set by the Basel Committee on Banking Supervision (Basel Committee)[4] and by FATF,[5] countries must assure that their financial institutions have appropriate customer identification and due diligence procedures in place. These procedures apply to a financial institution's individual and corporate customers alike. These rules or procedures ensure that financial institutions maintain adequate knowledge about their customers and their customers' financial activities. Customer

---

2. http://www.fatf-gafi.org/pdf/SRecTF_en.pdf.
3. http://www.fatf-gafi.org/pdf/Meth-2004_en.PDF.
4. Basel Core Principles for Effective Banking Supervision and Customer Due Diligence for Banks, principle 15, at http://www.bis.org/publ/bcbs30.pdf.
5. *The Forty Recommendations*, Rec. 5, http://www.fatf-gafi.org/pdf/40Recs-2003_en.pdf. *The Forty Recommendations* are reprinted in Annex IV and the *Special Recommendations* in Annex V of this Reference Guide.

identification requirements are also known as "know your customer" (KYC) rules,[6] a term employed by the Basel Committee.[7]

KYC policies not only help financial institutions detect, deter, and prevent money laundering and terrorist financing, they also confer tangible benefits on the financial institution, its law-abiding customers, and the financial system as a whole. In particular, KYC practices:

- Promote good business, governance, and risk management among financial institutions;
- Help maintain the integrity of the financial system and enable development efforts in emerging markets;
- Reduce the incidence of fraud and other financial crime; and
- Protect the reputation of the financial organization against the detrimental effect of association with criminals.[8]

1. Scope of Customer Identification and Due Diligence

The customer identification and due diligence procedures employed by a financial institution must also apply to its branches and majority-owned subsidiaries—both domestically and internationally—provided local law is not in conflict.[9] Where local law prohibits implementation, relevant authorities in the home country should be informed that these procedures cannot be applied by their host country institutions. Host country supervisors should make efforts to change such laws and regulations in the local jurisdiction.[10] Absent any legal restrictions in the host country, when two different levels of

---

6. Basel Committee, Core Principle for Effective Banking Supervision, Principle 15 states, "Banking supervisors must determine that banks have adequate policies, practices and procedures in place, including strict "know-your-customer" rules, that promote high ethical and professional standards in the financial sector and prevent the bank being used, intentionally or unintentionally, by criminal elements."
7. Basel Customer Due Diligence for Banks states: "Supervisors around the world are increasingly recognizing the importance of ensuring that their banks have adequate controls and procedures in place so that they know the customers with whom they are dealing. Adequate due diligence on new and existing customers is a key part of these controls." http://www.bis.org/publ/bcbs85.pdf.
8. Basel Customer Due Diligence for Banks (provision 9).
9. *The Forty Recommendations*, Rec. 22.
10. *Id.*

regulatory standards exist between the home and host country, the higher or more comprehensive, of the two standards should be applied.[11]

2. Who Is a Customer

The Basel Committee defines a customer as:

- A person or entity who maintains an account with a financial institution or on whose behalf an account is maintained (i.e., beneficial owners);
- Beneficiaries of transactions conducted by professional intermediaries(e.g., agents, accountants, lawyers); and
- A person or entity connected with a financial transaction who can pose a significant risk to the bank.[12]

A crucial aspect of customer identification is establishing whether the customer is acting on his, her or its own behalf, or whether there is a beneficial owner of the account that may not be identified in the documents maintained by the financial institution. If there is any reason to suspect that the customer is acting on behalf of another person or entity, appropriate due diligence measures should be instituted.

Beneficial ownership is also difficult in the case of legal entities or corporations where there is tiered ownership involved. Tiered ownership involves one corporation owning or controlling one or more other corporate entities. In some cases, there can be numerous corporations each, in turn, owned by another corporation and, ultimately, owned or controlled by a parent corporation. When corporations or legal entities are involved, appropriate due diligence measures should be employed to determine the identity of the actual parent or controlling entity.

---

11. Basel Customer Due Diligence for Banks (provision 66).
12. *Id.* (provision 21).

3. Customer Acceptance and Identification Procedures

Financial institutions should develop and enforce clear customer acceptance and identification procedures for clients and those acting on behalf of clients.[13] These procedures should include the development of high-risk-customer profiles. Such profiles would include standard risk indicators such as personal background, country of origin, possession of a public or high-profile position, linked accounts, and type and nature of business activity.[14] When crafting customer acceptance polices, financial institutions must take great care to strike the appropriate balance between risk aversion regarding criminal activities and the willingness to take on new clients. As a general rule, the rigidity of the acceptance standards should be commensurate with the risk profile of a potential customer. It is strongly recommended that only senior management should render decisions on customers whose profiles suggest they pose a high risk of money-laundering activities.[15]

Financial institutions should design their customer acceptance policies so that the socially disadvantaged are not excluded. Nor should these customer acceptance policies in any way restrict the general public's access to financial services.[16] This is particularly important for countries moving toward a broader use of financial instruments, including the use of checks, credit or debit cards, electronic and other payment mechanisms, and shifting away from a cash-based economy.

Accounts should be opened only after the new customer's identity has been satisfactorily verified.[17] No customer should be permitted to open or maintain an account using an anonymous or fictitious name.[18] This prohibition also applies to a numbered account if that account is accessed by use of a number or code once the account does not require the customer identification procedures using official documentation.[19] Numbered accounts are only permitted when the same customer identification procedures and supporting documentation (with record keeping) are employed. Under these guidelines,

---

13. *Id.* (provision 20).
14. *Id.*
15. *Id.*
16. *Id.*
17. *Id.* (provision 22). *The Forty Recommendations*, Rec. 5.
18. *The Forty Recommendations*, Rec.5, and Basel Customer Due Diligence for Banks, (provision30).
19. *Id.*

financial institutions must check and verify their customers' official identifying document. The best documents for verifying the identity of potential or actual customers are those that are the most difficult to reproduce.[20] In this regard, countries should require the use of "official" documents issued by appropriate authorities such as a passport, driver's license, personal identification or tax identification document.

In those instances where an agent is representing a beneficiary (e.g., through trusts, nominees, fiduciary accounts, corporations, and other intermediaries), financial institutions need to take reasonable measures to verify the identity and nature of the persons or organizations on whose behalf an account is being opened or for whom a transaction is being completed.[21] Financial institutions need to verify the legality of such entities by collecting the following information from potential customers:

- Name and legal form of customer's organization;
- Address;
- Names of the directors;
- Principal owners or beneficiaries;
- Provisions regulating the power to bind the organization;
- Agent(s) acting on behalf of organization; and
- Account number (if applicable).[22]

In cases of fund transfers, such as money remittances, financial institutions should include accurate and meaningful originator information (name, address, and account number) and pass this information along the payment chain with the fund transfer.[23]

A client's identity should be confirmed through due diligence procedures in cases where he or she is an occasional customer who has exceeded the designated threshold or when there is any doubt of that customer's actual identity.[24] The same would apply in the event of the occasional corporate customer.

---

20. Basel Customer Due Diligence for Banks (provision 23).
21. *The Forty Recommendations*, Rec. 5.
22. *Id.*, Rec. 5.
23. *Special Recommendations*, Spec. Rec. VII.
24. Basel Customer Due Diligence for Banks, provision 53; and FATF, *The Forty Recommendations*, Rec. 11.

Customer identification is an ongoing process that requires, as a general rule, financial institutions to keep up-to-date records on all relevant client information. Records should be updated in the event, for example, of significant transactions, changes in customer documentation standards, material changes in an account's operation, and the realization that current records are insufficient.[25] A country's financial institution supervisors are strongly encouraged to assist financial institutions in developing their own customer acceptance and identification procedures.

4. Low and High Risk Accounts and Transactions

The customer due diligence measures described above should be applied in accordance with the risk attached to the type of customer and transaction. This general principle is central to both the FATF Recommendations and the Basle Committee paper on Customer Due Diligence. For higher risk categories, enhanced measures should be taken and some particular cases are discussed below. For lower risk categories, a country may allow its financial institutions to apply reduced or simplified measures. FATF and the Basel Committee have identified some examples of such customers or transactions, but this is not exhaustive and it is a matter for a country's discretion. Examples of such lower risk customers are financial institutions, public companies and government enterprises.[26] Examples of such transactions are pooled accounts, pension schemes, and small scale insurance policies.[27]

Nevertheless, there is an expectation that customers should always be identified and some basic steps taken to verify identity. The reduced or simplified measures might apply to the extent of the verification process and/or the amount of information collected about the purpose and nature of the business relationship and transactions.[28]

A particular issue on which risk is a factor concerns establishing the identity of customers who already had accounts before verification of identity for new customers became a requirement. Neither the Basel Committee

---

25. Basel Customer Due Diligence for Bank (provision 24).
26. See *The Forty Recommendations*, Interpretive Notes to Rec. 5, paragraphs 9 and 10.
27. See *The Forty Recommendations*, Interpretive Notes to Rec. 5, paragraphs 11 and 12.
28. See *The Forty Recommendations*, Interpretive Notes to Rec. 5, paragraph 9.

nor FATF requires a comprehensive program to be instituted to verify the identity of existing customers or conduct other due diligence measures.[29] However, it is required that financial institutions should verify identity and carry out further due diligence on existing customers depending on materiality and risk.

5. Circumstances Requiring Increased Due Diligence

In certain cases, *The Forty Recommendations* provide that certain enhanced due diligence measures should be taken in addition to those performed in the normal course by financial institutions. The following discusses those cases requiring additional due diligence procedures.

a. Politically Exposed Persons

FATF defines Politically Exposed Persons (PEPs) as:

> Individuals who are or have been entrusted with prominent public functions in a foreign country, for example Heads of State or of government, senior politicians, senior government, judicial or military officials, senior executives of State owned corporations, important political party officials. Business relationships with family members or close associates of PEPs involve reputational risks similar to those with PEPs themselves. The definition is not intended to cover middle ranking or more junior officials in the forgoing categories.[30]

This definition covers only those customers who have public functions in a "foreign" country. Thus, it does not apply to "domestic" PEPs. However, FATF encourages countries to extend extra due diligence to domestic PEPs, but requires that extra due diligence be applied to foreign PEPs.[31]

---

29. See *The Forty Recommendations*, Interpretive Notes to Rec. 5, paragraph 8.
30. *The Forty Recommendations*, Glossary, Politically Exposed Persons.
31. *The Forty Recommendations*, Interpretive Notes to Rec. 6.

The additional due diligence measures consist of the following:

- Identifying PEPs;
- Approval at senior management level to account opening;
- Establishing the source of wealth and funds;
- Enhanced ongoing monitoring.

Actually finding out whether a customer is a PEP is often the biggest challenge for a financial institution given the definition of the term. No official organization issues a list of such individuals, but various commercial entities maintain and regularly update such lists.

b. Cross-Border Correspondent Banking Relationships

Cross-border correspondent banking relationships are another source of potentially high risk accounts for financial institutions. Such relationships could be a way for entities or persons from countries with lax arrangements to gain access to the global financial system without undergoing proper due diligence procedures. Before entering into correspondent banking relationships with a cross-border institution, a bank should:

- Establish the nature of the respondent bank's business, its reputation, and the quality of its supervision;
- Assess the AML/CFT controls of the respondent bank;
- Obtain senior management approval for the relationship;
- Document respective responsibilities;
- If "payable-through-accounts" are to be a feature of the business relationship, assure that the respondent bank verifies the identity and conducts ongoing due diligence of its customers.[32]

Correspondent banking relationship with institutions located in countries classified by FATF as "non-cooperative countries and territories"

---

32. *The Forty Recommendations*, Rec. 7.

(NCCTs) should be avoided.[33] No transactions should be undertaken with "shell banks" (i.e., a bank that is incorporated in a jurisdiction in which it has no physical presence and that is not affiliated with a regulated financial group).[34]

c. Non Face-to-Face Customers

As technology develops, the phenomenon of "non face-to-face" customers and business relationships is growing as customers use the telephone and internet to obtain financial services without necessarily visiting the provider. There is no intention on the part of the international standard setters to obstruct such developments, which give customers greater choice and services as well as benefit the economy. Financial institutions and others providing such services need to be aware that the AML/CFT risks are rather different with respect to such customers and need to take appropriate steps to deal with them.[35]

 While FATF raises the issue of increased risk with such accounts, it does not provide any guidance on which steps should be taken to address such increased risks. Thus, it is left to each country's discretion to establish appropriate policies and procedures.

d. Introduced Business

In some countries, financial businesses have customers "introduced" to them by intermediaries or third parties and will not have carried out any due diligence on these customers. In such circumstances, financial institutions should do three things.[36] First, the institution should make sure that the introducer is subject to customer due diligence requirements and that its compliance with such due diligence requirements is subject to supervision. Second, the

---

33. For the complete list of FATF's "no cooperative" jurisdictions, see http://www.fatf-gafi.org/ NCCT_en.htm.
34. *The Forty Recommendations*, Rec. 18. See also Basel Customer Due Diligence for Banks (Provision 51).
35. *Id.*, Rec. 8.
36. *Id.*, Rec. 9.

institution should make certain that the introducer has collected sufficient information about identity and other relevant due diligence documentation about the customer. Third, the institutions should make sure that the introducer can make that information available on request without delay.

The introducer can be domestic or international. Where it is an international party that is the introducer, the financial institution needs to be especially vigilant that the above requirements are met. Several countries, which permit introduced business, require that the introducer should be an individual or an institution that is subject to AML controls, is supervised by a regulatory body with responsibility for compliance with AML controls, and is located in a country that complies with FATF standards.

e. Other High Risk Business

FATF also draws attention to two other categories of transactions that require special attention. First, there are complex, unusual large transactions and unusual patterns of transactions which have no apparent economic or visible lawful purpose.[37] The background and purpose of such transactions should, as far as possible, be examined and the findings recorded. Where the financial institution cannot discover such information and/or is uneasy about the business, it should consider declining the business and/or making a suspicious transaction report.

Second, there are countries that have been identified as non-compliant with FATF recommendations that merit special attention. While transactions with such countries are not prohibited, financial institutions should pay special attention to them and, when there is doubt about their purpose, investigate further and record the outcome.[38] If the financial institution is not satisfied that the transaction is *bona fide* it should consider declining the business and/or making a suspicious transaction report.

---

37. *Id.*, Rec. 11.
38. *Id.*, Rec. 21.

6. Extending Due Diligence to Vendors and Others

The supply-chain structure of many businesses has become increasingly complex and interconnected with the advance in global commerce. Consequently, many financial institutions have found it necessary to exercise greater diligence over the vendors, suppliers, and agents of organizations as well as with employees and correspondent banks of financial institutions. Each country's financial institution supervisors may wish to consider implementing policies that incorporate these trends in due diligence, especially when such relationships may be considered higher risk as described above.

7. Insurance Sector Measures

The International Association of Insurance Supervisors (IAIS) maintains its own guidelines for customer identification and due diligence; the insurance industry must adhere to these in addition to the relevant requirements of *The Forty Recommendations* discussed above. The IAIS guidelines recommend that insurance companies:

- Establish to their "reasonable satisfaction" that every party relevant to the insurance application actually exists. For large numbers of subjects (e.g., group life policies and pensions), it may be sufficient to use a limited group such as the principal shareholders or main directors;
- Verify all underlying principals as well as their relationship with the policyholders—the principals and not the policyholders should be questioned regarding the nature of the relationship;
- Prohibit anonymous and fictitious accounts;
- Verify claims, commissions, and other money administered to no policyholders (e.g., partnerships, companies);
- Increase due diligence when the policyholder's financial flows or transaction patterns change in significant, unexpected, or unexplained ways;
- Increase due diligence regarding the purchase and sale of second-hand endowment policies and the use of single-unit-linked policies; and

- Monitor reinsurance or retrocession on a regular basis as a way to ensure payments to bona fide reinsurance entities at rates justified by the risk level.[39]

8. Security Sector Measures

The International Organization of Securities Commissions (IOSCO) has not established separate customer identification or due diligence requirements for securities firms, brokers, or collective investment entities. Although IOSCO has not established such specific requirements, the customer identification requirements of *The Forty Recommendations* (as described more fully in the Methodology[40]) do apply to the securities sector.

9. Measures for Designated Non-Financial Businesses and Professions

These requirements for customer due diligence, as well as those relating to record keeping, apply to designated non-financial businesses and professions in a more limited manner than to financial institutions. The following discussion outlines the applicable circumstances where due diligence procedures apply to these entities and persons.

a. Casinos

Due diligence procedures for financial institutions apply when casino customers engage in financial transactions equal to or exceeding USD/EUR 3000. Examples of such transactions include buying or cashing-in casino chips, opening accounts, wire transfers, and currency exchange. This does not mean that every gambling transaction has to be monitored or recorded for 5 years.[41]

---

39. See IAIS, Anti–Money Laundering Guidance Notes, http://www.iaisweb.org/02money.pdf.
40. http://www.fatf-gafi.org/pdf/Meth-2004_en.PDF.
41. *The Forty Recommendations*, Rec. 12, paragraph a. The applicable recommendations are Recs. 5, 6, and 8–11.

b. Real Estate Agents

Transactions for a client concerning the buying and selling of real estate require due diligence procedures. However, identification and other customer due diligence need only be conducted when a transaction takes place and only with respect to the party who is the client of the estate agent.[42] In many countries, the client will be the seller, rather than the buyer.

c. Dealers in Precious Metals and Stones

Cash transactions, equal to or exceeding USD/EUR 15,000, are to be covered by the due diligence requirements.[43]

d. Lawyers, Notaries, Other Independent Legal Professional, and Accountants

Identification and due diligence requirements apply to transactions prepared or carried out for a client with respect to the following specific activities:

- Buying and selling of real estate;
- Managing of client money, securities or other assets;
- Management of bank, savings or securities accounts;
- Organization of contributions for the creation, operation or management of companies;
- Creation, operation or management of legal persons or arrangements, buying and selling of business entities.[44]

The key phase is "prepare for or carry out transactions." This means that merely providing advice on how to undertake such a transaction is not covered. Identification and customer due diligence (and record keeping) are required after the professional becomes involved in carrying out the transaction, which includes the preliminary work on drawing up the transaction as

---

42. *Id.*, Rec. 12, paragraph b.
43. *Id.*, Rec. 12, paragraph c.
44. *Id.*, Rec. 12, paragraph d.

well as its execution. These are situations in which lawyers and accountants are functioning as "gatekeepers" to the financial system by providing services that would permit clients to engage in potential money laundering or terrorist financing transactions.

e. Trust and Company Service Providers

Due diligence procedures are applicable to transactions for a client prepared for and carried out in relation to the following specific activities:

- Acting as a formation agent of legal persons;
- Acting as (or arranging for anchor person to act as) a director or secretary of a company, a partner of a partnership of a similar position in relation to other legal persons;
- Providing a registered office; business address or accommodation, correspondence or administrative address for a company, a partnership or any other legal person or arrangement;
- Acting as (or arranging for another person to act as) a trustee or an express trust; or
- Acting as (or arranging for another person to act as) a nominee shareholder for another person.[45]

In some countries the above-described transactions are performed by lawyers. To be consistent with the criteria for lawyers set out above, the relevant test is again "prepare for and carry out," which excludes merely providing advice, but includes preliminary work on carrying out a specific transaction.

---

45. *Id.*, Rec. 12, paragraph e.

B. Record Keeping Requirements

1. Financial Institutions

Financial institutions should keep customer identity and transaction records for a minimum of five years following the termination of an account.[46] Institutions may be required to retain records for longer than five years if required by their regulators. Contents of the records should be made readily available to authorities upon request and, further, be of sufficient detail to permit the prosecution for criminal behavior.[47]

Maintaining records is important for both prevention and detection of money laundering and terrorist financing purposes. If a potential customer knows that records are being maintained, the customer may not be as likely to try to use the institution for these illegal purposes. Record maintenance also helps detect those involved and provides a financial trail to help competent authorities pursue those involved.

The following information should be included when recording a customer's transaction:

- Name of the customer and/or beneficiary;
- Address;
- Date and nature of the transaction;
- Type and amount of currency involved in the transaction;
- Type and identifying number of account; and
- Other relevant information typically recorded by the financial institution.[48]

2. Insurance Sector

The IAIS maintains its own set of record keeping requirements; the insurance entities must adhere to these, in addition to the relevant guidelines of *The Forty Recommendations*. The insurance entity must also obtain the following information (where applicable) when recording a customer's transaction:

---

46. *The Forty Recommendations*, Rec. 10.
47. *Id.*
48. *Id.*

- Location completed;
- Client's financial assessment;
- Client's need analysis;
- Payment method details;
- Benefits description;
- Copy of documentation used to verify customer identity;
- Post-sale records associated with the contract through its maturity; and
- Details of maturity processing and claim settlement (including "discharge documentation").[49]

Financial institution supervisors must verify that all representatives for insurance companies are licensed under appropriate insurance law and jurisdiction.[50] Representatives may retain documents on behalf of an insurance entity, but the integrity of the records rests on the insurance entity as the product provider.[51] In such cases, a clear division of responsibility between the insurance entity and its representative is necessary.[52]

3. Securities Sector

The IOSCO has established its own set of record keeping requirements, which securities firms should follow in addition to adhering to the applicable general requirements of *The Forty Recommendations* discussed above. IOSCO requires that the national centralized authority on financial crime or other competent authority ensure that intermediaries maintain records as needed demonstrating their adherence to the regulatory rules.[53] These records should be legible, understandable, and comprehensive, and should include all transactions involving collective investment assets and transactions.[54]

---

49. See IAIS Anti–Money Laundering Guidance Notes.
50. *Id.*
51. *Id.*
52. *Id.*
53. See IOSCO Principles for the Supervision of Operators of Collective Investment Schemes (CIS Sept. 1997), available at http://www.iosco.org/pubdocs/pdf/IOSCOPD69.pdf.
54. *Id.*

4. Designated Non-Financial Businesses and Professions

Record keeping requirements for designated non-financial businesses and professions apply in the same circumstances as are applicable to customer identification and customer due diligence requirements.[55] See section A.9, above, Customer Due Diligence and Identification, Measures for Designated Non-Financial Businesses and Professions.

C. Suspicious Transactions Reporting

If a financial institution suspects or has reasonable grounds to suspect that funds are the proceeds of a criminal activity, or are related to terrorist financing, it should report its suspicions to the applicable financial intelligence unit.[56] Moreover, banks should be required to report suspicious activities and significant incidents of fraud to the supervisors, and supervisors do need to ensure that appropriate authorities have been alerted.[57] Financial institutions, when filing suspicious activity reports (STRs), should not, under any circumstances, notify a customer that his/her behavior has been reported as suspect to authorities.[58] From that point on—which is to say, upon notification—financial institutions should comply fully with instructions from government authorities, including the production of records.[59]

1. Suspicious Transactions: What Is Involved

Suspicious transactions have certain broad characteristics, including, most obviously, transactions that depart from normal patterns of account activity. Any complex or unusually large transactions—in addition to any unusual patterns of transactions absent an apparent economic, commercial, or lawful purpose—are suspect and, therefore, merit further investigation by the finan-

---

55. *The Forty Recommendations*, Rec. 12.
56. *The Forty Recommendations*, Rec. 13.
57. Basel Core Principle 15, Description 31.
58. *The Forty Recommendations*, Rec.14.
59. *Id.*, Recs.10 and 28.

cial institution and, if necessary, by the appropriate authorities.[60] To assist financial institutions in screening for suspicious transactions, these financial institutions should establish risk-sensitive limits to monitor particular classes or categories of accounts. Specific examples of suspicious activity (e.g., very high account turnover inconsistent with balance size) are useful for individual financial institutions and should be provided to them in some form by supervisors.[61]

Financial institutions and their employees should always be vigilant for suspicious transactions. While the following are indications of suspicious transactions, the listing is not exhaustive:

- General Signs

    - Assets withdrawn immediately after they are credited to an account.
    - A dormant account suddenly becomes active without any plausible reason.
    - The high asset value of a client is not compatible with either the information concerning the client or the relevant business.
    - A client provides false or doctored information or refuses to communicate required information to the bank.
    - The arrangement of a transaction either insinuates an unlawful purpose, is economically illogical or unidentifiable.

- Signs Regarding Cash Transactions

    - Frequent deposit of cash incompatible with either the information concerning the client or his business.
    - Deposit of cash immediately followed by the issuance of checks or transfers towards accounts opened in other banks located in the same country or abroad.
    - Frequent cash withdrawal without any obvious connection with the client's business.

---

60. *Id.*, Rec.11.
61. *Id.*, Rec. 25; See also Basel Customer Due Diligence for Banks, (provision 53).

- Frequent exchange of notes of high denomination for smaller denominations or against another currency.
- Cashing checks, including travelers' checks, for large amounts.
- Frequent cash transactions for amounts just below the level where identification or reporting by the financial institution is required.

- Signs Regarding Transactions on Deposit Accounts

  - Closing of an account followed by the opening of new accounts in the same name or by members of the client's family.
  - Purchase of stocks and shares with funds that have been transferred from abroad or just after cash deposit on the account.
  - Illogical structures (numerous accounts, frequent transfers between accounts, etc.).
  - Granting of guarantees (pledge, bonds) without any obvious reason.
  - Transfers in favor of other banks without any indication of the beneficiary.
  - Unexpected repayment, without a convincing explanation, of a delinquent loan.
  - Deposit of checks of large amounts incompatible with either the information concerning the client or the relevant business.

2. "Safe Harbor" Provisions for Reporting

"Safe harbor" laws help to encourage financial institutions to report all suspicious transactions. Such laws protect financial institutions and employees from criminal and civil liability when reporting suspicious transactions to competent authorities in good faith. These legal provisions should provide financial institutions, and their employees or representatives, protection against lawsuits for any alleged violation of confidentiality or secrecy laws provided that the suspicious report was filed in good faith (i.e., it was not frivolous nor malicious).[62]

---

62. *The Forty Recommendations*, Rec. 14.

3. Scope of Reporting Obligation

An STR is a way of alerting authorities to the possibility that a particular transaction could involve money laundering or terrorist financing and should, therefore, be investigated. In most cases, the reporting financial institution will not have evidence that the transaction represents the proceeds of crime, and is less likely to know of what specific crime might be involved. The financial institution will simply be aware that the transaction is unusual and not consistent with the normal type of transaction on the account. Most likely, it will not be aware of the source of the funds or the reason for the transaction and cannot inquire of the customer without the risk of tipping-off the customer. In such situations, the institution should submit a suspicious transaction report and leave it to the authorities to further investigate.

Because reporting institutions will usually not know the underlying basis of the transaction, a suspicious transaction reporting system should base the requirement to report on "suspicion" that funds may be related to a criminal offense. It is not necessary to require the reporting institution to investigate the transaction or have actual evidence that the funds relate to criminal activity.

4. Fiscal Crimes

Some countries do not classify fiscal crimes, such as tax evasion, as a money laundering predicate offense. Thus, laundering the proceeds of tax evasion is not necessarily a money laundering offense. However, financial institutions should still report transactions that they find suspicious and leave it to the authorities to determine whether money laundering is involved. Otherwise, there is a risk that customers would attempt to explain away transactions related to money laundering predicates as the proceeds of tax evasion and pressure institutions not to file STRs.

5. Insurance Sector

The IAIS has established its own set of guidelines for reporting suspicious transactions.[63] The insurance industry should follow these, in addition to the requirements of *The Forty Recommendations* noted above. Insurance companies should report suspicious activity to the financial intelligence unit or other national centralized authority. The following are insurance sector-specific cases of suspicious transactions meriting additional investigation:

- Unusual or disadvantageous early redemption of an insurance policy;
- Unusual employment of an intermediary in the course of some usual transaction or financial activity (e.g., payment of claims or high commission to an unusual intermediary);
- Unusual payment method; and
- Transactions involving jurisdictions with lax regulatory instruments regarding money laundering and/or terrorist financing.[64]

6. Securities Sector

The IOSCO has not established separate suspicious activity reporting requirements for securities firms, brokers, or collective investment entities. Although IOSCO has not established separate or additional requirements in this area, the suspicious activity reporting requirements of *The Forty Recommendations* do apply to the securities sector.

7. Designated Non-Financial Businesses and Professions

Under the 2003 revision of *The Forty Recommendations*, designated non-financial businesses and professionals are now required to file suspicious transactions reports, but on a more limited basis than their obligation to identify customers and carry out due diligence.[65]

---

63. See IAIS Anti-Money Laundering Guidance Notes.
64. *Id.*
65. *The Forty Recommendations*, Rec. 16.

For lawyers, notaries, other independent legal professionals and accountants, there is only an obligation to file an STR only when they engage in a financial transaction for, or on behalf of, a client. This is narrower than the obligation to identify clients and conduct due diligence upon them in two respects:

- The reporting obligation covers only "financial transactions," not all transactions; and
- There is a reporting obligation only at the point at which the professional engages in a financial transaction for his or her client.[66]

There is no obligation to report in legally privileged circumstances. Individual countries determine when such reporting obligations arise, but the privilege normally covers information obtained either in ascertaining the legal position of a client or representing the client in proceedings. Countries may provide that members of this group may report to their respective self-regulatory organizations (SRO), rather than the FIU, provided the SRO cooperates with the FIU.[67]

Dealers in precious metals and precious stones are required to file STRs only when they engage in a cash transaction with a customer equal to or exceeding the USD/EUR 15,000 threshold.[68]

Trust and company service providers are required to file STRs only in circumstances where they engage in transactions on behalf of a client.[69] As a consequence, any transaction, not just a financial transaction, that is suspicious should be reported. The reporting is limited, however, to situations where the trust or company service provider actually carries out the transaction; mere providing advice or preparing a transaction is not reportable.

---

66. *Id.*, Rec. 16, paragraph a.
67. *Id.*, Interpretive Note to Rec. 16.
68. *Id.*, Rec. 16, paragraph b.
69. *Id.*, Rec. 16, paragraph c.

D. Cash Transaction Reporting

Countries should consider the possible benefits of requiring all cash transactions that exceed a fixed threshold amount to be reported.[70] It is not mandatory, however, that a country have such a requirement. Cash transaction reporting has significant resource and privacy implications, which countries need to take into account in considering the issue. Each country or jurisdiction establishes its own reporting threshold based upon its own circumstances. For example, the United States requires that financial institutions record and report to designated authorities all transactions involving currency or bearer instruments in excess of $10,000.[71]

Other countries require reporting at similar levels. Such thresholds may be established by statute, or by regulation under the authority of the appropriate government supervisory agency. Depending on circumstances in a country, such requirements may also apply to non-financial businesses and professionals, such as casinos, antique or automobile dealers, lawyers, accountants or other situations where large purchases are paid for in cash.

Relevant authorities should take great care in designating a country's threshold level; it must be high enough to screen out insignificant transactions yet low enough to detect transactions potentially connected with financial crime. In addition, countries may wish to add exemptions to reporting requirements for transactions where reporting is burdensome to the system and not particularly productive for enforcement purposes.

In addition, certain entities can represent a low risk for engaging in money laundering, and, therefore, may be eligible for exemption. These entities include governments, certain financial institutions or corporations that are reasonably assumed to be corruption-free, and customers that make frequent, large cash transactions due to the nature of their businesses. Such exceptions should be reviewed on a regular basis to determine if the exception remains appropriate, both as a general rule and for specific entities, under relevant circumstances.

---

70. *The Forty Recommendations*, Rec. 19.
71. See, for example, U.S. Bank Secrecy Act of 1970.

1. Multiple Cash Transactions

Cash reporting requirements also apply to same-day multiple transactions, a practice called "smurfing." If the consolidated transaction amount exceeds the designated reporting threshold, financial institutions need to report the entire series of transactions.[72] This safeguard against smurfing—whereby many individual transactions involving multiple accounts at a financial institution manage to take place just below the country's reporting threshold—is a vital part of the effort to prevent money laundering and terrorist financing. Criminals and terrorists obviously resort to their own countermeasures to avoid detection by software programs. This is why it is absolutely crucial for the relevant authorities to use proactive analysis in detecting criminal and terrorist financial activity.

Of course, a transaction can also be reported as a suspicious transaction that does not meet the threshold or multiple transactions test. For example, a single deposit of 9,900 may be considered suspicious, under various circumstances when the country has a reporting threshold of 10,000 because it suggests structuring of transactions by a customer in order to evade the reporting requirements.

2. Cross Border Movements

Money launderers engage in cross-border transfers of cash, bearer negotiable instruments and high-value commodities as a scheme for laundering funds. It is important that countries have a mechanism in place to detect when such transfers may be used for money laundering or terrorist financing purposes.

Authorities should consider establishing a minimum reporting limit for cross-border movements of currency, other negotiable instruments, and high-value commodities (i.e., precious metals or gems). Unusual or suspicious international movement of such goods, their point of origin and destination should be reported to the country's customs service or other appropriate authorities.[73]

---

72. Basel Customer Due Diligence for Banks, (provision 16).
73. *The Forty Recommendations*, Rec. 19.

3. Modern Money Management Techniques

The monitoring capabilities of financial institutions and government officials have benefited from the movement away from cash and currency transfers toward checks, payment cards, direct deposit, and book-entry recording of securities. These transactions leave a helpful paper trail when wrongdoing is suspected and permit competent authorities to make investigations. Success in investigations depends upon accurate and complete record keeping. For this reason, the use of these modern money management and payment transfer methods is highly encouraged.[74]

E. Balancing Privacy Laws with Reporting and Disclosure Requirements

The reporting of information, e.g., suspicious transactions and cash transactions, or the disclosure of records by a financial institution to a competent authority, necessarily involves information that is normally treated confidentially under a country's bank secrecy or privacy laws.

In requiring the reporting or disclosure of such information for AML and CFT purposes, a country needs to make appropriate exceptions in its privacy laws or otherwise specifically authorize the reporting and disclosure for those limited purposes. FATF specifically provides that financial institution privacy laws should be drafted so as not to inhibit the implementation of any of its recommendations.[75] At the same time, a country needs to build in protections to assure that confidentiality will be observed, except where public policy needs, such as prosecution for money laundering, outweigh the overall need to protect privacy of financial information. By assuring confidentiality and privacy in the overall scheme, a country protects reporting and disclosure from abuse. In doing so, a country encourages maximum cooperation and proper reporting and disclosure by those entities and persons subject to such requirements.

---

74. *Id.*, Recs. 20 and 28.
75. *Id.*, Recs. 4 and 28.

F. Internal Controls, Compliance, and Audit

Countries should require all financial institutions covered by their AML and CFT laws to establish and maintain internal policies and procedures to prevent their institutions from being used for purposes of money laundering and terrorist financing.[76] Internal policies and procedures will vary among different institutions and different types of institutions, but they should nevertheless all consider the size, scope, and nature of that institution's operation.

Internal procedures include ongoing training that keeps employees informed and up-to-date about developments on AML and CFT. Employee training needs to (1) describe the nature and processes of money laundering and terrorist financing; (2) explain AML/CFT laws and regulatory requirements; and (3) explain an institution's policies and systems with regard to reporting requirements regarding suspicious activity, with emphasis on customer identification, due diligence and reporting requirement.

In addition, financial institutions should screen job applicants for possible intent to use their institutions to launder money and/or to finance terrorism.[77]

The designation of an AML/CFT compliance officer at the management level, by each financial institution, is recommended.[78] Such a compliance officer helps to ensure that appropriate management attention is devoted to the institution's compliance efforts.

An audit function is also a required internal policy and procedure that needs to be established; the audit function should be separate from the compliance administration function, in order to test and assure the adequacy of the overall compliance function.[79]

G. Regulation and Supervision—Integrity Standards

The foregoing discussions deal with AML and CFT preventative measures that should be applied by national authorities to financial institutions and certain

---

76. *Id.*, Rec. 15..
77. *Id.*
78. *Id.*, Interpretive Note to Rec. 15.
79. *Id.*

designated non-financial businesses and professions. It is not sufficient for national authorities to impose those requirements in legislation. Countries also need to take measures to ensure that they are implemented in practice. Like many other elements of the international standards, the extent of regulation and supervision should be based on the money laundering and terrorist financing risk to the institution in question. The framework established by the standard setters envisages different types of regulation and supervision for:

- Core Principle Institutions,
- Other Financial Institutions, and
- Designated Non Financial Businesses and Professions.

The regulations and supervision recommendations regarding integrity standards of *The Forty Recommendations* are discussed in detail in Chapter V, under Supervision and Regulation—Integrity Standards.

H. Legal Entities and Arrangements

Each country should take appropriate measures to prevent the unlawful use of corporations and other forms of legal entities by money launderers and those who finance terrorism.[80] Such measures should include accurate and timely information about the beneficial ownership and control of legal entities; such information should be accessed in an expeditious manner by competent authorities. In addition, in countries where bearer shares of securities are permissible, appropriate measures should be taken to assure that such bearer instruments are not abused for money laundering or terrorist financing purposes.[81]

A country should also take appropriate measures to assure that trust and similar legal arrangements are not misused by those involved in money laundering or terrorist financing.[82] Such preventative measures should include access to details about the settler, trustee and beneficiaries of these types of legal arrangements.[83]

---

80. *Id.*, Rec. 33.
81. *Id.*
82. *Id.*, Rec. 34.
83. *Id.*

Chapter VII

The Financial Intelligence Unit

Those involved in the fight against money laundering and terrorist financing must have access to certain kinds of financially related information in order to conduct financial investigations. In this regard, the financial intelligence unit (FIU) plays an increasingly important role in this process.[1]

Money launderers manipulate their illicit proceeds in an endeavor to conceal or disguise their true nature, source, location, disposition, and movement, with the ultimate objective of integrating these proceeds into, and through, the legitimate economy.[2] Those who finance terrorism seek to conceal the source of the funds and disguise the illicit use of funds in support of terrorism. Financial investigations are assisted greatly by a country's compre-

---

1. For a comprehensive discussion on FIUs, see *Financial Intelligence Units, An Overview 2004*, (*FIUs Overview*) by the International Monetary Fund and World Bank, available (read-only) at www.amlcft.org.
2. United Nations Convention against Illicit Traffic in Narcotic Drugs and Psychotropic Substances (1988) (Vienna Convention), art. 3(b)(i) & (ii). http://www.incb.org/e/conv/1988/.

hensive regime that requires the reporting of certain information and record keeping, and that facilitates information sharing among competent authorities, both domestically and internationally. The primary goals of financial investigations are to identify, trace, and document the movement of funds; to identify and locate assets that are subject to law enforcement measures; and to support the prosecution of criminal activity.

Financial investigations seek to discover the financial trail left by criminals. As part of this process, investigators analyze financial institution account records, real estate records, documents on liens and judgments, corporate registries, brokerage and mutual fund accounts, insurance contracts and a full spectrum of other financial and business relations records. Illicit financial operations have recently grown more sophisticated and complex, requiring traditional investigators to acquire new and specialized financial intelligence tools.

The Financial Action Task Force on Money Laundering (FATF), which is recognized as the international standard setter for anti-money laundering (AML) and combating the financing of terrorism (CFT), provides in *The Forty Recommendations on Money Laundering* (*The Forty Recommendations*), that each country should establish an FIU.[3] Further, FATF urges countries to impose measures on financial institutions and certain non-financial businesses and professions requiring them to maintain records on the identities of their clients and their transactions, and to report any suspicious transactions.[4] Information generated by these reporting and record keeping requirements is to be reported to the country's FIU and is used to reconstruct transactions, to establish the link between individual clients and a particular business, to prove the "state of mind" of an individual, and finally, to identify the role of an individual in a criminal or terrorist financing activity.

Information reporting and record keeping requirements generate substantial financial data, much of which is not easily useable by competent authorities without further analysis. If a country's AML and CFT institutional frameworks are to be at all effective, the country must institute a reliable, efficient system for processing, analyzing, and disseminating this information. Without such a system in place, law enforcement has a much

---

3. *The Forty Recommendations*, Rec. 26., http://www.fatf-gafi.org/pdf/40Recs-2003_en.pdf.
4. *Id.*, Recs. 10–22.

more difficult time detecting criminal or terrorist financial dealings. The pressing need for effective data analysis of possible financial crime explains, in part, the proliferation of FIUs and the growing importance of their roles in the international effort to prevent, detect and prosecute money laundering and terrorist financing.[5]

A. Definition of a Financial Intelligence Unit

The Egmont Group of Financial Intelligence Units (Egmont Group), which is the international standard setter for FIUs, adopted the following definition of an FIU in November 1996:

> A central, national agency responsible for receiving (and, as permitted, requesting), analyzing, and disseminating to the competent authorities, disclosures of financial information (i) concerning suspected proceeds of crime, or (ii) required by national legislation or regulation, in order to counter money laundering.[6]

The United Nations Convention against Transnational Organised Crime (2000) (Palermo Convention) adopted this definition, stating, "Each state Party...shall...consider the establishment of a financial intelligence unit to serve as a national center for the collection, analysis and dissemination of information regarding potential money laundering."[7]

Expanding on this definition, FATF requires countries to establish an FIU, which has these three essential functions, i.e., the collector or "repository" of reported information, analysis and financial information sharing,[8] for detecting and countering money laundering and terrorist financing. The FATF

---

5. As of June 2004, 94 countries have established financial intelligence units that are members of the Egmont Group. The Egmont Group, Financial Intelligence Units of the World, available at http://www.egmontgroup.org/.
6. The Egmont Group is an informal organization of financial intelligence units named after the location of the group's first meeting at the Egmont-Arenberg Palace in Brussels. The goal of the group is to provide a forum for FIUs to improve support to their respective national anti–money laundering programs. See Egmont Group, "Information Paper on Financial Intelligence Units and the Egmont Group," available at http://www.egmontgroup.org/info_paper_final_092003.pdf. See also Chapter III, the Egmont Group.
7. The *Palermo Convention*, Article 7(1)(b).
8. *The Forty Recommendations*, Recs. 36, 37 and 40.

also has a general requirement that all national authorities exchange informa-tion and co-operate with their domestic and international counterparts.[9]

In 2004, the Egmont Group revised its definition of an FIU to include specifically the combating of terrorist financing.[10] The current definition of an FIU as follows:

> A central, national agency responsible for receiving (and as permitted, requesting), analyzing and disseminating to competent authorities, disclosures of financial information:
>
> i. concerning suspected proceeds of crime and potential financing of terrorism, or
>
> ii. required by national legislation or regulation, in order to com-bat money laundering and terrorist financing.[11]

As a result, the Egmont Group's definition of an FIU is entirely consis-tent with *The Forty Recommendations*.

B. Core Functions

FIUs vary from country to country, but all of them share three core func-tions; they receive, analyze and disseminate information to combat money laundering and terrorist financing. The dissemination of financial informa-tion should be done on both a domestic and international basis.

Because money laundering is often a cross-border activity, it is important for FIUs to join forces with other national intelligence units. Thus, even the best domestic laws and regulations against money laundering, including those for an FIU, need an effective international information sharing mechanism in order to combat effectively money laundering and terrorist financing.

---

9. *Id.*, Recs. 26 and 31.
10. The Egmont Group, Revised Statement of Purpose (June 23, 2004), http://www.egmontgroup. org/.
11. *Id.*

1. Centralized Repository of Reported Information

Financial institutions must report all suspicious activity reports and other required disclosures (such as cash transaction reports) to their country's FIU.[12] The centralization of this "repository function"—designating the FIU as the recipient of financial disclosures—is a prerequisite for an effective preventive national and international framework against money laundering.[13]

The use of a centralized repository for the reporting of information and required disclosures ensures that all of the relevant information is in one place, facilitating the processing of information and analysis on a consistent basis. Centralization also ensures greater efficiency in information gathering.

2. Analytical Function

FIUs are more than mere databases for financial information required to be submitted by legislation or national regulatory authorities. FIUs must analyze the data they receive because so many suspicious transaction reports (STRs) and other financial disclosures often appear to be innocent transactions. Ordinary deposits, withdrawals, fund transfers, or the purchase of a security or an insurance policy may, however, be important pieces of information in detecting and prosecuting money laundering and terrorist financing.

Only through examination and analysis can FIUs detect criminal financial transactions. Distinguishing truly suspect transactions from those that are only benignly unusual requires informed analysis. Without it, the most sophisticated data gathering in the world will not be productive.

These analytical functions require countries to vest their FIUs with the necessary legal authority, proper human resources, and sufficient technical capacity. In particular, the FIU's analytical functions require extended powers to access information. These powers should include: access to certain commercial or government databases; the authority to request additional information from reporting entities and other sources as necessary; and access to

---

12. *The Forty Recommendations*, Recs. 13 and 19, paragraph 6.
13. See *FIUs Overview*, Chapter 3, Receiving Transaction Reports.

advanced intelligence techniques and apparatus, such as wire tapping and covert operations, subject to domestic legal principles.

Each country must balance very real privacy concerns against the FIU's need for an effective analytical function. While utilizing publicly available commercial databases does not raise privacy concerns, authorizing centralized intelligence units to request additional information does. The same caution applies to FIU surveillance and other intelligence techniques. Financial institution privacy laws should be drafted so as not to interfere with there functions of the FIU, yet protect the privacy of information.[14]

FIUs perform three specialized analytical functions: tactical, operational and strategic.[15]

a. Tactical Analysis

Tactical analysis is the process of collecting the data needed to build a case and to provide the accompanying facts behind the commission of a criminal offense. Although tactical analysis may be performed on all incoming reports, it is likely that STRs will provide the most directly useful information.

Tactical analysis includes the matching of data received from reporting institutions and others with data held by the FIU or accessible to it. Such data includes lists of names, addresses, phone numbers, and data in the other reports forwarded by reporting institutions. While some reporting institutions produce the simplest form of tactical information themselves, FIUs add to these reports related information on the reported client or transaction that they have in their databases.

Upon receipt of an STR, staff of the FIU will look for additional information on the subject, the company, the transactions, or other elements involved in a particular case to provide the basis for further analysis. The main sources of such additional information are:

- The FIU's own data,
- Publicly available sources,

---

14. *The Forty Recommendations*, Rec. 4.
15. *Id.*, Chapter 3, Analyzing Reports.

- Governemnt-held databases,
- Aditional information from reporting entities and other entities, and
- Other FIUs.[16]

b. Operational Analysis

Operational analysis uses tactical information to formulate different hypotheses on the possible activities of a suspected criminal. Operational analysis supports the investigative process. It uses all sources of information available to the FIU to produce activity patters, new targets, relationships among the subject and his or her accomplices, investigative leads, criminal profiles, and, where possible indications of possible future behavior.

One technique of operations analysis is financial profiling. This provides the analyst with methods for developing indicators of concealed income of an individual, a group of individuals, or an organization. It is an effective indirect method of gathering, organizing, and presenting evidence related to the financial status of subjects. The relevance of the profile is to show that the target cannot demonstrate a legitimate source for the difference between his or her outflow of cash versus the income. The tracing of a person's assets may also provide leads linking the subject with predicate offenses.

Through operational analysis, the information received by the FIU is developed into operational intelligence, which can be transmitted to law-enforcement agencies or prosecutors for further action.[17]

c. Strategic Analysis

Strategic analysis develops knowledge to be used for the future work of the FIU. The main characteristic of strategic intelligence is that it is not related to individual cases, but rather to new issues or trends. The scope of any strategic analysis varies greatly depending upon the FIU's mandate. It may consist of the identification of evolving criminal patterns in a particular group or

_____
16. *Id.*
17. *Id.*

the provision of broad insights into emerging patterns of criminality at the national level.

Strategic analysis is developed after all available information has been collected and analyzed. It requires a wider range of data than operational analysis, as well as experienced analysts. The data comes from reports provided by the reporting entities, the FIU's own operational intelligence and tactical information, public sources, law enforcement and other governmental agencies. At a broader level, strategic analysis may suggest the need to impose reporting and other AML/CFT obligations on new entities or enhance existing reporting requirements.[18]

3. Domestic Information Sharing

If it suspects money laundering or the financing of terrorism, the FIU should have the authority to share, or route, financial information and intelligence to other domestic authorities for investigation or action. The FIU should also be authorized to cooperate and coordinate its actions with the other domestic authorities devoted to the detection, prevention and prosecution of money laundering and terrorist financing.

The importance of timely information sharing with the proper authorities cannot be overstated. Effective measures against money laundering rely on getting the available information to the appropriate authority. For most FIUs, the sharing of information usually follows some analysis of reported financial disclosures. For other FIUs, especially those that receive an enormous volume of financial disclosures, the financial disclosures are made available to law enforcement authorities immediately; these FIUs conduct analysis on financial disclosures and other financial information upon request of law enforcement as needed at a later time. In either case, the key is for the FIU to provide the competent authority with financial intelligence as quickly as possible so that the competent authority can pursue the leads provided by the FIU.[19]

Domestic coordination is vital. The FIU has to be an essential partner in domestic coordination and could even be empowered to assume the lead role

18. *Id.*
19. *Id.*, Chapter 3, Dissemination Reports.

in coordinating the relevant authorities that fight money laundering—which is to say, the FIU, regulators and supervisors of the financial sector, the police, the judicial authorities, and other relevant ministries or administrations.[20]

4. International Information Sharing

Because so much of money laundering and terrorist financing are cross-border activities, FIUs must be able to share financial intelligence with other FIUs worldwide in order to be effective partners in the international fight against these crimes. A core feature of an FIU is its ability to cooperate in an efficient and rapid manner with all of its foreign counterparts. Information sharing at the international level should occur through direct and secure communication with the competent foreign authorities.[21]

C. Types or Models of FIUs

Countries generally choose one of four basic models in establishing or improving the operations of an FIU:

a. The *administrative model*, which is either attached to a regulatory/ supervisory authority, such as the central bank or the ministry of finance, or as an independent administrative authority;

b. The *law enforcement model*, whereby the agency is attached to a police agency, whether general or specialized;

c. The *judicial* or *prosecutorial model*, where the agency is affiliated with a judicial authority or the prosecutor's office; or

d. The *hybrid model*, which is some combination of the above three.

These variations arise primarily from different country circumstances and from the lack of an internationally accepted model, when the first such units were established in the early 1990s. For example, in some countries, the function of the FIU as an additional tool for law enforcement organiza-

---

20. *The Forty Recommendations*, Rec. 31.
21. See Chapter VIII of this Reference Guide, International Cooperation.

tions in combating money laundering and associated crimes was emphasized, and this led to the establishment of the FIU in an investigative or prosecutorial agency. Other countries emphasized the need for a "buffer" between the financial institutions and the police and, consequently, their FIUs were established outside of these agencies.

It should be emphasized, however, that the four classifications are, to a certain degree, arbitrary and that there are other ways of classifying FIUs. Discussed below is a description of each model, advantages and disadvantages (although this listing is not exhaustive) and examples of countries that use the model.

1. Administrative

Administrative-type FIUs are usually part of the structure, or under the supervision of, an administration or an agency other than law-enforcement or judicial authorities.[22] Sometimes, the administrative type constitutes a separate agency, placed under the supervision of a ministry or administration (autonomous) or not placed under such supervision (independent). The main rationale for such an arrangement is to establish an "buffer" between the financial sector (and, more generally, non-financial businesses and professionals subject to reporting obligations) and the law enforcement authorities in charge of financial crime investigations and prosecutions.

The advantages of an administrative-type FIU are:

- The FIU acts as an interface between the financial and other sectors subject to reporting obligations, on the one hand, and law-enforcement authorities, on the other hand; this avoids the creation of direct institutional links between reporting parties and law enforcement agencies, while bringing disclosures to the attention of law enforcement agencies.
- Financial institutions and others are more confident about disclosing information if they know that dissemination will be limited to cases of money laundering and terrorist financing and will be based on the FIU's own analysis, rather than the reporting institution's limited information.

---

22. *FIUs Overview*, Establishing an FIU.

- The FIU is a "neutral," technical, and specialized interlocutor for the reporting parties.
- If the FIU is placed in a regulatory agency, it is the natural interlocutor of the financial institutions.
- Information can be easily exchanged with all types of FIUs.

The disadvantages are:

- Because the FIU is not part of the law enforcement administration, there may be a delay in applying law enforcement measures, such as freezing a suspicious transaction or arresting a suspect, on the basis of financial disclosures.
- The FIU usually does not have the range of legal powers that law enforcement agencies and judicial authorities have to obtain evidence.
- The administrative-type FIUs (unless that are truly independent) are more subject to the direct supervision of political authorities.[23]

Examples of countries with administrative-type FIUs include Andorra, Aruba, Australia, Belgium, Bolivia, Bulgaria, Canada, Colombia, Croatia, the Czech Republic, France, Israel, the Republic of Korea, Liechtenstein, Malta, Monaco, the Netherlands, the Netherlands Antilles, Panama, Poland, Romania, Russia, Slovenia, Spain, Ukraine, the United States, and Venezuela.[24]

By making an administrative authority a "buffer" between the financial institution and other reporting sectors and the law enforcement sectors, authorities can more easily enlist the cooperation of reporting institutions, which are often conscious of the drawbacks vis-à-vis their clients of having direct institutionalized links with law enforcement agencies. Administrative-type FIUs are often preferred by the banking sector. They may also appeal to other institutions and professionals that have been added to the list of reporting entities for the same reasons.

---

23. *Id.*
24. *Id.*

2. Law Enforcement

In some countries, the emphasis on the law-enforcement aspects of the FIU led to the creation of the FIU as part of a law enforcement agency, since this was the easiest way to establish a body with appropriate law-enforcement powers without having to design a new entity and a new legal and administrative framework.[25]

Operationally, under this arrangement, the FIU will be close to other law enforcement units, such as a financial crimes unit, and will benefit from their expertise and sources of information. In return, information received by the FIU can be accessed more easily by law enforcement agencies and can be used in any investigation, thus increasing its usefulness. Exchanges of information may also be expedited through the use of existing national and international criminal information exchange networks.

The advantages of a law enforcement type of FIU are:

- It is built on an existing infrastructure, so there is no need to set up a new agency.
- Maximum law enforcement use can be made of financial disclosure information.
- There is quick law enforcement reaction to indicators of money laundering and other crimes.
- Information can be exchanged using the extensive network of international criminal information exchange networks (such as Interpol).
- There is relatively easy access to criminal intelligence and to the intelligence community at large.

The disadvantages are:

- This type of FIU tends to be more focused on investigations than on prevention measures.
- Law enforcement agencies are not a natural interlocutor for financial institutions; mutual trust must be established, which may take some

___
25. *Id.*

time, and law enforcement agencies may lack the financial expertise required to carry out such a dialogue.

- Gaining access to a financial institutions' data (other that the reported transactions) usually requires the launching of a formal investigation.
- Reporting institutions may be reluctant to disclose information to law enforcement if they know the information could be used in the investigation of any crime (not just money laundering and the financing of terrorism).
- Reporting institutions may be reluctant to disclose information to law enforcement on transactions that are no more than "suspicions."

Examples of law enforcement FIUs include Austria, Estonia, Germany, Hungary, Iceland, Ireland, Slovakia, Sweden, and the United Kingdom.

Also, a law enforcement-type of FIU will normally have all the powers of the law enforcement agency itself, without the need for separate, specific legislative authority. These powers include the power to freeze transactions and seize assets (with the same degree of judicial supervisions as applies to other law enforcement powers in the country).

3. Judicial or Prosecutorial

This type of FIU is generally established within the judicial branch of the country and most frequently under the prosecutor's jurisdiction. Such an arrangement is typically found in countries with a continental law tradition, where the public prosecutors are part of the judicial system and have authority over the investigatory bodies.[26]

Judicial or prosecutorial-type FIUs can work well in countries where banking secrecy laws are so strong that a direct link with the judicial or prosecutorial authorities is needed to ensure the cooperation of financial institutions.

The advantages of a judicial or prosecutorial-type FIU are:

---

26. *Id.*

- They usually possess a high degree of independence from political interference.
- The disclosure of information is provided directly to the agency authorized to investigate or prosecute the crime.
- The judiciary's powers (e.g., seizing funds, freezing accounts, conducting interrogations, detaining people, conducting searches) are immediately brought into play.

The disadvantages are:

- Generally, the same disadvantages of law enforcement-type FIUs apply to judicial or prosecutorial-type FIUs except for the reluctance to disclose information upon "suspicion."
- This type of FIU may have difficulty exchanging information with non-judicial or prosecutorial FIUs.[27]

Examples of judicial or prosecutorial FIUs include Cyprus and Luxembourg.[28]

4. Hybrid FIUs

This last category encompasses FIUs that contain different combinations of the arrangements described in the other three categories. This hybrid type of arrangement is an attempt to obtain the advantages of the different types of FIUs put together in one organization. Some FIUs combine the features of administrative-type and law enforcement-type of FIUs, while others combine the powers of the customs office with those of the police. It may be noted that in some FIUs, staff from various regulatory and law enforcement agencies work in the FIU, while continuing to exercise the powers of their agency of origin. Among the countries that have established "hybrid" FIUs are Denmark, Jersey, Guernsey, and Norway.[29]

---

27. *Id.*
28. *Id.*
29. *Id.*

D. Possible Additional Functions

In addition to its core function responsibilities, an FIU could be given a number of other funtions, regardless of which model is utilized.

1. Supervisory and Regulatory Responsibilities

The FIU could be granted the power to supervise financial institutions and non-financial businesses and professions with regard to their compliance with record keeping and reporting requirements.[30] In such cases, the FIU could also be authorized to impose sanctions or penalties against such entities and persons for failing to comply with their reporting or recordkeeping obligations—for example, meaningful fines and/or license suspensions. Furthermore, the FIU could be authorized to promulgate regulations necessary for the implementation of laws against money laundering and terrorist financing.

Some authority within the country needs to be responsible for these compliance matters. In most countries, this responsibility belongs to the supervisory authority of each financial sector, non-financial business or profession. But, because the FIU is the unique recipient of financial intelligence, in addition to which it analyzes financial intelligence, the FIU is well placed to monitor compliance with AML and CFT obligations. Some countries have opted to give the AML/CFT compliance responsibility to the FIU. In certain countries, some reporting entities and persons are not subject to any supervision other than that of the FIU, which makes it the most suitable body to address the compliance issues raised in this context.

In addition, the FIU could be authorized to issue regulations for the financial and other reporting sectors with regard to the implementation of laws against money laundering. Giving such responsibilities to the FIU, however, should take into account issues of balancing AML/CFT needs with other supervisory concerns. To be effective, an FIU must receive adequate resources and appropriate government support for the FIU to accomplish its core functions and any additional responsibilities. If the FIU's staffing capacity is lim-

---

30. *Id.*, Other FIU Functions

ited, additional supervisory or regulatory functions could undermine its core functions.

2. Investigations

Countries may grant their FIUs the function of providing investigative support to other law enforcement agencies in the course of ongoing investigations on money laundering. In this case, the FIU would be expected to share information with investigative authorities upon request. These powers may entail the exercise of additional powers that would enable the FIU to request additional information from financial institutions or even to carry out investigations, including identifying potential assets, to be frozen, seized, or confiscated.

3. Enforcement and Blocking of Assets

Countries may also grant their FIU the power to take provisional measures to deal effectively with cases where urgent action is needed. Because the FIU is a crucial governmental point for identifying suspicious transactions, it is logical to grant the FIU provisional powers to preserve assets that might become subject to confiscation. Such measures could include the temporary freezing of assets as well as other measures that restrain any legal disposition of these assets.

Such provisional powers require, however, that the FIU be able to investigate and identify any assets vulnerable to confiscation under the laws against money laundering and terrorist financing. In doing so, however, particular care should be taken to assure that the FIU has sufficient resources to perform its core functions—that is, receiving and analyzing the suspicious-transaction reports, as well as sharing information with domestic and international counterparts.

Where provisional powers of blocking transactions and/or freezing assets are authorized, such powers are usually limited in terms of the duration of the blocking or freezing. Freezing or seizing assets usually requires judicial authorities or a government authority outside the FIU.[31]

4. Training

Because of focused and multidisciplinary expertise of an FIU, it could easily serve as the governmental unit to advise and train personnel from financial institutions in measures to fight money laundering and terrorist financing.

Again, countries must consider resource limitations in deciding whether to attach this function to the FIU. Capacity, funding and expertise are crucial concerns in this area, since demand for such services could become extensive.

5. Research

The FIU is in a unique position to provide research to its government based upon its experience of receiving, analyzing an disseminating financial information on money laundering and terrorist financing. This is especially true if the FIU is given a broad mandate with regard to strategic analysis, as discussed above in this chapter. Its strategic function could easily be expanded to authorize separate research and reports on its findings.

As with so many functions, the addition of research and the scope of that research depend upon funding, staffing and expertise. Without such resources, the core functions of the FIU could suffer.

E. Organizing the FIU

There are numerous decisions that have to be made in establishing the FIU or enhancing the operations of an existing FIU.

---

31. *Id.*

1. Choosing the Right Model

Good decisions about the proper model to adopt for an FIU proceed from equally sound knowledge about a country's cultural and economic characteristics and its legal and law enforcement traditions. Although no single model will work for all countries, some criteria are essential; the discussion below is given in the form of questions:

- Will or does the FIU possess relevant capacity and expertise in financial operations? If not, what is needed?
- What is the relationship between the proposed or existing FIU and the financial industry in the domestic context? What would enhance that relationship?
- Will or does the institution possess a culture conducive to protecting the confidentiality of financial information and to mitigating potential harm to individual privacy?
- Will or does the proposed FIU possess the actual legal authority, technical capacity, and experience to provide appropriate and timely international cooperation?
- Would the legal framework applicable to the proposed or existing FIU allow it to take part in the international administrative type of cooperation and would the legal framework allow for rapid, efficient, spontaneous and/or "upon request" international information exchanges relating to suspicious transactions?

2. Capacity Considerations

Financial investigations are only as good as the individual investigators and the technological infrastructure that supports the financial intelligence efforts. A country must make policy determinations on how the FIU can make the best use of the financial analytical skills of its staff members. In this regard, the country must also determine the best institutional setting for these skills—the central bank, ministry of finance, the police, the judiciary. Fashioning an FIU as a wholly separate agency from a country's existing regulatory, administrative, or law enforcement agencies could also have serious resource implications.

3. Staffing Considerations

Recruitment policies have implications for matters relating to resources, privacy, and institutional effectiveness. The relative rarity of investigatory financial expertise means that staffing considerations should be driven by the multidisciplinary nature of financial investigations in order to make recruitment as diverse as possible.

Staff background and the terms of employment are both important. On the one hand, treasury or finance ministry officials, banking supervisors, and customs officers could bring their respective financial expertise and their understanding of transactions involving reporting entities. On the other hand, police or judicial officers bring useful law enforcement experience, particularly if the FIU has been granted law enforcement powers.

The terms of employment also impact the degree of independence, and the degree of confidentiality in the work of the FIU. The rarity of the high level skills/experience required of FIU analysts means that some countries might opt for staffing their units with experts seconded from other agencies. Although this is a less-costly staffing option—and probably one that is more conducive to effective information sharing—governments need to weigh the privacy and longer term implications of such decisions.

F. Privacy Safeguards

FIUs are repositories, as well as guardians, of highly sensitive information, a fact that calls for constant vigilance regarding legal and systemic safeguards.

1. The Main Policy Tension: Privacy Versus Efficiency

Certain policy tensions emerge as FIUs take shape; these stem mostly from the ambitious goals of AML and CFT laws and regulations, which compete with or erode rival privacy interests.[32]

---

32. The Egmont Group's statement of purpose, in the preamble, provides that it is "mindful of...the sensitive nature of disclosures of financial information." The Group also holds that "FIUs should work to encourage that national legal standards and privacy laws are not conceived

Laws against money laundering have emerged, in part, as a response to the obstacles that bank secrecy laws posed to supervisory and law enforcement efforts. In some jurisdictions, strong bank secrecy requirements have frequently defeated investigative efforts to obtain financial information required to detect crimes and regulatory breaches, or for tracing or confiscating assets. Such a result is contrary to the FATF recommended structure, which provides that financial institution privacy laws should not inhibit any of the FATF recommendations.[33] Cumbersome procedures also hamper investigative efforts to gather information and/or evidence abroad. With financial globalization, such concerns have become even more acute. AML/CFT laws can be seen as an attempt to ensure efficient information exchange and evidence gathering, both domestically and internationally, as prerequisites for effective regulatory and criminal law enforcement in today's globalized economy.

The very sensitive and confidential nature of financial information means that FIUs need to institute stringent procedural safeguards for their important financial evidence gathering and information sharing functions. Effective law enforcement rests on efficient and speedy access to financial information. But this law enforcement need pushes against the boundaries of financial privacy concerns, raising legitimate concerns about the potential for abuse.

In its roles as repository, processor, and clearinghouse of financial information relating to the crime of money laundering and terrorist financing, FIUs are at the forefront of this debate about efficiency versus privacy. This tension is reflected in the choices countries make about the structure, functions, powers, and procedures of their financial intelligence units. Countries need to make realistic assessments of the costs to privacy inherent in each of the choices they make about the FIU's authorities and restrictions.

2. Confidentiality Principle

Imposing the confidentiality principle on FIUs is one of the most important protections against abuse of financial information privacy. This principle will

---

so as to inhibit the exchange of information, in accordance with these principles, between or among FIUs; see The Egmont Group, Principles for Information Exchange between Financial Intelligence Units for Money Laundering Cases, (June 13, 2001), Principle 7. http://www.egmontgroup.org/princ_info_exchange.pdf.
33. *The Forty Recommendations*, Rec. 4

also enable the FIU to exercise its functions as an intermediary between the reporting parties and the criminal justice system.

In cases where the FIU is part of another agency, such as the police or the office of the public prosecutor, the unit is usually governed by a general duty of confidentiality. In the absence of such a general duty, however, a specific duty of confidentiality should be expressed in the legal provisions governing and creating the FIU, and should be enforced by criminal and/or effective civil sanctions.[34] The duty of confidentiality may also be contained in domestic privacy laws of general application.

The FIU's duty of confidentiality, however, should be drafted so as not to restrict unduly the possibility of providing feedback to the reporting entities, as feedback is important both for the relationship between the FIU and the financial intermediaries and for enabling the reporting institutions to develop efficient reporting mechanisms.[35] Confidentiality requirements should be drafted in a way that does not inhibit international cooperation among FIUs.[36]

3. Specialty Principle

To complement the duty of confidentiality, FIUs can adopt a "specialty principle," which serves to limit the use of information reported to it by financial institutions and others, or as requested by the FIU from reporting parties. If an FIU is prohibited from using information provided to it for any purpose other than fighting money laundering and terrorist financing (and related crimes), countries can develop a sense of trust between reporting institutions and other parties and the FIU.

The specialty limitation necessarily depends on what it means to "fight money laundering and terrorist financing." The restriction could be drafted to mean the financial information managed by the FIU could be used only for the performance of the agency's duties, as described in the law that estab-

---

34. Guy Stessens, *Money Laundering: A New International Law Enforcement Model* (Cambridge, England, and New York, New York, United States: Cambridge University Press, 2000), 191.
35. See section G, Information and Feedback, of this Chapter. See also FATF, Providing Feedback to reporting Financial Institutions and Other Persons: Best Practice Guidelines, ¶ 6, available at http://www.fatf-gafi.org/pdf/FEEDB_en.pdf.
36. The Egmont Group, Principles of Information Exchange between Financial Intelligence Units for Money Laundering Cases (June 13, 2001), Principle 7.

lished the FIU. It could also be expressed in a specific statutory or regulatory stipulation regarding the conditions for the dissemination of information by the FIU.

The specialty principle should be drafted in sufficiently broad language so that the FIU is not prevented from enforcing the laws and regulations against money laundering and terrorist financing. This should also allow for information supplied to the FIU to be used to enforce laws and regulations relating to the underlying predicate offense or offenses. In addition, if the specialty principle applies to international information exchanges among FIUs, it should be drafted so as not to inhibit or damage the efficiency of international cooperation among FIUs.[37]

Breaches of the specialty limitation should be sanctioned by procedural laws about inadmissibility of the evidence before the courts, and/or by some form of civil or statutory liability for breach of confidentiality.

4. Independence and Accountability

Countries must assure the independence of the FIU from political influence, as well as independence from the competent or other supervisory authority in deciding which transactions to analyze or what information to disseminate. Independence provides another measure of protection against the abuse or misuse of financial disclosures. Independence is not an absolute concept, there will always be some measure of accountability, but the FIU should not be subject to abuse or undue influence from other government authorities. This sense of independence further supports a sense of trust between the FIU and reporting financial entities, which, in turn, promotes the prevention and detection of money laundering and terrorist financing.

This independence could be guaranteed in several ways. In certain instances it could be accomplished by creating the FIU as a separate agency with an autonomous budget and staff without accountability to any agencies that might be inclined to use the system beyond its proper limits. This inde-

---

37. *Id.*, at Principles of Information Exchange between Financial Intelligence Units for Money Laundering Cases (June 13, 2001), Principles 11 and 12.

pendence should, however, be accompanied by proper accountability mechanisms, such as parliamentary reporting, audits, and/or judicial oversight.

G. Information and Feedback

It is important that the FIU work closely with reporting entities and persons, as well as a country's competent authorities, to fight money laundering and terrorist financing. Consistent with its privacy obligations, the FIU should provide feedback about money laundering and terrorist financing trends and typologies that will assist financial institutions and non-financial businesses and persons to improve their AML/CFT practices and controls and, in particular, their reporting of suspicious transactions. It is a frequent criticism by reporting institutions that they receive little or no feedback from their FIUs about the usefulness of their reports. Thus, reporting entities have no guidance about whether their approach to reporting is helpful in the fight against money laundering and terrorist financing.

While there are obviously constraints on what an FIU can tell a reporting institution about a particular report (especially if that report involves an ongoing enquiry), it should be possible for the FIU to give general feedback to institutions about the quality and usefulness of their reports. FIUs will also have collected data, which once analyzed, should produce useful information about developments and trends in money laundering. This should be shared with reporting entities and persons so that they know what to look out for in designing their AML/CFT systems. Feedback about particular case histories, once any investigation and legal proceedings are over, should also prove useful.

The FATF now provides that all competent authorities, including FIUs, should establish guidance and provide feedback.[38] Authorities can expect this issue to feature prominently in AML/CFT assessments. FIUs will also need to maintain comprehensive statistics on STRs received and disseminated.[39]

---

38. *The Forty Recommendations*, Rec. 25.
39. *Id.*, Rec. 32.

Chapter VIII

International Cooperation

O rganized crime and other large and highly profitable criminal activities are increasingly being perpetrated on a cross-border basis. This is particularly the case for money-laundering operations, where criminals use the open international financial system to benefit from free movement of capital throughout the world in order to hide the illicit origins of the proceeds of their crime and further their illicit activities. In the context of fighting money laundering from the global standpoint, rapid exchanges of information and effective international cooperation among the various agencies in countries throughout the world have become a prerequisite to success.

International cooperation is needed more and more at all stages (i.e., the financial intelligence gathering, investigative and prosecution stages) of anti money laundering (AML), investigations. At the financial intelligence gathering stage of a money laundering case, for instance, financial intelligence units (FIUs) need to exchange information with their foreign counterparts in order to be able to analyze properly suspicious activity reports and other financial disclosures. The same can be said for the investigating stage in order for the police to investigate successfully money laundering cases. The ability to exchange rapidly information with their foreign counterparts, without undue obstacles or delay, is increasingly becoming a key feature of any FIU, law enforcement or prosecution authority.

In addition, having in mind that money launderers are always looking for safe havens with lax, ineffective or corrupt AML and combating the financing of terrorism (CFT) regimes, or those with limited international cooperation capabilities, countries will find that having a proper international cooperation framework in place helps them to prevent, detect and prosecute money laundering in their own domestic financial system.

A. Prerequisites for Effective International Cooperation

In order for countries to be able to use the existing channels of international cooperation, they need to meet several prerequisites, including: (1) building a comprehensive and efficient domestic capacity; (2) ratifying and implementing the international conventions regarding money laundering and terrorism financing; and (3) complying with the recommendations of the Financial Action Task Force on Money Laundering (FATF), i.e. *The Forty Recommendations on Money Laundering* (*The Forty Recommendations*)[1] and the nine *Special Recommendations on Terrorist Financing* (*Special Recommendations*),[2] as well as with other sector-specific international standards.

1. Prerequisite Conditions for International Cooperation: Building a Comprehensive and Efficient Domestic Capacity

Naturally, putting in place all the necessary authorities and providing them with all the necessary powers, responsibilities, staffing and budget so that

---

1. *The Forty Recommendations* at http://www.fatf-gafi.org/pdf/40Recs-2003_en.pdf. Reprinted in Annex IV of this Reference Guide.
2. *Special Recommendations* at http://www.fatf-gafi.org/pdf/SRecTF_en.pdf. Reprinted in Annex V of this Reference Guide.

they can perform efficiently their duties is a prerequisite for a country to be able to cooperate at the international level with its partners.[3]

Among others, in order to have an effective AML/CFT framework, a country should have established administrative supervisory authorities to oversee financial institutions in each sector, as well as an FIU—that is, a central authority charged with receiving and analyzing suspicious transaction activities(STA) and other types of mandatory reporting (such as cash transaction reports) for the purpose of fighting money laundering and terrorist financing.

Similarly, on the criminal justice system side, countries should have effective police services with specialized skills and training in money laundering and terrorist financing investigations, as well as a functioning, non corrupt judicial/prosecutorial system.

Properly building and staffing these authorities provide the foundation for an effective and comprehensive framework for fighting money laundering and terrorist financing at both the domestic and international levels.

2. Ratifying and Implementing the International Conventions

All countries should sign and ratify the relevant conventions adopted by the United Nations (UN): In particular, countries should sign and ratify the *UN Convention Against Illicit Traffic in Narcotic Drugs and Psychotropic Substances* (1988) (*Vienna Convention*),[4] the *UN Convention for the Suppression of the Financing of Terrorism* (1999),[5] and the *UN Convention Against Transnational Organized Crime* (2000) (*Palermo Convention*).[6] These actions are part of FATF's recommendations.[7]

In addition, countries should sign and ratify the other AML and CFT conventions adopted by organizations in their respective region, such as the Council of Europe's Convention on Laundering, Search, Seizure

---

3. *The Forty Recommendations*, Rec. 36.
4. The *Vienna Convention*, http://www.incb.org/e/conv/1988/.
5. UN Convention for the Suppression of the Financing of Terrorism, http://www.un.org/law/cod/finterr.htm.
6. The *Palermo Convention*, http://www.unodc.org/palermo/convmain.html.
7. *The Forty Recommendations*, Rec. 1, and Special Recommendations, Spec. Rec. I.

and Confiscation of the Proceeds from Crime (1990) (the Strasbourg Convention).[8]

Countries should implement fully all of the provisions of these conventions in their domestic laws, including those related to the criminalization of money laundering and international cooperation, which will enable them to take part in the mutual legal assistance arrangements provided by these conventions.[9]

3. Complying with the FAFT Recommendations and Other Sector Specific International Standards

Countries should comply with the existing international standards for fighting organized crime, money laundering, and combating the financing of terrorism. These standards include the FATF recommendations, which apply to all aspects of a country's laws and regulations against money laundering and the financing of terrorism. It includes as well the Core Principles for Effective Banking Supervision adopted by Basel Committee on Banking Supervision (the Basel Committee), and its Customer Due Diligence Principles; Other standards have been set by the International Association of Insurance Supervisors (IAIS), the International Organization of Securities Commissions (IOSCO) and the Egmont Group.

Each of these standard setters requires that each country establish international channels of cooperation with their foreign partners. For instance, FATF recommends that "each country should make efforts to improve a spontaneous or upon request international information exchange relating to suspicious transactions, persons and corporations involved in those transactions between competent authorities."[10] In addition to general principles on international cooperation against money laundering, specific conditions apply to the international cooperation between FIUs, financial supervisory authorities, and between law enforcement and judicial authorities.

---

8. *The Forty Recommendations*, Rec. 35.
9. *Id.*, at Rec. 36.
10. *Id.*, at Rec. 40.

B. General Principles of International Cooperation Against Money Laundering

According to the relevant international standards, the following general principles should be implemented by countries in order to ensure that effective gateways for the exchange of information and the provision of international cooperation exist at each stage of a money laundering or terrorist financing investigation:

- When an authority in country A has information officially requested by an authority in country B, the requested country-A authority should be in a position to provide the information promptly to the requesting authority in country B.

- When an authority in country A has information it knows would be useful for an authority in country B, the country-A authority should be able to provide the information spontaneously and promptly to the country-B authority.

- When an authority in country A is requested by a country-B authority to obtain information or a document, or to conduct an investigation or an inquiry, or to perform a particular action useful in the context of an analysis, investigation, or prosecution of money laundering, the requested country-A authority should be in a position to perform the requested action (naturally if this action is permitted by rules regulating the performance of its duties at the domestic level).[11]

This exchange of information with, or provision of assistance and cooperation to, a foreign authority should not be subject to unduly restrictive conditions. It is generally accepted however that the requested authority can subject its assistance to certain conditions. For example, the requested authority could subject its assistance to the following conditions and stipulate that the requesting authority:

- Perform similar functions as the requested authority (specialty principle);
- Describe in its request the purpose and the scope of information to be used, and the information, once transmitted by the requested authori-

---

11. *Id.*, at Recs. 36 and 40.

ty, should be treated by the requesting authority according to the scope of its request (transparency);

- Is subject to confidentiality provisions similar to those applicable to the requested authority (confidentiality); and
- Is itself in a position to exchange information with the requested authority (reciprocity).

C. International Cooperation Between FIUs

Because money laundering is a cross-border activity, the detection of money laundering operations often depends on information sharing among FIUs in different countries and on their ability to cooperate, efficiently and speedily, with their foreign counterparts. In addition, countries should be aware of the possible consequences of choosing a particular organizational structure when establishing their FIU.

1. The Core Features of FIU International Cooperation

An FIU's ability to cooperate at the international level depends on a principle of mutual recognition among entities performing the same duties and on a foundation of mutual trust.[12] The consequence is that each FIU should possess certain core features in accordance with the Egmont Group definition and act in accordance with the Egmont principles. This would enable the entity to qualify and to be treated as an FIU by other FIUs. These features are described in Chapter VII, the Financial Intelligence Unit.

In addition, each FIU should be authorized by law to share financial information and other relevant financial intelligence with its foreign counterparts. In particular, the FIU should be able to cooperate and exchange information either on its own initiative or upon request. This could be achieved on the basis of reciprocity or formal mutual agreement, such as memorandum of understanding (MOU). Finally, the requested FIU should

---

12. Revised Statement of Purpose, The Egmont Group (Julyne 123, 20031), http://www.egmont group.org/statement_of_purpose.pdf.

be authorized to produce, and be capable of producing, promptly any available information or analysis that may be relevant to an investigation by the requesting FIU.

2. Conditioning the FIU's Ability to Cooperate at the International Level

The FIU's ability to cooperate at the international level should not be subject to unduly restrictive conditions (see Part B of this Chapter for legislative restrictions). Adequate safeguards—including confidentiality provisions—should be in place to ensure that information exchanges between FIUs are consistent with fundamental domestic and internationally agreed-on principles of privacy and data protection.[13] At a minimum, every country should ensure that information received from a foreign FIU is treated with and protected by the same confidentiality provisions that apply to similar information obtained from domestic sources.[14]

3. The Relationship Between Different Organizational Models and International Cooperation

An FIU should be authorized to cooperate at the international level with all its foreign counterparts, regardless of their internal and organizational structure. This point is particularly important in light of the diverse organizational structures that exist among FIUs worldwide. Indeed, while most FIUs, as financial intelligence gathering bodies, are attached to administrative authorities, such as ministries of finance, treasury departments, regulatory/ supervisory authorities, or other ad hoc administrative structures, other FIUs are attached to police units. Some are even attached to prosecutors' offices. In addition, even if most FIUs share the same responsibilities, there could be some other structural differences among them, as well as certain legal/procedural differences. Therefore, the rules governing the ability of a particular FIU to cooperate to the fullest extent at the international level have to take

---

13. *The Forty Recommendations*, Rec. 40.
14. Principles for Information Exchange Between financial Intelligence Units for Money Laundering Cases, Annex to Statement of Purpose, The Egmont Group.

this diversity into account. In other words, the rules need to be sufficiently flexible so that FIUs can exchange information with all its counterparts, regardless of their nature or organizational structure.[15]

The question for a country is (1) whether there are or should be restrictions on sharing financial information; (2) if so, how much information should be shared; and (3) what type of information should be shared. Thus, policy makers must be aware that choosing a particular organizational model may have direct and/or indirect consequences on the FIU's ability to cooperate at the international level. For instance, creating a purely judiciary-based FIU may hamper international cooperation with other countries that do not have a judicial FIU. Indeed, in many countries, fundamental or constitutional legal principles do not allow judicial authorities to have access to the same international cooperation or information-exchange channels as the administrative authorities or the police. In certain countries, these legal principles oblige the judicial authorities to cooperate at the international level only in accordance with the judicial cooperation procedures (mutual legal assistance mechanisms), which are governed by treaties and principles that may contain a number of restrictive conditions. Such conditions may inhibit the comprehensive and rapid exchange of information with other FIUs at the intelligence stage.

D. International Cooperation Between Financial Supervisory Authorities

It is widely recognized that financial supervisors (banking insurance and securities) should be authorized to cooperate—spontaneously or upon request—with their foreign counterparts with respect to AML/CFT analysis and regulatory investigations. The general principles of international cooperation, as described above in Part B, apply to these particular information exchange channels. In the supervisory context, this cooperation takes place in each specific sector between the relevant supervisors.

---

15. *The Forty Recommendations*, Recs. 40.

1. Cooperation Between Banking Supervisors

With respect to information sharing, the Basel Committee has issued additional principles, which apply to all banking supervisors. These principles have been established in the Customer Due Diligence paper, issued by the Basel Committee in October 2001. In particular, branch supervisors of banking groups should not be constrained from sharing consolidated reports pertaining to deposits, "borrower concentration," or notification of funds under management if the home country supervisor needs this information.[16]

The host jurisdiction should permit foreign home-country supervisors or auditors to carry out on-site inspections to verify compliance with home country "Know Your Customer" (KYC) procedures and policies at the local branch level and among subsidiaries of foreign banks. This will require are view of customer files and random sampling of accounts.[17]

Foreign home-country supervisors, or auditors, should have access, in the host jurisdiction, to information on individual customer accounts, to the extent necessary. This is to say, to the extent that permits supervisors to properly evaluate the due diligence standards being applied to customer identification, as well as to evaluate the risk management practices in place.[18]

Finally, supervisors should have safeguards in place to ensure that information regarding individual accounts obtained through cooperative arrangements is used exclusively for lawful supervisory purposes, and can be protected by the recipient in a satisfactory manner.[19]

2. Cooperation Between Securities Supervisors

IOSCO has issued additional principles that apply to all securities supervisors. The securities supervisor should have authority to share both public and nonpublic information with domestic and foreign counterparts.[20]

---

16. Basel Committee on Banking Supervision, *Customer Due Diligence, for Banks*, October 2001, para. 68. http://www.bis.org/publ/bcbs85.pdf.
17. *Id.*
18. *Id.*
19. *Id.*
20. International Organization of Securities Commissioners (IOSCO), Core Principle No. 11. http://www.iaisweb.org/358coreprinicplesmethodologyoct03revised.pdf. For further information, see the IOSCO Multilateral MOU (May 2002).

Cooperative mechanisms should be in place at the international level to facilitate the detection and deterrence of cross-border misconduct and assist in the discharge of licensing and supervisory responsibilities. Among these are memoranda of understanding.[21]

International cooperation can provide assistance in: (1) obtaining public or nonpublic information, for example, about a license holder, a listed company, shareholder, beneficial owner, or a person exercising control over a license holder or company; banking, brokerage, or other records; (2)arranging for voluntary cooperation from those who may have information about the subject of an inquiry; (3) procuring information under compulsion—either or both the production of documents and oral testimony or statements; (4) providing information on the regulatory processes in a jurisdiction; or (5) securing court orders, for example, or other urgent court injunctions.[22]

Information-sharing arrangements, whether formal or informal, should consider providing assistance in obtaining or providing (1) public or non-public information, for example, about a license holder, listed company, shareholder, beneficial owner or a person exercising control over a license holder or company; (2) banking, brokerage or other records; (3) voluntary cooperation from those who may have information about the subject of an inquiry; (4) information under compulsion—either or both the production of documents and oral testimony or statements; and (5) information on the regulatory process in a jurisdiction, or in obtaining court orders, for example, urgent injunctions.[23]

3. Cooperation Between Insurance Supervisors

Insurance supervisors have no formal rules governing cooperation with each other for specific AML purposes. This does not mean that they do not share information to the extent permitted by their respective jurisdictions. In any

---

21. IOSCO, Principles, Sec. 9.4. See also IOSCO Principles, Sec. 11.10, and IOSCO Public Document No. 52, Discussion Paper on International Cooperation in Relation to Cross-Border Activity of Collective Investment Schemes, IOSCO Technical Committee, June 1996.

22. IOSCO Principles, Sec. 9.4; IOSCO, "Report on Issues Raised for Securities and Futures Regulators by Under-regulated and Uncooperative Jurisdictions," Public Document No. 41,IOSCO Technical Committee, October 1994.

23. IOSCO, Principles, Sec. 9.3.

event, the general principles of international cooperation, as described above, should apply in the insurance sector.

E. International Cooperation Between Law Enforcement and Judicial Authorities

International cooperation among prosecutorial and judicial authorities is vital to any framework that hopes to be comprehensive and efficient against money laundering activities. Almost no prosecution of money laundering can succeed without the support of a foreign jurisdiction at one point of the investigation.[24]

International cooperation depends upon the signing and ratification of all the relevant conventions agreed by the United Nations and other regional international organizations. Indeed, these conventions often provide the necessary legal basis to exchange information with and undertake actions on behalf of foreign judicial authorities.

The general principles in this area are the same as those described in Part B, above. The unique nature of judicial international cooperation means that a number of additional and/or entirely specific principles have been established in this area. These principles come from the various United Nations conventions, as well as from the FATF recommendations.

It should be emphasized that varying constitutional requirements should be respected and addressed when negotiating arrangements among sovereign judicial authorities. In addition, care has to be taken not to allow suspects to take refuge in the non-extraditable category of "political crimes" in AML/CFT cases, especially when influential persons are involved.

1. Basic Principles

Laws and procedures should encourage and facilitate mutual legal assistance in AML/CFT law-enforcement matters, particularly with regard to the use of compulsory measures. These include the production of records by financial institutions and other persons; the search of persons and premises; the track-

---

24. *The Forty Recommendations*, Rec. 36.

ing of property and the identification of assets; and the seizure of assets and obtaining evidence for use in AML/CFT investigations and prosecutions and in related actions in foreign jurisdictions.[25]

Appropriate laws and procedures must provide for effective mutual legal assistance in AML/CFT investigations or proceedings where the requesting jurisdiction is seeking: (1) the production or seizure of information, documents, or evidence (including financial records) from financial institutions, other entities, or natural persons; (2) searches of financial institutions, other entities, and domiciles; (3) the taking of witnesses' statements; and (4) the tracking, identifying, freezing, seizure, and confiscation of assets laundered or intended to be laundered, the proceeds of money laundering and assets used for or intended to be used for the financing of terrorism, as well as the instrumentalities of such offenses, or assets of corresponding value.[26]

Treaties or other formal arrangements (and informal mechanisms) must be in place to support international cooperation; such as through the use of bilateral or multilateral mutual legal assistance.[27] Institutional and other arrangements should permit law enforcement authorities to exchange information with their international counterparts regarding the subjects of investigations; such arrangements should be based on agreements in force and by other mechanisms for cooperation. In addition, national authorities should record the number, source, and purpose of requests for such information exchange, as well as its resolution.

Countries should provide its relevant law enforcement and judicial authorities with adequate financial, human, and technical resources so that they can ensure adequate oversight, conduct investigations, and respond promptly and fully to requests for assistance received from other countries.

2. Additional Principles

To the greatest extent possible, differing standards in the requesting and requested jurisdictions concerning the "mental intent" of the offense under domestic law should not affect the ability to provide mutual legal assistance.[28]

---

25. *Id.*, at Rec. 40.
26. *Id.*, at Rec. 38.
27. *Id.*, at Rec 27.
28. *Id.*, at Rec 36.

Assistance should be provided in investigations and proceedings where persons have committed both laundering and the predicate offenses, as well as in investigations and proceedings where persons have committed money laundering only.

Authorities should be authorized to conduct cooperative investigations (including controlled delivery of confidential information) along with other countries' appropriate competent authorities; assurance should be offered that adequate safeguards are in place.[29]

Arrangements should permit the effective cross-border coordination of seizure and forfeiture, including, where permissible, authorizing the sharing of confiscated assets with other countries when confiscation is directly or indirectly a result of coordinated law enforcement actions.[30]

Finally, procedures should allow for the extradition of individuals charged with a money-laundering, terror-financing, or related offense or for prosecution of the accused domestically when he or she is not extraditable.[31]

F. Considerations for Fiscal Matter Offenses

In general, countries should ensure that their competent authorities provide the widest possible range of international cooperation to their foreign counterparts. As noted above (Section B), countries are entitled to place certain conditions on their assistance, although they must avoid placing unduly restrictive conditions upon their assistance. A condition that may be applied to mutual legal assistance or extradition is dual criminality, although countries are encouraged to render such help even in the absence of dual criminality.

Some countries do not criminalize certain fiscal offenses, such as tax evasion, as offenses for money laundering predicate and, thus, may not be able to provide assistance if another country requests it in the context of an enquiry concerning the laundering of the proceeds of a fiscal crime. However, if fiscal matters are only a part of the request and it has a non-fiscal component as well, provided the non-fiscal component includes a money laundering predicate, the requested country should provide assistance.

---

29. *Id.*, at Rec 27.
30. *Id.*, at Rec 38.
31. *Id.*, at Rec 39

Chapter IX

Combating the Financing of Terrorism

The terrorist attacks on the United States on September 11, 2001, increased the importance of preventing, detecting and suppressing the financing of terrorism and terrorist acts on the part of the international community. In October of 2001, the Financial Action Task Force on Money Laundering (FATF) expanded its mission beyond anti-money laundering (AML) to include the worldwide effort of combating the financing of terrorism (CFT).

To achieve these goals, FATF adopted the original eight *Special Recommendations on Terrorist Financing* (*Special Recommendations*) at the same time that it amended its mission. In October 2004, FATF adopted new Special Recommendation IX regarding cash couriers. Like its earlier efforts, *The Forty Recommendations on Money Laundering* (*The Forty Recommendations*), FATF's *Special Recommendations* are not suggestions, but rather mandates for action by every country, not just FATF members, if that country is to be viewed as complying with international standards for

CFT.[1] Countries may also wish to consult the Methodology on AML/CFT for information on how the *Special Recommendations* are evaluated.[2] Moreover, FATF specifically invited all countries to adopt the *Special Recommendations* and participate in its self-assessment exercise.[3] Implementation of the *Special Recommendations*, together with *The Forty Recommendations*, sets out the basic framework to detect, prevent and suppress terrorist financing.

The *Special Recommendations* are still relatively new. Thus, experience with interpreting and implementing them is somewhat limited. At first, FATF adopted general Guidance Notes to help explain the *Special Recommendations*.[4] As it has gained experience over time, FATF has issued formal and more authoritative Interpretive Notes for several of the *Special Recommendations*.[5] In addition, FATF has issued Best Practices guidance for several of the *Special Recommendations*.[6] Finally, FATF has issued *Guidance for Financial Institutions in Detecting Terrorist Financing* as a means of helping financial institutions learn about mechanisms used to finance terrorism.[7]

A. Ratification and Implementation of United Nations Instruments

The first *Special Recommendation* consists of two parts.[8] The first part provides that "each country is to take immediate steps to ratify and to implement fully the United Nations Convention for the Suppression of the Financing of Terrorism (1999)."[9] Assessors of compliance with this recom-

---

1. *Special Recommendations*, http://www.fatf-gafi.org/pdf/SRecTF_en.pdf. The Special Recommendations and Guidance Notes are reprinted in Annex V of this Reference Guide.*The Forty Recommendations*, http://www.fatf-gafi.org/pdf/40Recs-2003_en.pdf. *The Forty Recommendations* are reprinted in Annex IV of this Reference Guide.
2. http://www.fatf-gafi.org/pdf/Meth-2004_en.pdf.
3. elf-Assessment Questionnaire on Terrorist Financing, http://www.fatf-gafi.org/SAQTF_en.htm.
4. Guidance Notes for the Special Recommendations on Terrorist Financing (Guidance Notes) are reprinted in Annex VI of this Reference Guide, http://www.fatf-gafi.org/pdf/TF-SAGU-IDE20020327_en.pdf.
5. The Interpretive Notes for *Special Recommendations* II, III, VI and VII are reprinted in Annex VI of this Reference Guide. For Spec. Rec. II, http://www.fatf-gafi.org/pdf/INSR2_en.PDF and for Spec. Recs. III, VI and VII, http://www.fatf-gafi.org/TFInterpnotes.htm#Special%20Recommendation%20III.
6. For Spec. Rec. III, http://www.fatf-gafi.org/pdf/SR3-BPP_en.pdf; for Spec. Rec. VI, http://www.fatf-gafi.org/pdf/SR6-BPP_en.pdf; for Spec Rec. VIII, http://www.fatf-gafi.org/pdf/SR8-NPO_en.pdf.
7. http://www.fatf-gafi.org/pdf/GuidFITF01_en.pdf.
8. *Special Recommendations*, Spec. Rec. I.
9. See http://www.un.org/law/cod/finterr.htm. See also Chapter III, United Nations.

mendation pay particular attention to the specific action that a country has taken to implement the various provisions of this convention.

The second part of the first *Special Recommendation* requires each country to implement fully United Nations (UN) Security Council Resolutions dealing with terrorist financing, particularly Security Council Resolution 1373.[10] While the *Special Recommendations* specifically mention Resolution 1373,[11] all such resolutions dealing with terrorist financing should be addressed by a country. Moreover, the universe of such resolutions is likely to change over time. Listed below, are the Security Council Resolutions currently listed as important in the "Methodology for Assessing Compliance with the FATF 40 Recommendations and the FATF 8 Special Recommendations":[12]

- S/RES/1267 (1999)[13]
- S/RES/1333 (2000)[14]
- S/RES/1363 (2001)[15]
- S/RES/1390 (2002)[16]
- S/RES/1455 (2003)[17]
- S/RES/1526 (2004)[18]

As with all UN conventions, actual implementation is the key to compliance for FATF purposes. Implementation means that a country has taken all appropriate and necessary measures in order to make the provisions of the UN Convention and the UN Security Council Resolutions effective, i.e. legally binding within its borders.[19] These necessary measures may be accomplished by law, regulation, directive, decree or another appropriate legislative or executive action, according to the country's constitutional and legal framework.[20]

---

10. *Special Recommendations*, Spec. Rec. I.
11. http://www.state.gov/p/io/rls/othr/2001/5108.htm.
12. http://www.fatf-gafi.org/pdf/Meth-2004_en.PDF.
13. http://www.un.org/Docs/scres/1999/sc99.htm.
14. http://www.un.org/Docs/scres/2000/sc2000.htm.
15. http://www.un.org/Docs/scres/2001/sc2001.htm.
16. http://www.un.org/Docs/scres/2002/sc2002.htm.
17. http://www.un.org/Docs/sc/unsc_resolutions03.html.
18. http://www.un.org/Docs/sc/unsc_resolutions04.html.
19. FATF, Guidance Notes, Paragraph 5.
20. *Id.*

Of the UN Security Council Resolutions dealing with terrorist financing, the one that is specifically mentioned in this Recommendation is Resolution 1373.[21] This resolution obligates all UN member countries to:

- Criminalize actions to finance terrorism;
- Deny all forms of support for terrorist groups;
- Suppress the provision of safe haven or support for terrorists, including freezing funds or assets of persons, organizations or entities involved in terrorist acts;
- Prohibit active or passive assistance to terrorists; and
- Cooperate with other countries in criminal investigations and sharing information about planned terrorist acts.[22]

B. Criminalizing the Financing of Terrorism and Associated Money Laundering

The second of the *Special Recommendations* contains two elements, which require that each country should:

- Criminalize the financing of terrorism, terrorist acts and terrorist organizations; and
- Establish terrorist offenses as predicate offenses of money laundering.[23]

FATF has issued an Interpretive Note describing how a country should implement *Special Recommendation II*.[24] This recommendation requires each country to criminalize the financing of terrorism, terrorist acts and terrorist organizations whether the funds were derived illegally (in which case the action should be a predicate offence for money laundering under the second element of the recommendation) or legally. The legislation should be specific in terms of criminalizing the financing of terrorism. It is not enough

---

21. *Special Recommendations*, Spec. Rec. I.
22. S/RES/1371 (2001), http://www.un.org/Docs/scres/2001/sc2001.htm.
23. *Special Recommendations*, Spec. Rec. II.
24. http://www.fatf-gafi.org/pdf/INSR2_en.PDF.

to criminalize "aiding and abetting" or "attempting" or "conspiracy."[25] This concept is not always clear enough in some legal systems. The legislation should also cover any person who collects or provides funds with the intention that the funds should be used for terrorism; it is not necessary to establish or prove that the funds were actually used for terrorism.[26]

C. Freezing and Confiscating Terrorist Assets

Under the third *Special Recommendation*, each country should implement measures to freeze the "funds or other assets of terrorists, those who finance terrorism and terrorist organizations in accordance with the UN resolutions."[27] Furthermore, each country should take appropriate action to authorize competent authorities within the country "to seize and confiscate property that are the proceeds of, or used in, or intended or allocated for use in, the financing of terrorism, terrorist acts or terrorist organizations."[28]

FATF has issued a formal Interpretive Note for the implementation of *Special Recommendation III*.[29] In addition, FATF has also issued a set of Best Practices that should help countries understand how to best implement the requirements of this recommendation.[30]

In this recommendation, there are three basic concepts that may have different meanings in different countries: freezing, seizure and confiscation (or forfeiture). "Freezing" means that a competent authority within a country has the authorization to block or restrain specific funds or assets and, thereby, prevent those funds or assets from being moved or otherwise dispersed.[31] The "frozen" funds or assets remain the property of the owner and remain under the administration of the financial institution (or other entity) and under the control of existing management. The goal of freezing assets is to eliminate control over the assets by the owner so that the assets cannot be used for any prohibited purpose.

---

25. *Id.*
26. *Id.*
27. *Special Recommendations*, Spec. Rec. III.
28. *Id.*
29. http://www.fatf-gafi.org/pdf/INSR3_en.pdf.
30. http://www.fatf-gafi.org/pdf/SR3-BPP_en.pdf.
31. FATF, Interpretive Note for Spec. Rec. III, at Paragraph 7a.

"Seizure" means that the competent government authority has the authorization to take control of the specified funds or assets.[32] Under seizing, the assets or funds remain the property of the original owner, but possession, administration and management of the assets is taken over by the relevant competent authority. "Confiscation" or "forfeiture" means that the competent authority has authorization to transfer ownership of the specified funds or assets to the country itself.[33] Confiscation usually occurs when there is a criminal conviction or judicial decision that determined that the assets or funds were derived from criminal activity, or were intended to be used in violation of law.

The freezing of terrorist funds under the authority of the relevant UN resolutions should be done by administrative action without the need for further legislative or judicial procedures. Because implementation of U.N. Security Council resolutions is a binding legal obligation on member states, it should be possible for all countries to act immediately. Indeed it is very important that freezing action is immediate because if there is any delay, the funds are likely to be removed from the jurisdiction.

The United Nations 1267 Committee issues a consolidated list of individuals and organizations whose funds are ordered frozen under the various UNSCRs on Al-Qaeda, the Taliban and Osama bin-Laden.[34] The freezing order relates both to those individuals and organizations and anyone acting for them. The list is updated from time to time and a consolidated list is published on the UN website.

Under *Special Recommendation III*, countries should also have in place mechanisms to freeze funds of individuals or organizations involved in terrorism. This is also a general requirement under Security Council Resolution 1373. The Counter Terror Committee (CTC), acting under Resolution 1373, does not issue a list but gives the authority to individual countries to designate the persons and entities whose funds should be frozen. Countries should take into account the freezing action taken by other countries under Resolution 1373.[35] While there is no obligation to follow freezing action taken by other countries, such lists should be examined and, where appro-

---

32. *Id.*, at Paragraph 7b.
33. *Id.*, Guidance Notes, at Paragraph 7c.
34. http://www.un.org/Docs/sc/committees/1267/1267ListEng.htm.
35. FATF, Interpretive Note to Spec. Rec. II, at Paragraph I.

priate, imitated. Countries should take such action on the basis of reasonable grounds or reasonable belief that the designated entity or individual is involved in financing terrorism.

D. Reporting Suspicious Transactions Related to Terrorism

Under the fourth of the *Special Recommendations*, financial institutions, that "suspect or have reasonable grounds to suspect that funds are linked or related to, or are to be used for terrorism, terrorist acts or by terrorist organizations" should report promptly their suspicions to the competent authorities.[36]

This requirement applies to both financial institutions, as defined in *The Forty Recommendations*, and to the non-financial businesses and professions that are now defined in *The Forty Recommendations* (see Chapter 5).[37] These reporting requirements must be consistent in the application of the country's AML and CFT laws.

This recommendation involves reporting under two alternative circumstances: when there is a "suspicion" that funds are linked to terrorist financing; and when there are "reasonable grounds to suspect" that funds are linked to terrorist financing. The distinction between the two is the certainty that forms the standard for the required reporting of a transaction.[38] The "suspect" standard is a subjective standard and is the same as that used in FATF's AML recommendations.[39] The "reasonable grounds to suspect" standard is consistent with the AML recommendation, but is somewhat broader than the pure "suspect" standards and, thereby, requires reporting under a broader set of circumstances. Countries can satisfy this reporting requirement based upon either the "suspicion" or "having reasonable grounds to suspect" standard.[40]

---

36. *Special Recommendations*, Spec. Rec. IV.
37. FATF, Guidance Notes, at Paragraph 19.
38. FATF, Guidance Notes, at Paragraph 21.
39. *The Forty Recommendations*, Rec. 1513, which provides: "If financial institutions suspect that funds stem from a criminal activity," they should promptly report their suspicions.
40. FATF, Guidance Notes, at Paragraph 21.

E. International Cooperation

The fifth of the *Special Recommendations*, provides that each country should afford another country, through mutual legal assistance mechanism or other mechanisms, "the greatest possible measure of assistance in connection with criminal, civil enforcement, and administrative investigations, inquiries and proceedings relating to the financing of terrorism, terrorist acts and terrorist organizations."[41] Each country should also take all appropriate measures to assure that it does not provide safe havens for individuals charged with financing terrorism, terrorist acts or terrorist organizations, and should have procedures in place to extradite such persons, if possible.[42]

The first part of this recommendation mandates the exchange of information through mutual legal assistance mechanisms or means other than mutual legal assistance. "Mutual legal assistance" means the authority to provide a full range of legal assistance, including the taking of evidence; the search and seizure of documents or items relevant to criminal proceedings or criminal investigations; and the ability to enforce a foreign restraint, seizure, confiscation or forfeiture order in a criminal matter.[43] Exchange of information by means "other than through mutual legal assistance" means any other arrangement, including an exchange occurring through financial intelligence units (FIUs) or other governmental agencies that exchange information bilaterally pursuant to memoranda of understanding (MOUs), exchange of letter or otherwise.[44]

The second part of this recommendation concerns the concepts of "safe haven" and "extradition." These terms have the same meanings as the terms "safe haven,"[45] as used in UN Security Resolution 1373,[46] and "extradite,"[47] as used in the UN *International Convention for the Suppression of the Financing of Terrorism.*[48] With regard to extradition, countries should assure that "claims of political motivation are not recognized as a ground

---

41. *Special Recommendations*, Spec. Rec. V.
42. *Id.*
43. FATF, Guidance Notes, at Paragraph 24.
44. *Id.*, at Paragraph 25.
45. *Id.*, at Paragraph 26.
46. UN Security Resolution 1373 (2001), at paragraph 2 (c).
47. *Id.*
48. UN Convention of Suppression of the Financing of Terrorism, at Article 11, http://www.un.org/law/cod/finterr.htm.

for refusing requests to extradite persons alleged to be involved in terrorist financing."[49] This concept and phrasing are from the *UN Convention on Suppression of the Financing of Terrorism.*[50]

F. Alternative Remittance Systems

Under the sixth *Special Recommendation*, each country should take actions to ensure that individuals and legal entities that provide for "the transmission of money or value" are licensed or registered and subject to the same standards, i.e., *The Forty Recommendations*, that apply to other financial institutions.[51] In addition, those entities that perform such services illegally should be subject to administrative, civil or criminal sanctions.[52] Such requirements should apply the transmission on money or value through an informal transfer system.

FATF has issued an Interpretive Note as well as a set of Best Practices on *Special Recommendation VI*, in order to provide formal guidance and general assistance, respectively, to countries on how to implement this recommendation.[53]

Formal money remittance or transfer services are often provided by a distinct category of non-bank financial institutions, through which funds are moved on behalf of individuals or legal entities through a dedicated network or through the regulated banking system. For purposes of determining compliance with *The Forty Recommendations*, these money transmitters, which are included within the definition of the term "financial institutions," should be subject to a country's AML/CFT laws, and should be licensed or registered.[54]

The "money or value transfer system" refers to a type of financial service through which funds or value are moved from one geographic location to another through informal and unsupervised networks or mechanisms.[55] In many jurisdictions, these informal systems have traditionally operated out-

---

49. FATF, Guidance Notes, at Paragraph 26.
50. Article 14 of Convention.
51. *Special Recommendations*, Spec. Rec. VI.
52. *Id.*
53. http://www.fatf-gafi.org/pdf/INSR6_en.PDF and http://www.fatf-gafi.org/pdf/SR6-BPP_en.pdf.
54. *The Forty Recommendations*, Glossary, Financial Institutions.
55. FATF, Guidance Notes, at paragraph 31, and Interpretive Note at paragraph 4.

side the regulated financial sector, as described above. Such informal systems include the Black Market Peso Exchange, *hundi* or *Hawala* systems.[56]

The goal of *Special Recommendation VI* is to assure that countries impose AML and CFT requirements on all forms of money/value transfer systems.[57] Thus, at a minimum, a country should ensure that all money and value transmission services, including informal ones, are subject to specific FATF and international standards.[58] Furthermore, a corollary requirement of this special recommendation is that a competent authority be designated to license or register all such informal money/value transmission services and to require these entities to have adequate programs to guard against money laundering and terrorist financing.[59] Such a requirement is consistent with *The Forty Recommendations*.[60]

The international community is not, through this recommendation, attempting to eliminate informal money value transfer systems. In many cases, these systems provide a valuable service to people who cannot easily access the formal financial sector. However, there have been cases where such systems have been used to launder money and transfer funds to terrorists and this recommendation aims to apply AML/CFT controls to them. This recommendation also requires the compliance of such entities, but does not subject them to the same kind of requirements for regulation and supervision as an institution subject to the Basel Committee on Banking Supervision, International Association of Insurance Supervisors or International Organization of Securities Commissions.

G. Wire Transfers

Under the seventh *Special Recommendation*, each country should take appropriate actions to require covered financial institutions, including money remit-

---

56. For a discussion on this subject, see Bank/Fund papers on these issues (See Chapter X, Analysis of the Hawala System and Remittance System Studies). See also, FATF-XI Typologies Report (2000) (http://www.fatf-gafi.org/pdf/TY2000_en.pdf), and Asia Pacific Group Report on Underground Banking and Alternative Remittance Systems (2001) (http://www.apgml.org/content/typologies_reports.jsp).
57. FATF, Guidance Notes, at paragraph 29, and Interpretive Note, paragraph 2.
58. *The Forty Recommendations*, Recs. 4–25.
59. *Id.*, Rec. 23.
60. *Id.*

ters, to include accurate and meaningful originator information (name, address and account number) on fund transfers and related messages that are sent, and further require that the information should remain with the transfer or related message throughout the payment chain.[61] In addition, such financial institutions should conduct enhanced scrutiny of, and monitor for suspicious activity funds transfers that do not contain complete originator information.[62]

The implementation of this recommendation has proven somewhat complex and FATF has produced a rather lengthy Interpretative Note to clarify the requirements of *Special Recommendation VII*.[63] There is no set of Best Practices applicable to this recommendation.

The objective of this recommendation is to obtain information on who is sending wire transfers so that funds sent for illegal purposes can be identified along with their senders.[64] The information requirements depend upon whether the transfer is cross-border or domestic. Cross-border transfers need to be accompanied by the name, account number (or unique reference number where there is no account e.g. one-off transactions), and address.[65] An identity number or customer identification number or date and place of birth can be substituted for the address if there are fears about revealing the address of a customer. Providing this information on the wire transfer will enable information about the sender to be obtained much more quickly and easily if there is an international money laundering or terrorist financing investigation than if it has to be the subject of lengthy inquiries.

Domestic transfers need only to be accompanied by the account number, provided there is the ability to trace the rest of the information about the organization within three days of the sender institution receiving a request, either from the beneficiary institution or the authorities. Countries may exempt transactions of up to EUR/USD 3,000 from those requirements.[66]

Beneficiary financial institutions should be able to identify wire transfers that do not show meaningful information. This is not a requirement to examine every transaction and it is very unlikely that the beneficiary institutions would be able to carry out any investigation about the accuracy of the

61. *Special Recommendations*, Spec. Rec. VII.
62. *Id.*
63. http://www.fatf-gafi.org/pdf/INSR7_en.PDF.
64. *Id.* At paragraph 1.
65. *Id.*, at paragraph 8 and 9.
66. http://www.fatf-gafi.org/pdf/INSR7_en.PDF.

information. The originator of the funds transfers are not their customers. However, institutions should have systems in place to examine a sample of wire transfers. Where there is incomplete information institutions should consider filing a suspicious transaction report. Where a financial institution sends messages that do not include the required originator information, the beneficiary institution should reconsider the business relationship with the originator.[67]

H. Non-Profit Organizations

According to the eighth *Special Recommendation*, each county should review the adequacy of its laws and regulations regarding non-profit organizations, in order to determine whether they can be used for terrorist financing purposes.[68] In particular, a country should ensure that its non-profit organizations cannot be misused:

- By terrorist organizations posing as legitimate ones;
- To exploit legitimate entities as conduits for terrorist financing, including to avoid asset freezing measures; or
- To conceal or obscure the clandestine diversion of funds intended for legitimate purposes to terrorist organizations.[69]

There is no Interpretive Note on this recommendation, however, in an effort to help countries protect their non-profit institutions from abuse, FATF has issued a set of international best practices entitled, Combating the Abuse of Non-Profit Organizations.[70]

The goal of this recommendation is to prevent non-profit organizations (i.e., those organized for charitable, religious, educational, social or fraternal purposes), as well as other legal entities and arrangements, from being misused by terrorists.[71] In this regard, the recommendation is rather general because the different entities categorized as non-profit organizations take

---

67. *Id.*, at paragraphs 11–14.
68. *Special Recommendations*, Spec. Rec. VIII.
69. *Id.*
70. http://www.fatf-gafi.org/pdf/SR8-NPO_en.pdf (11 October 2002).
71. FATF, Guidance Notes, at Paragraph 39.

various legal forms and the nature of their operations varies from jurisdiction to jurisdiction.[72]

In an effort not to require adherence to a rigid set of rules that may be of little or no meaning in certain jurisdictions, the recommendation consists of general guidance and goals to be achieved, rather than specific requirements. There are three areas for attention by countries under the recommendation:

- *Ensure financial transparency.* Such organizations should have transparent financial records and conduct their activities in a way that can be audited and funds accounted for. Accounts should be published and disbursements of funds should be done through accounts with established financial institutions.
- *Programmatic verification.* The organizations should know who receives funds and how they are spent and should take active steps to monitor these things. This is especially important when the recipients are in another country.
- *Administration.* There should be good records kept for the activities of the organization and there should be clear governance structures and internal accountability.

I. Cash Couriers

The objective of the ninth *Special Recommendation*, which was adopted in October of 2004, is to ensure that terrorists and other criminals cannot finance their activities or launder the proceeds of their crimes through the transportation of currency and monetary instruments from one country to another.[73] Persons or entities that carry cash and cash equivalents across national borders are often referred to as "cash couriers."

Special Recommendation IX has essentially four specific requirements regarding cash courier activities. First, each country should have a system in place to detect the physical cross-border transportation of currency and bearer negotiable instruments.[74] Second, each country should provide its compe-

---

72. *Id.*
73. Interpretative Note to Special Recommendation IX, at Paragraph 1.
74. *Special Recommendations*, Spec. Rec. IX.

tent authorities with legal authority to stop or restrain currency and bearer negotiable instruments that are either: (i) suspected of being related to terrorist financing or money laundering; or (ii) misrepresented in a required declaration or disclosure. Third, this *Special Recommendation* further requires that each country have effective, proportionate, and dissuasive sanctions in place for persons making a false declaration or disclosure regarding a cross-border transportation of currency or bearer negotiable instrument(s). Fourth and finally, there is the requirement for each country to adopt measures permitting it to confiscate currency and bearer negotiable instruments that are related to terrorist financing or money laundering.

FATF adopted a formal Interpretative Note to accompany *Special Recommendation IX* at the same time that it adopted this recommendation.[75] The Interpretative Note provides a reasonably thorough definition of the terms used in the recommendation as well as a reasonably thorough description of how a country may implement the requirements of this recommendation. FATF also adopted an International Best Practices paper, entitled "Detecting and Preventing the Cross-Border Transportation of Cash by Terrorists and Other Criminals," to accompany this recommendation.[76] A country may also wish to consult the best practices paper, which was adopted in February of 2005, for purposes of how to implement the requirements of *Special Recommendation IX*.

According to the Interpretative Note, "bearer negotiable instruments" means:

- monetary instruments in bearer form, such as travelers' checks;
- negotiable instruments (including checks, promissory notes and money orders) that are in bearer form, endorsed to a fictitious payee, or otherwise in such a form that title passes upon delivery; or
- incomplete instruments (including checks, promissory notes and money orders) that are signed, but do not include the payee's name.[77]

It should be noted that, for purposes of this *Special Recommendation*, gold, precious metals and precious stones are specifically excluded from the

---

75. Interpretative Note to Special Recommendation IX.
76. http://www.fatf-gafi/50/63/3442418.pdf.
77. Interpretative Note to Special Recommendation IX, at Paragraph 3.

meaning of the term "bearer negotiable instruments."[78] Disclosures, declarations or other representations regarding these items may, nonetheless, be covered under a country's legal requirements, such as its customs laws or regulations, but it is not necessary to cover them in order to comply with this recommendation.[79]

"Physical cross-border transportation" means any in-bound or out-bound physical transportation of currency or bearer negotiable instruments from one country to another. It includes: physical transportation (i) by a natural person, or in that person's luggage or vehicle; (ii) shipment through containerized cargo; or (iii) mailing by a natural or legal person.[80]

Under the Interpretative Note, a country may satisfy the recommendation's requirement to have detection measures in place through the use of one of two systems: a declaration system or a disclosure system.[81] With a "declaration system," all persons making a physical cross-border transportation of currency or bearer negotiable instrument(s) having a specified threshold value (maximum value may not exceed EUR/USD 15,000) or more, would be required to submit a truthful declaration to designated competent authorities regarding the value of such transfer and other relevant information. The predetermined threshold should be set sufficiently low to meet the objectives of the recommendation.[82]

With a "disclosure system," all persons making a cross-border transportation of currency or bearer negotiable instrument(s) would be required to make a truthful disclosure to designated competent authorities upon request regarding the value of the transfer and other relevant information.[83] In this regard, a country should ensure that competent authorities are authorized to make their requests on a targeted basis, either upon intelligence or suspicion, or on a random basis.

It is important to note that a country needs to have a detection system in place for both in-coming and out-going transportations, but does not have to use the same type of system for in-coming and out-going transportations.[84]

---

78. *Id.*, at footnote 1.
79. *Id.*
80. *Id.*, at Paragraph 5.
81. *Id.*, at Paragraph 9.
82. *Id.*, at Paragraph 9a.
83 *Id.*, at Paragraph 9b.
84. *Id.*, at Paragraphs 9 and 10a.

Thus, for example, a country could have a declaration system for in-coming transportations and a disclosure system for out-going transportations, and vice-versa.

A false declaration or disclosure is defined to mean:

- a misrepresentation of the value of the currency or bearer negotiable instrument(s) being transported,
- a misrepresentation of any relevant data that is asked for in the required declaration or disclosure or otherwise requested by competent authorities, or
- the failure to make a declaration or disclosure as required.[85]

Upon discovery of either a false declaration or false disclosure, the designated competent authority should have the legal authority to request and obtain additional information from the person with regard to the origin of the subject currency or bearer negotiable instrument(s) and the intended use of such currency or instruments.[86]

Regardless of which system is utilized, information obtained through the declaration and/or disclosure processes should be made available to the financial intelligence unit (FIU).[87] In addition, the declaration and/or disclosure process should permit the greatest possible range of international cooperation and assistance in accordance with *The Forty Recommendations*, specifically Recommendations 35 through 40, and *Special Recommendation V*.[88] In this regard, where declarations or disclosures above the maximum threshold are made, where false declarations or disclosures are discovered, or where there are suspicions of money laundering or terrorist financing, relevant information should be retained, including the amount of currency or bearer instrument(s) declared, disclosed or discovered, and the identification data of the persons.[89]

With regard to persons carrying out the physical transportation of currency or bearer negotiable instruments that are actually related to terrorist financing or money laundering, such currency or bearer negotiable

---

85. *Id.*, at Paragraphs 6 and 7.
86. *Id.*, at Paragraph 10b.
87. *Id.*, at Paragraph 10c.
88. *Id.*, at Paragraph 10f.
89. *Id.*

instruments should be subject to measures, including legislative ones, consistent with *The Forty Recommendations* (Recommendation 3) and *Special Recommendation III*, that would permit their confiscation.[90] Prior to such a determination, where there is either a: (i) suspicion of terrorist financing or money laundering; or (ii) false declaration or disclosure, competent authorities should have the legal authority to stop or restrain the subject currency and/or bearer negotiable instrument(s) for a reasonable time to determine whether there is evidence of terrorist financing.[91]

Finally, countries are encouraged to implement *Special Recommendation IX* subject to safeguards to ensure the proper use of information received and without restricting either trade payments between countries for goods and services or the freedom of capital movements in any way.[92]

J. Self-Assessment Questionnaire on Terrorist Financing

In order to focus on issues of interpretation and implementation with regard to the *Special Recommendations*, FATF issued a Self Assessment Questionnaire on Terrorist Financing (SAQFT).[93] The SAQFT was initially used only by FATF members. Upon completion of the initial assessment of the SAQFT, FATF issued the Guidance Notes on the *Special Recommendations* and the SAQTF. The SAQTF is also available on the FATF website and may be used by any country for its own assessment purposes.[94]

---

90. *Special Recommendation IX* and Interpretative Note to Special Recommendation IX, at paragraph 11.
91. Interpretative Note to Special Recommendation IX, at paragraph 10e.
92. Interpretative Note to Special Recommendation IX, at paragraph 10e.
93. http://www.fatf-gafi.org/SAQTF_en.htm.
94. *Id.*

Chapter X

World Bank and International Monetary Fund Initiatives to Fight Money Laundering and Terrorist Financing

A. Awareness Raising
1. The Global Dialogue Series
2. Country Assistance Strategy

B. Development of a Universal AML/CFT Assessment Methodology
1. Twelve-Month Pilot Program
2. Reports on the Observance of Standards and Codes
3. Revision of the Universal Methodology

C. Building Institutional Capacity
1. Organization of Training Conferences
2. Delivery of Technical Assistance to Individual Countries

D. Research and Analysis
1. Analysis of the Hawala System
2. Alternate Remittance System Studies
3. World Bank AML/CF Website
4. FIU Handbook
5. Reference Guide

The missions of the World Bank (Bank) and the International Monetary Fund (IMF or Fund) are fundamentally different. Nonetheless, both organizations have identical goals with regard to anti-money laundering (AML) and combating the financing of terrorism (CFT). Moreover, the Bank and the Fund work jointly in all of their efforts to achieve those goals.

The basic mission of the Bank is to fight poverty throughout the world. The Bank helps countries strengthen their development efforts by providing loans and technical assistance for institutional capacity building, as well as loans for improvements in the infrastructure and environment of developing countries. The mission of the Bank includes providing resources, sharing knowledge and forging partnerships in the public and private sectors.[1]

In essence, the mission of the IMF is macro-economic and involves financial stability surveillance throughout the world. IMF goals include:

---

1. About the World Bank, http://www.worldbank.org.

- Promoting international monetary cooperation;
- Facilitating the expansion and balanced growth of international trade;
- Promoting foreign currency exchange stability; and
- Assisting in the establishment of multilateral systems of payments.

In addition, the Fund promotes international monetary stability by making loans to countries to permit them to correct maladjustments in their balance of payments without resorting to measures that may destroy national or international prosperity.[2]

In April 2001, the two Boards of Executive Directors of the World Bank and the IMF recognized that money laundering is a problem of global concern that affects major financial markets and smaller ones.[3] Taking into account that money laundering has potentially devastating economic, political and social consequences for countries that are in the process of developing domestic economies and building strong financial institutions, the Bank recognized that money laundering can impose important costs upon developing countries. The IMF recognized that money laundering has a full range of macroeconomic consequences, including unpredictable changes in money demand, risks to the soundness of financial institutions and financial systems, and increased volatility on international capital flows and exchange rates due to unanticipated cross border transfers.

Following the events of September 11, 2001, the World Bank and IMF Boards of Executive Directors adopted action plans to enhance efforts for AML/CFT. Furthermore, the Boards recognized, in July and August 2002, *The Forty Recommendations on Money Laundering* (*The Forty Recommendations*) and the eight *Special Recommendations on Terrorist Financing* (*Special Recommendations*), issued by the Financial Action Task Force on Money Laundering (FATF), as the relevant international standards for AML/CFT. The Boards added AML and CFT to the list of areas that are useful for their operational work and started a 12-month pilot program using

2. About the IMF, http://www.imf.org.
3. For a more detailed discussion of the actions of the Bank and the Fund, see Intensified Work on Anti-Money Laundering and Combating the Financing of Terrorism. Joint Progress Report on Work of the IMF and World Bank, http://www.imf.org/external/np/mae/aml/2002/eng/092502.htm.

a universal, comprehensive AML/CFT assessment methodology in November 2002.

Over the course of the pilot program, the Fund and the Bank conducted assessments in 33 jurisdictions and FATF and the FATF-style regional bodies (FSRBs) conducted assessments in an additional eight jurisdictions. The Boards of the Fund and the Bank reviewed the outcome of the pilot program in March 2004. They concluded that the pilot had been successful and welcomed the deepening of international attention that it had led to on AML/CFT issues and the good collaboration that had taken place with FATF and the FATF-style regional bodies (FSRBs). At that time, the Boards resolved to make AML/CFT work a permanent part of their activities; to continue their collaboration with the FATF; to endorse the revised FATF recommendations as the new standard for which Reports on the Observance of Standards and Codes (ROSCs) are prepared and the revised Methodology to assess that standard; and to devote additional resources to this work in the future. The Fund and Bank expect to conduct approximately 20 assessments per year using the same Methodology used by FATF and the FSRBs.

A. Awareness Raising

1. The Global Dialogue Series
The first step in establishing or improving a country's institutional framework for AML and CFT is to raise the awareness level within the country's leadership about the issues, to demonstrate the implications for the country's future, to share the experiences that other countries have had, and to inform the country about available resources and assistance. Toward that goal, the World Bank and IMF have established a series of Regional Policy Global Dialogues on AML/CFT. These are organized through interactive videoconferences for member countries within a given geographic region enabling government officials from those countries, staff of the Bank and Fund, FATF-Style Regional Bodies (FSRBs), regional development banks and other international organizations to discuss and exchange information. The issues discussed center upon:

- Identifying the challenges faced by countries in the struggle against illicit money flows;

- Sharing the lessons of success;
- Identifying specific problems for countries in that region; and
- Understanding the types of assistance countries need to combat money laundering and terrorist financing.

Some of the key questions addressed in the Global Dialogue Series are:

- How can the World Bank and IMF help countries strengthen their response to money laundering and terrorist financing?
- How does money laundering and terrorist financing fit into the broader context of corruption and poor governance?
- What has been the response of governments?
- What are the current challenges for regulators?
- What is the appropriate institutional structure for each country in implementing an effective program to fight money laundering and terrorist fighting?
- What are the future challenges in combating money laundering and terrorist financing in participating countries?

To answer those questions, senior policymakers in the participating countries offer their views on the economic costs of criminal abuse of financial systems, particularly money laundering and the financing of terrorism. Other points for discussion include practical means of sustaining economic development and financial market integrity in the face of such threats. The dialogue helps countries to learn from each other by drawing on their particular experiences as well as the broader experience of international experts.

2. Country Assistance Strategy

The Bank is integrating the results of the Financial Sector Assessment Program (FSAP) into the broader range of development measures considered in the Country Assistance Strategy (CAS), which sets out the priorities for the Bank's program for a given country on a three-year basis in consultation with the government of that country. Following systematic reviews of FSAP findings, AML/CFT assistance has already been included in more than 30

CASs prepared since March 2002. Technical assistance is given high priority in countries where weaknesses in the integrity of the AML/CFT regime may pose significant governance and development risks. CASs also address AML/CFT issues in greater detail in countries that have been deficient in meeting international standards and best practices.

The Fund has integrated AML/CFT components into its Article IV surveillance.[4] In addition to Financial System Stability Assessment (FSSA) reports to the Executive Board (which summarize the outcome of FSAPs, including the AML/CFT assessments), results from the AML/CFT questionnaire have been incorporated in more than 70 Article IV discussions since January 2002.

B. Development of a Universal AML/CFT Assessment Methodology

Over the course of 2002, the Bank and IMF worked in close collaboration with FATF and other international standard setters, i.e., the Basel Committee on Banking Supervision (Basel Committee), International Association of Securities Commissioners (IOSCO), International Association of Insurance Supervisors (IAIS) and the Egmont Group, to produce a single, comprehensive AML/CFT assessment methodology. This methodology was agreed and endorsed by FATF at its October 2002 Plenary meeting. The methodology consisted of 120 criteria covering each of the FATF *Forty* and *Special Recommendations*, including implementation of criminal law enforcement.[5] It covered the legal and institutional AML/CFT framework for a country, including the establishment of financial intelligence units (FIUs). The methodology also covered relevant United Nations (UN) Security Council Resolutions and international conventions and other measures of international standard setters. It provided an in-depth assessment of the preventive measures for financial institutions.

Following the revision of *The Forty Recommendations* in June 2003, the Bank and Fund worked with the FATF and FSRBs to produce a revised assessment methodology. This was endorsed by the FATF in February 2004

---

4. About the IMF, http://www.imf.org.
5. Methodology on AML/CFT, http://www.fatf-gafi.org/pdf/Meth-2004_en.PDF.

and by the Bank and Fund Boards in March 2004. It incorporates over 200 "essential criteria" against which countries will be assessed for their compliance with the FATF standards and some "additional criteria" which, although not part of the standard against which compliance is rated, comprise international best practices and will be part of the assessment. There are considerably more criteria than in the previous version of the methodology, reflecting the extension of the standards agreed in 2003.

The methodology will be used by the international organizations in their evaluations of AML/CFT controls carried out as part of their overall assessments of a country's compliance with international financial standards in the FSAP and OFC processes. They will result in a ROSC for AML/CFT, which will be reported to the Executive Boards of the Bank and the Fund. The methodology will also be used by the FATF and FSRBs in their mutual evaluations. FATF and the FSRBs will prepare a ROSC as part of their mutual evaluatios, which will be recognized by the Bank and the Fund.

The process is one in which the FATF, FSRBs, the Bank, and the Fund each carry out assessments using the same methodology and agree to recognize each others reports. The organizations work together to establish a sensible schedule for assessments, which fits in with the FSAP/OFC schedule of the international financial institutions and FATF/FSRB mutual evaluation timetables. It is expected that the Fund and the Bank will conduct approximately 20 assessments per year, and that FATF and the FSRBs will conduct about the same number. This schedule should allow every country to receive a full assessment approximately once every five years.

C. Building Institutional Capacity

1. The Organization of Training Conferences

The Bank and Fund hold targeted training conferences on specific AML/CFT issues, utilizing public officials involved in AML/CFT from a particular region. For example, during 2002, two technical assistance conferences took place: one in Montevideo, Uruguay, and one in Moscow, Russia.

The Moscow conference is illustrative of the type of information presented. The focus of the conference was the creation of operational Financial Intelligence

Units (FIUs). The conference was aimed at those countries that either do not have operational FIUs or that have just started operating them. The primary aim of the conference was to involve experts from Eastern European countries that have recently achieved AML/CFT compliance standards, and allow officials from those countries to present their experience and best practices.

The conference was also a useful mechanism to help countries and organizations that provide AML/CFT technical assistance understand where the most urgent needs are, and to enable them to make personal contacts with government officials of those countries so future assistance might be more readily and easily provided.

The conference was successful in demonstrating the importance of attention to AML/CFT issues, and presenting the various requirements of international standards in such a manner that officials from participating countries could understand. It also demonstrated the specific steps necessary to begin taking action in their respective countries. Additionally, government officials were able to make personal contacts with experts in the field as well as their counterparts in their own neighboring countries, which makes obtaining advice and assistance in implementing AML/CFT less burdensome.

A further workshop was held in South Africa in May 2004, involving the 14 member countries of the Eastern and Southern Africa Anti-Money Laundering Group (ESAAMLG). It was organized by ESAAMLG with the participation of the Bank and Fund and included experts from several other international organizations and countries. The aim of the workshop was to inform policy makers from the ESAAMLG countries of the basic elements of a national strategy to counter money laundering and terrorist financing and work with them to develop their strategies to tackle the major AML/CFT issues in each country. The participants worked at the meeting to produce outline strategies which were then to be further developed in the country before being finalized and presented to the ESAAMLG plenary in August 2004.

2. Delivery of Technical Assistance to Individual Countries

The Bank and the Fund are providing various forms of technical assistance (TA) to countries that want to establish or improve their AML/CFT regimes.[6] Since April of 2001, these TA efforts have increased. The Bank and Fund use the findings from the FSAPs and separate AML/CFT reviews as a means of determining what TA is needed and prioritizing the TA.

For developing countries, AML/CFT TA is included in a jurisdiction's CAS, which sets out the priorities for the Bank's assistance program on a three-year basis in consultation with the government of the country. In particular, TA is given high priority in countries where weakness in the integrity of the AML/CFT may pose significant governance and developmental risks.

The focus of the Bank's and the Fund's TA for AML/CFT is on:

- Formulation of AML/CFT laws and regulations that meet international best practices;
- Implementation of laws, regulations, policies and procedures by financial sector supervisors and other similar competent authorities charged with responsibility for enforcement of AML/CFT measures;
- Establishment of legal frameworks for financial intelligence units (FIUs) that meet international best practices;
- Development of training and awareness programs to address AML/CFT concerns in the public and private sectors;
- Collaboration with other parties in multinational training programs; and development of computer-based training materials.

In the two-year period leading up to the March 2004 decision by the Bank and Fund boards to make AML/CFT a permanent part of their work programs, the Bank and Fund delivered 85 country-specific technical assistance projects reaching 63 countries and 32 regional projects reaching over 130 countries.

---

6. Intensified Work on AML/CFT, paragraphs 39 and 40. See http://finsec.worldbank.org/assets/images/AML-CFT_Methodology_SecM2002-0554.pdf.

D. Research and Analysis

1. Analysis of the Hawala System

The Bank and the Fund conducted a study on the operational characteristics of informal funds transfer systems (IFTs), commonly referred to as *Hawalas*.[7] The study examines the historical and socioeconomic context within which *Hawalas* have evolved. In this regard, their growth is rooted primarily in the facilitation of trade between distant geographic locations at a time when conventional banking instruments were either weak or nonexistent.

The study also analyzes the operational features of IFTs for both legitimate and illegitimate purposes. These operational features are mainly speed, lower transaction costs, ethnic and cultural convenience and familiarity, versatility and potential anonymity. In addition, IFTs have prospered in countries where financial institutions are inefficient and financial policies are restrictive. Finally, like any underground economic activity, IFTs have implications for monetary control; influencing exchange rate operations; distorting economic data, (and, thereby, statistical information available to policy makers); and reducing taxes on income and services.

The study further discusses the implications for regulatory and supervisory responses to this type of activity. Recommendation VI of FATF's *Special Recommendations* recommends that countries treat Hawalas and other IFTs as part of the regulated system, subject to many of the same AML/CFT requirements as covered financial institutions.[8] More countries are subjecting these entities to licensing or registration in accordance with the FATF recommendation.

2. Alternative Remittances Systems Studies

In September of 2002, the Asia-Pacific Economic Cooperation (APEC) Finance Ministers established a working group on alternative remittance systems (ARS) to examine the economic, structural and regulatory factors

---

7. http://www1.worldbank.org/finance/html/amlcft/docs/IFTS_IMF/IFTS_Contents.pdf.
8. http://www.fatf-gafi.org/pdf/SRecTF_en.pdf.

that encourage the use of ARS in the APEC economies. In support of the project, the World Bank prepared a report that creates a framework for estimating the magnitude of remittances flows, analyzes incentives for formal versus informal channels, and examines the role of formal financial sectors in the provision of remittance services that are compliant with international AML/CFT standards.[9]

As part of the APEC ARS Initiative follow-up, and as part of an effort to increase the World Bank's involvement in studying the important topic of ARSs for all of its clients, comparative case studies have been planned for specific economies. Research findings and conclusions of these case studies will be shared as part of the exchange of ideas and experiences. This is an ongoing project; the findings from different studies will be reported and available on the Bank's AML/CFT website.

3. World Bank AML/CFT Website

The Bank operates a website specifically for AML/CFT purposes.[10] This website contains up-to-date information about the Bank's programs and efforts to combat money laundering and terrorist financing. It also contains reference materials and publications, such as this Reference Guide. The website may be accessed at www.amlcft.org. Those wishing to contact the Bank on AML/CFT matters should write aml@worldbank.org.

4. FIU Handbook

In 2004, the Fund and the Bank jointly published a handbook on virtually all aspects of the establishment and operation of financial intelligence units (FIUs). The handbook is entitled *Financial Intelligence Unit, An Overview.*[11]

---

9. See http://www.amlcft.org, APEC Symposium on Remittances.
10. http://www.amlcft.org.
11. The handbook is available for purchase from the IMF. It is also available for viewing (read-only) on the Bank's AML/CFT website, http://www.amlcft.org.

The handbook covers a wide array of topics relating to FIU, including:

- Key steps for establishing an FIU,
- Basic models of operation,
- Core functions,
- Additional functions, and
- International assessments.

5. The Reference Guide

This Reference Guide on AML and CFT is a product of the Bank's and Fund's efforts to fight money laundering and terrorist financing. When policy makers looked at the AML/CFT material available to a country, particularly a developing country with limited experience in the area, it quickly became apparent that there was no single source that could be used to address all the issues. Hence, the Bank and Fund commissioned this Reference Guide as a means to make all relevant information available from a single and comprehensive source.

The first edition was published in 2003 and made available in five languages (English, French, Russian, Arabic and Spanish). This second edition has been prepared as an update, following the revision of *The Forty Recommendations* in June 2003,[12] the revised Methodology for assessments in 2004,[13] other changes in relevant materials, and subsequent developments in Fund and Bank AML/CFT programs and activities.

The Reference Guide is available on the Bank's website, http://www.aml cft.org/, and will also be translated into other languages.

---

12. http://www.fatf-gafi.org/pdf/40Recs-2003_en.pdf.
13. http://www1.worldbank.org/finance/html/amlcft/methodology.htm.

Annex I

Websites for Key Organizations, Legal Instruments, and Initiatives

Basel Committee on Banking Supervision—Bank For International Settlements

- http://www.bis.org/ (BIS Home Page)
- http://www.bis.org/bcbs/ (Basel Committee on Banking Supervision)
- http://www.bis.org/publ/bcbs30.pdf (Core Principles for Effective Banking Supervision)
- http://www.bis.org/publ/bcbs61.pdf (Core Principles Methodology)
- http://www.bis.org/publ/bcbs85.htm#pgtop (Customer Due Diligence for Banks)
- http://www.bis.org/publ/bcbsc137.pdf (Prevention of Criminal Use of the Banking System for the Purpose of Money Laundering—December 1988)

Commonwealth Secretariat

- http://www.thecommonwealth.org/ (Main site)

- http://www.thecommonwealth.org/dynamic/Country.asp (Commonwealth countries)

Council Of Europe

- http://www.coe.int/portalT.asp (Main page)
- http://conventions.coe.int/Treaty/en/Treaties/Html/141.htm (Convention on Laundering, Search, Seizure and Confiscation of the Proceeds from Crime—The Strasbourg Convention, 8.XI.1990)

Egmont Group For Financial Intelligence Units (FIUs)

- http://www.egmontgroup.org/ (Main page)
- http://www.egmontgroup.org/list_of_fius_062304.pdf (Countries with operational Financial Intelligence Units)
- http://www.egmontgroup.org/statement_of_purpose.pdf (Statement of Purpose of the Egmont Group of Financial Intelligence Units, Guernsey, 2004)
- http://www.egmontgroup.org/info_paper_final_092003.pdf (Information Paper on Financial Intelligence Units and the Egmont Group)
- http://www.egmontgroup.org/procedure_for_being_recognised.pdf (Procedure for being recognized as member country)
- http://www.fincen.gov/fiuinaction.pdf (List of AML cases)

European Union

- http://europa.eu.int/ (Main page)
- http://www.imolin.org/eudireng.htm (Council Directive on Prevention of use of Financial System for the Purpose of Money Laundering (91/308/EC))
- http://www.imolin.org/EUdir01e.htm (Directive 2001/97/EC of the European Parliament and of the Council of 4 December 2001 amending Council Directive 91/308/EC on prevention of the use of the financial system for the purpose of money laundering.)

Financial Action Task Force on Money Laundering (FATF)

- http://www.fatf-gafi.org (Welcome page)

- http://www.fatf-gafi.org/MLaundering_en.htm (Money Laundering)
- http://www.fatf-gafi.org/pdf/40Recs-2003_en.pdf (*The Forty Recommendations 2003*)
- http://www.fatf-gafi.org/pdf/SRecTF_en.pdf (*The Special Recommendations* 2001)
- http://www1.oecd.org/fatf/TerFinance_en.htm (Terrorist Financing)
- http://www1.oecd.org/fatf/pdf/PB9906_en.pdf (Policy Brief Money Laundering)
- http://www.fatf-gafi.org/FATDocs_en.htm(Money Laundering Methods and Trends)
- http://www1.oecd.org/fatf/pdf/GuidFITF01_en.pdf (Guidance for financial institutions in Detecting Terrorist Financing)
- http://www1.oecd.org/fatf/Initiatives_en.htm (Other International Anti-Money Laundering and Combating Terrorist Financing Initiatives)
- http://www.fatf-gafi.org/pdf/SR8-NPO_en.pdf (Combating the Abuse of Non-Profit Organisations: International Best Practices (11 October 2002)
- http://www1.oecd.org/fatf/pdf/PR-20021220_en.pdf (FATF statements and documents on NCCT, Press Release, December 20, 2002, FATF decides to impose counter-measures on Ukraine; no counter-measures to apply to Nigeria at this time)
- http://www1.oecd.org/fatf/pdf/INSR7-Consult_en.pdf (FATF issues for public consultation a proposal of an Interpretative Note to Special Recommendation VII: Wire Transfers (11 October 2002))
- http://www1.oecd.org/fatf/pdf/FEEDB_en.pdf (FATF Best Practice Guidelines on Providing Feedback to Reporting Financial Institutions and Other Persons (25 June 1998))
- http://www1.oecd.org/fatf/pdf/AR2004_en.PDF (Annual Report (2003–2004))
- http://www.fatf-gafi.org/SAQTF_en.htm. (Self-assessment questionnaire)
- http://www1.oecd.org/fatf/NCCT_en.htm (Non-Cooperative Countries and Territories)

FATF-Style Regional Bodies

Asia/Pacific Group on Money Laundering

- http://www.apgml.org (Main site)

- http://www.apgml.org/content/member_jurisdiction.jsp (Member Jurisdictions)
- http://www.apgml.org/content/observer_jurisdiction.jsp (Observer Jurisdictions)
- http://www.apgml.org/content/organisations.jsp (Observer Organisations)

Caribbean Financial Action Task Force

- http://www.cfatf.org (Main site)
- http://www1.oecd.org/fatf/Ctry-orgpages/org-cfatf_en.htm (Co-operating and Supporting Nations and Observers)
- http://www.cfatf.org/about/about.asp?PageNumber=1 (Membership)
- http://www.cfatf.org/eng/recommendations/cfatf/ (Caribbean Financial Action Task Force—CFATF 19 Recommendations, 1990)
- http://www.cfatf.org/eng/kingdec/index.pdf (Kingston Declaration on Money Laundering—November 5–6, 1992)

MONEYVAL (Council of Europe Select Committee of Experts on the Evaluation of Anti-Money Laundering Measures (PC-R-EV Committee), (Now known as MONEYVAL)

- http://www.coe.int/T/E/Legal_affairs/Legal_cooperation/Combating_ economic crime/Money_laundering/ (Main site)
- http://www1.oecd.org/fatf/Ctry-orgpages/org-pcrev_en.htm (Membersand Observers)

Eastern and Southern Africa Anti-Money Laundering Group (ESAAMLG)

- http://www.esaamlg.org (Main site)
- http://www1.oecd.org/fatf/Ctry-orgpages/org-esaamlg_en.htm (Members and Observers)

Financial Action Task Force of South America (GAFISUD)

- http://www.gafisud.org (Main site)
- http://www.gafisud.org (See members and observers)

International Association of Insurance Supervisors

- http://www.iaisweb.org/ (Main page)
- http://www.iaisweb.org/framesets/pas.html (Overview of IAIS principles, standards and guidance papers)
- http://www.iaisweb.org/132_176_ENU_HTML.asp (Member countries and jurisdictions)

International Monetary Fund

- http://www.imf.org/ (Main page)
- http://www.imf.org/external/np/mae/aml/2002/eng/092502.htm (Intensified Work on Anti-Money Laundering and Combating the Financing of Terrorism (AML/CFT) (September 2002)
- http://www.imf.org/external/np/mae/am/2002/eng/092523.htm (Comprehensive Methodology on AML/CFT)

International Organization of Securities Commissioners

- http://www.iosco.org/iosco.html (Main page)
- http://www.iosco.org/pubdocs/pdf/IOSCOPD125.pdf (IOSCO Objectives and Principles of Securities Regulation) (2002)
- http://www.iosco.org/docs-public/1997-authorisation_of_collective. html (Authorisation of Collective Investment Schemes (CIS) and Related Services. A Report of the Technical Committee) (1997)
- http://www.iosco.org/library/index.cfm?whereami=resolutions (A Directory of Resolutions Passed by the International Organisation of Securities Commissions)
- http://www.iosco.org/docs (Principles for the Supervision of Operators of Collective Investment Schemes (September, 1997))

Organization of American States–CICAD

- http://www.oas.org/main/english/ (Main page)
- http://www.cicad.oas.org/en/?CICAD%20-%New.htm (Summit of the Americas, Ministerial Conference Concerning the Laundering of Proceeds and Instrumentalities of Crime – Buenos Aires, Argentina, December 2, 1995. See Money Laundering, see Documents, see Plan of Action of Buenos Aires.)

- http://www.cicad.oas.org/Desarrollo_Juridico/eng/legal-regulations-money.htm (Model Regulations Concerning Laundering Offenses Connected to Illicit Drug Trafficking and Other Serious Offenses (1998)

United Nations

- http://www.un.org
- http://www.undcp.org/ (Office on Drugs Control and Crime)
- http://www.un.org/Overview/unmember.html (List of Member Sates)
- http://www.unodc.org/pdf/lap_money-laundering-proceeds_2000.pdf (United Nations International Drug Control Programme (UNDCP) Money Laundering and Proceeds of Crime Bill 2000)
- http://www.incb.org/e/conv/1988/ (United Nations Convention Against Illicit Traffic in Narcotic Drugs and Psychotropic Substances (1988) (*Vienna Convention*))
- http://www.undcp.org/adhoc/palermo/convmain.html (United Nations Convention against Transnational Organized Crime (2000) (The *Palermo Convention*))
- http://www.unodc.org/unodc/crime_cicp_signatures_convention.html (Signatories–Convention against Transnational Organized Crime)
- http://www.un.org/law/cod/finterr.htm (United Nations International Convention for the Suppression of the Financing of Terrorism (1999))
- http://www.untreaty.un.org/ENGLISH/Status/Chapter_xviii/treaty11.asp (Status–Convention of the Suppression of the Financing of Terrorism)
- http://www.un.org/aboutun/charter/index.html (UN Charter)
- http://untreaty.un.org/English/Terrorism.asp (United Nations Treaty Collection Conventions on Terrorism)
- http://www.imolin.org/ml99eng.htm (United Nations Model Legislation on Laundering, Confiscation and International Cooperation in Relation to the Proceeds of Crime (1999))
- http://www.un.org/terrorism/ (UN Action against Terrorism)
- http://www.un.org/sc/ctc (Counter-Terrorism Committee)
- http://www.unodc.org/unodc/treaty_adherence.html (List of member countries)
- http://www.imolin.org/imolin/en/pocf03.html (United Nations Model Money Laundering, Proceeds of Crime and Terrorist Financing Bill 2003)

- http://www.imolin.org/imolin/en/tfbill03.html (United Nations Model Terrorist Financing Bill 2003)

United Nations–International Money Laundering Information Network

- http://www.imolin.org/ (Main page)
- http://www.imolin.org/imolin/gpml.html(United Nations Global Program Against Money Laundering)
- http://www.imolin.org/conventi.htm (Standards, Conventions and Legal Instruments)
- http://www.imolin.org/model.htm (Model Laws/Regulation)
- http://www.imolin.org/map.htm (National legislation relating to money laundering (map))
- http://www.imolin.org/reference.htm (Reference)
- http://www.imolin.org/current.htm (Current Events in the Anti-Money Laundering Arena)
- http://www.imolin.org/calendar.htm (Calendar of Events)

United Nations–Security Council Resolutions

- http://www.un.org/documents/scres.htm

Wolfsberg Group of Banks

- http://www.wolfsberg-principles.com/index.html (The Wolfsberg Group of Banks)
- http://www.wolfsberg-principles.com/privat-banking.html (Global Anti-Money-Laundering Guidelines for Private Banking)
- http://www.wolfsberg-principles.com/wolfsberg_statement.html (The Suppression of the Financing of Terrorism)
- http://www.wolfsberg-principles.com/corresp-banking.html (The Wolfsberg Anti-Money Laundering Principles for Correspondent Banking)

The World Bank Group

- http://www.worldbank.org/
- http://www.amlcft.org (Financial Market Integrity website on anti-money laundering and terrorist financing)

Annex II

Other Useful Websites and Resources

Websites

European Central Bank

- http://www.ecb.int/

The Financial Crimes Enforcement Network (FinCEN)

- http://www.fincen.gov/af_main.html

Financial Stability Forum)

- http://www.fsforum.org/

Interpol

- http://www.interpol.com/Public/Terrorism/default.asp (Interpol's involvement in the fight against international terrorism)

The Money Laundering Compliance Website

- http://www.countermoneylaundering.com/

Organisation for Economic Co-operation and Development

- http://www.oecd.org/ (Home page)

U.S. Department of the Treasury, Comptroller of the Currency, Administrator of National Banks

- http://www.occ.treas.gov/launder/origc.htm (Money Laundering: A Banker's guide to Avoiding Problems)

U.S. State Department—Country Summaries

- http://www.state.gov/documents/organization/8703.pdf (Money Laundering and Financial Crimes)

The World Customs Organization

- http://www.wcoomd.org/ie/index.html (Main page)

Other Resources

- Guy Stessens. 2000. *Money Laundering :A New International Law Enforcement Model.* Cambridge, England, and New York, New York, United States: Cambridge University Press.
- Herbert Morais. 2002. "The War Against Money Laundering, Terrorism and the Financing of Terrorism," *LAWASIA Journal.* This publication is produced by the Law Association for Asia and the Pacific, Darwin, Australia, although is not currently available online (http://www.lawsocnsw.asn.au/publications.htm). Contact the LAWASIA secretariat. A much shorter version of this article, under the title "Behind the Lines in the War on Terrorist Funding," was published in the *International Financial Law Review*, December 2001.

Annex III

United Nations Anti-Terrorist Conventions Referred to in the International Convention for the Suppression of the Financing of Terrorism

1. Convention for the Suppression of Unlawful Seizure of Aircraft, done at The Hague on 16 December 1970.
2. Convention for the Suppression of Unlawful Acts against the Safety of Civil Aviation, done at Montreal on 23 September 1971.
3. Convention on the Prevention and Punishment of Crimes against Internationally Protected Persons, including Diplomatic Agents, adopted by the General Assembly of the United Nations on 14 December 1973.
4. International Convention against the Taking of Hostages, adopted by the General Assembly of the United Nations on 17 December 1979.
5. Convention on the Physical Protection of Nuclear Material, adopted at Vienna on 3 March 1980.
6. Protocol for the Suppression of Unlawful Acts of Violence at Airports Serving International Civil Aviation, supplementary to the Convention for the Suppression of Unlawful Acts against the Safety of Civil Aviation, done at Montreal on 24 February 1988.

7. Convention for the Suppression of Unlawful Acts against the Safety of Maritime Navigation, done at Rome on 10 March 1988.

8. Protocol for the Suppression of Unlawful Acts against the Safety of Fixed Platforms located on the Continental Shelf, done at Rome on 10 March 1988.

9. International Convention for the Suppression of Terrorist Bombings, adopted by the General Assembly of the United Nations on 15 December 1997.

Annex IV

The Financial Action Task Force Forty Recommendations on Money Laundering and Interpretative Notes

A. Legal Systems

Scope of the criminal offence of money laundering

1.   Countries should criminalise money laundering on the basis of the *United Nations Convention against Illicit Traffic in Narcotic Drugs and Psychotropic Substances*, 1988 (the *Vienna Convention*) and the *United Nations Convention against Transnational Organized Crime*, 2000 (the *Palermo Convention*).

   Countries should apply the crime of money laundering to all serious offences, with a view to including the widest range of predicate offences. Predicate offences may be described by reference to all offences, or to a threshold linked either to a category of serious offences or to the penalty of imprisonment applicable to the predicate offence (threshold approach), or to a list of predicate offences, or a combination of these approaches.

Where countries apply a threshold approach, predicate offences should at a minimum comprise all offences that fall within the category of serious offences under their national law or should include offences which are punishable by a maximum penalty of more than one year's imprisonment or for those countries that have a minimum threshold for offences in their legal system, predicate offences should comprise all offences, which are punished by a minimum penalty of more than six months imprisonment.

Whichever approach is adopted, each country should at a minimum include a range of offences within each of the designated categories of offences.[1]

Predicate offences for money laundering should extend to conduct that occurred in another country, which constitutes an offence in that country, and which would have constituted a predicate offence had it occurred domestically. Countries may provide that the only prerequisite is that the conduct would have constituted a predicate offence had it occurred domestically.

Countries may provide that the offence of money laundering does not apply to persons who committed the predicate offence, where this is required by fundamental principles of their domestic law.

2. Countries should ensure that:

    a) The intent and knowledge required to prove the offence of money laundering is consistent with the standards set forth in the *Vienna* and *Palermo Conventions*, including the concept that such mental state may be inferred from objective factual circumstances.

    b) Criminal liability, and, where that is not possible, civil or administrative liability, should apply to legal persons. This should not preclude parallel criminal, civil or administrative proceedings with respect to legal persons in countries in which such forms of liability are available. Legal persons should be subject to effective, proportionate and dissuasive sanctions. Such measures should be without prejudice to the criminal liability of individuals.

Provisonal measures and confiscation

---

1. See the definition of "designated categories of offences" in the Glossary.

3.   Countries should adopt measures similar to those set forth in the *Vienna* and *Palermo Conventions*, including legislative measures, to enable their competent authorities to confiscate property laundered, proceeds from money laundering or predicate offences, instrumentalities used in or intended for use in the commission of these offences, or property of corresponding value, without prejudicing the rights of *bona fide* third parties.

Such measures should include the authority to: (a) identify, trace and evaluate property which is subject to confiscation; (b) carry out provisional measures, such as freezing and seizing, to prevent any dealing, transfer or disposal of such property; (c) take steps that will prevent or void actions that prejudice the State's ability to recover property that is subject to confiscation; and (d) take any appropriate investigative measures.

Countries may consider adopting measures that allow such proceeds or instrumentalities to be confiscated without requiring a criminal conviction, or which require an offender to demonstrate the lawful origin of the property alleged to be liable to confiscation, to the extent that such a requirement is consistent with the principles of their domestic law.

B. Measures to Be Taken by Financial Institutions and Nonfinancial Businesses and Professions to Prevent Money Laundering and Terrorist Financing

4.   Countries should ensure that financial institution secrecy laws do not inhibit implementation of the FATF Recommendations.

Customer due diligence and record-keeping

5.*   Financial institutions should not keep anonymous accounts or accounts in obviously fictitious names.

Financial institutions should undertake customer due diligence measures, including identifying and verifying the identity of their customers, when:

- establishing business relations;

---

*   Recommendations marked with an asterisk should be read in conjunction with their Interpretative Note.

- carrying out occasional transactions: (i) above the applicable designated threshold; or (ii) that are wire transfers in the circumstances covered by the Interpretative Note to Special Recommendation VII;
- there is a suspicion of money laundering or terrorist financing; or
- the financial institution has doubts about the veracity or adequacy of previously obtained customer identification data.

The customer due diligence (CDD) measures to be taken are as follows:

a) Identifying the customer and verifying that customer's identity using reliable, independent source documents, data or information.[2]

b) Identifying the beneficial owner, and taking reasonable measures to verify the identity of the beneficial owner such that the financial institution is satisfied that it knows who the beneficial owner is. For legal persons and arrangements this should include financial institutions taking reasonable measures to understand the ownership and control structure of the customer.

c) Obtaining information on the purpose and intended nature of the business relationship.

d) Conducting ongoing due diligence on the business relationship and scrutiny of transactions undertaken throughout the course of that relationship to ensure that the transactions being conducted are consistent with the institution's knowledge of the customer, their business and risk profile, including, where necessary, the source of funds.

Financial institutions should apply each of the CDD measures under (a) to (d) above, but may determine the extent of such measures on a risk sensitive basis depending on the type of customer, business relationship or transaction. The measures that are taken should be consistent with any guidelines issued by competent authorities. For higher risk categories, financial institutions should perform enhanced due diligence. In certain circumstances, where there are low risks, countries may decide that financial institutions can apply reduced or simplified measures.

---

2. Reliable, independent source documents, data or information will hereafter be referred to as "identification data."

Financial institutions should verify the identity of the customer and beneficial owner before or during the course of establishing a business relationship or conducting transactions for occasional customers. Countries may permit financial institutions to complete the verification as soon as reasonably practicable following the establishment of the relationship, where the money laundering risks are effectively managed and where this is essential not to interrupt the normal conduct of business.

Where the financial institution is unable to comply with paragraphs (a) to (c) above, it should not open the account, commence business relations or perform the transaction; or should terminate the business relationship; and should consider making a suspicious transactions report in relation to the customer.

These requirements should apply to all new customers, though financial institutions should also apply this Recommendation to existing customers on the basis of materiality and risk, and should conduct due diligence on such existing relationships at appropriate times.

6.* Financial institutions should, in relation to politically exposed persons, in addition to performing normal due diligence measures:

a) Have appropriate risk management systems to determine whether the customer is a politically exposed person.
b) Obtain senior management approval for establishing business relationships with such customers.
c) Take reasonable measures to establish the source of wealth and source of funds.
d) Conduct enhanced ongoing monitoring of the business relationship.

7. Financial institutions should, in relation to cross-border correspondent banking and other similar relationships, in addition to performing normal due diligence measures:

a) Gather sufficient information about a respondent institution to understand fully the nature of the respondent's business and to determine from publicly available information the reputation of the institution and the quality of supervision, including whether it has been subject to a money laundering or terrorist financing investigation or regulatory action.

b) Assess the respondent institution's anti-money laundering and terrorist financing controls.

c) Obtain approval from senior management before establishing new correspondent relationships.

d) Document the respective responsibilities of each institution.

e) With respect to "payable-through accounts", be satisfied that the respondent bank has verified the identity of and performed on-going due diligence on the customers having direct access to accounts of the correspondent and that it is able to provide relevant customer identification data upon request to the correspondent bank.

8. Financial institutions should pay special attention to any money laundering threats that may arise from new or developing technologies that might favour anonymity, and take measures, if needed, to prevent their use in money laundering schemes. In particular, financial institutions should have policies and procedures in place to address any specific risks associated with nonface to face business relationships or transactions.

9.* Countries may permit financial institutions to rely on intermediaries or other third parties to perform elements (a) – (c) of the CDD process or to introduce business, provided that the criteria set out below are met. Where such reliance is permitted, the ultimate responsibility for customer identification and verification remains with the financial institution relying on the third party.

The criteria that should be met are as follows:

a) A financial institution relying upon a third party should immediately obtain the necessary information concerning elements (a) – (c) of the CDD process. Financial institutions should take adequate steps to satisfy themselves that copies of identification data and other relevant documentation relating to the CDD requirements will be made available from the third party upon request without delay.

b) The financial institution should satisfy itself that the third party is regulated and supervised for, and has measures in place to comply with CDD requirements in line with Recommendations 5 and 10.

It is left to each country to determine in which countries the third party that meets the conditions can be based, having regard to information available on countries that do not or do not adequately apply the FATF Recommendations.

10.* Financial institutions should maintain, for at least five years, all necessary records on transactions, both domestic or international, to enable them to comply swiftly with information requests from the competent authorities. Such records must be sufficient to permit reconstruction of individual transactions (including the amounts and types of currency involved if any) so as to provide, if necessary, evidence for prosecution of criminal activity.

Financial institutions should keep records on the identification data obtained through the customer due diligence process (e.g. copies or records of official identification documents like passports, identity cards, driving licenses or similar documents), account files and business correspondence for at least five years after the business relationship is ended.

The identification data and transaction records should be available to domestic competent authorities upon appropriate authority.

11.* Financial institutions should pay special attention to all complex, unusual large transactions, and all unusual patterns of transactions, which have no apparent economic or visible lawful purpose. The background and purpose of such transactions should, as far as possible, be examined, the findings established in writing, and be available to help competent authorities and auditors.

12.* The customer due diligence and record-keeping requirements set out in Recommendations 5, 6, and 8 to 11 apply to designated non-financial businesses and professions in the following situations:

a) *Casinos*—when customers engage in financial transactions equal to or above the applicable designated threshold.

b) *Real estate agents*—when they are involved in transactions for their client concerning the buying and selling of real estate.

c) *Dealers in precious metals and dealers in precious stones*—when they engage in any cash transaction with a customer equal to or above the applicable designated threshold.

d) *Lawyers, notaries, other independent legal professionals and accountants* when they prepare for or carry out transactions for their client concerning the following activities:

- buying and selling of real estate;
- managing of client money, securities or other assets;
- management of bank, savings or securities accounts;
- organisation of contributions for the creation, operation or management of companies;
- creation, operation or management of legal persons or arrangements, and buying and selling of business entities.

e) Trust and company service providers when they prepare for or carry out transactions for a client concerning the activities listed in the definition in the Glossary.

Reporting of suspicious transactions and compliance

13.* If a financial institution suspects or has reasonable grounds to suspect that funds are the proceeds of a criminal activity, or are related to terrorist financing, it should be required, directly by law or regulation, to report promptly its suspicions to the financial intelligence unit (FIU).

14.* Financial institutions, their directors, officers and employees should be:

a) Protected by legal provisions from criminal and civil liability for breach of any restriction on disclosure of information imposed by contract or by any legislative, regulatory or administrative provision, if they report their suspicions in good faith to the FIU, even if they did not know precisely what the underlying criminal activity was, and regardless of whether illegal activity actually occurred.

b) Prohibited by law from disclosing the fact that a suspicious transaction report (STR) or related information is being reported to the FIU.

15.* Financial institutions should develop programmes against money laundering and terrorist financing. These programmes should include:

a) The development of internal policies, procedures and controls, including appropriate compliance management arrangements, and adequate screening procedures to ensure high standards when hiring employees.

b) An ongoing employee training programme.

c) An audit function to test the system.

16.* The requirements set out in Recommendations 13 to 15, and 21 apply to all designated nonfinancial businesses and professions, subject to the following qualifications:

a) Lawyers, notaries, other independent legal professionals and accountants should be required to report suspicious transactions when, on behalf of or for a client, they engage in a financial transaction in relation to the activities described in Recommendation 12(d). Countries are strongly encouraged to extend the reporting requirement to the rest of the professional activities of accountants, including auditing.

b) Dealers in precious metals and dealers in precious stones should be required to report suspicious transactions when they engage in any cash transaction with a customer equal to or above the applicable designated threshold.

c) Trust and company service providers should be required to report suspicious transactions for a client when, on behalf of or for a client, they engage in a transaction in relation to the activities referred to Recommendation 12(e).

Lawyers, notaries, other independent legal professionals, and accountants acting as independent legal professionals, are not required to report their suspicions if the relevant information was obtained in circumstances where they are subject to professional secrecy or legal professional privilege.

Other measures to deter money laundering and terrorist financing

17. Countries should ensure that effective, proportionate and dissuasive sanctions, whether criminal, civil or administrative, are available to deal with natural or legal persons covered by these Recommendations that fail to comply with anti-money laundering or terrorist financing requirements.
18. Countries should not approve the establishment or accept the continued operation of shell banks. Financial institutions should refuse to enter into, or continue, a correspondent banking relationship with shell banks. Financial institutions should also guard against establishing relations with respondent foreign financial institutions that permit their accounts to be used by shell banks.

19.* Countries should consider the feasibility and utility of a system where banks and other financial institutions and intermediaries would report all domestic and international currency transactions above a fixed amount, to a national central agency with a computerised data base, available to competent authorities for use in money laundering or terrorist financing cases, subject to strict safeguards to ensure proper use of the information.

20. Countries should consider applying the FATF Recommendations to businesses and professions, other than designated non-financial businesses and professions, that pose a money laundering or terrorist financing risk. Countries should further encourage the development of modern and secure techniques of money management that are less vulnerable to money laundering.

Measures to be taken with respect to countries that do not or insufficiently comply with the FATF Recommendations

21. Financial institutions should give special attention to business relationships and transactions with persons, including companies and financial institutions, from countries which do not or insufficiently apply the FATF Recommendations. Whenever these transactions have no apparent economic or visible lawful purpose, their background and purpose should, as far as possible, be examined, the findings established in writing, and be available to

help competent authorities. Where such a country continues not to apply or insufficiently applies the FATF Recommendations, countries should be able to apply appropriate countermeasures.

22. Financial institutions should ensure that the principles applicable to financial institutions, which are mentioned above are also applied to branches and majority owned subsidiaries located abroad, especially in countries which do not or insufficiently apply the FATF Recommendations, to the extent that local applicable laws and regulations permit. When local applicable laws and regulations prohibit this implementation, competent authorities in the country of the parent institution should be informed by the financial institutions that they cannot apply the FATF Recommendations.

Regulation and supervision

23.* Countries should ensure that financial institutions are subject to adequate regulation and supervision and are effectively implementing the FATF Recommendations. Competent authorities should take the necessary legal or regulatory measures to prevent criminals or their associates from holding or being the beneficial owner of a significant or controlling interest or holding a management function in a financial institution.

For financial institutions subject to the Core Principles, the regulatory and supervisory measures that apply for prudential purposes and which are also relevant to money laundering, should apply in a similar manner for anti-money laundering and terrorist financing purposes.

Other financial institutions should be licensed or registered and appropriately regulated, and subject to supervision or oversight for anti-money laundering purposes, having regard to the risk of money laundering or terrorist financing in that sector. At a minimum, businesses providing a service of money or value transfer, or of money or currency changing should be licensed or registered, and subject to effective systems for monitoring and ensuring compliance with national requirements to combat money laundering and terrorist financing.

24. Designated non-financial businesses and professions should be subject to regulatory and supervisory measures as set out below.

    a) Casinos should be subject to a comprehensive regulatory and supervisory regime that ensures that they have effectively implemented the necessary anti-money laundering and terrorist-financing measures. At a minimum:

        – casinos should be licensed;
        – competent authorities should take the necessary legal or regulatory measures to prevent criminals or their associates from holding or being the beneficial owner of a significant or controlling interest, holding a management function in, or being an operator of a casino
        – competent authorities should ensure that casinos are effectively supervised for compliance with requirements to combat money laundering and terrorist financing.

    b) Countries should ensure that the other categories of designated non-financial businesses and professions are subject to effective systems for monitoring and ensuring their compliance with requirements to combat money laundering and terrorist financing. This should be performed on a risk-sensitive basis. This may be performed by a government authority or by an appropriate self-regulatory organisation, provided that such an organisation can ensure that its members comply with their obligations to combat money laundering and terrorist financing.

25.*The competent authorities should establish guidelines, and provide feedback which will assist financial institutions and designated non-financial businesses and professions in applying national measures to combat money laundering and terrorist financing, and in particular, in detecting and reporting suspicious transactions.

C. Institutional and Other Measures Necessary in Systems for Combating Money Laundering and Terrorist Financing

Competent authorities, their powers and resources

26.* Countries should establish a FIU that serves as a national centre for the receiving (and, as permitted, requesting), analysis and dissemination of STR and other information regarding potential money laundering or terrorist financing. The FIU should have access, directly or indirectly, on a timely basis to the financial, administrative and law enforcement information that it requires to properly undertake its functions, including the analysis of STR.

27.* Countries should ensure that designated law enforcement authorities have responsibility for money laundering and terrorist financing investigations. Countries are encouraged to support and develop, as far as possible, special investigative techniques suitable for the investigation of money laundering, such as controlled delivery, undercover operations and other relevant techniques. Countries are also encouraged to use other effective mechanisms such as the use of permanent or temporary groups specialised in asset investigation, and co-operative investigations with appropriate competent authorities in other countries.

28. When conducting investigations of money laundering and underlying predicate offences, competent authorities should be able to obtain documents and information for use in those investigations, and in prosecutions and related actions. This should include powers to use compulsory measures for the production of records held by financial institutions and other persons, for the search of persons and premises, and for the seizure and obtaining of evidence.

29. Supervisors should have adequate powers to monitor and ensure compliance by financial institutions with requirements to combat money laundering and terrorist financing, including the authority to conduct inspections. They should be authorised to compel production of any information from financial institutions that is relevant to monitoring such compliance, and to impose adequate administrative sanctions for failure to comply with such requirements.

30. Countries should provide their competent authorities involved in combating money laundering and terrorist financing with adequate financial, human and technical resources. Countries should have in place processes to ensure that the staff of those authorities are of high integrity.

31. Countries should ensure that policy makers, the FIU, law enforcement and supervisors have effective mechanisms in place which enable them to co-operate, and where appropriate coordinate domestically with each other concerning the development and implementation of policies and activities to combat money laundering and terrorist financing.

32. Countries should ensure that their competent authorities can review the effectiveness of their systems to combat money laundering and terrorist financing systems by maintaining comprehensive statistics on matters relevant to the effectiveness and efficiency of such systems. This should include statistics on the STR received and disseminated; on money laundering and terrorist financing investigations, prosecutions and convictions; on property frozen, seized and confiscated; and on mutual legal assistance or other international requests for co-operation.

Transparency of legal persons and arrangements

33. Countries should take measures to prevent the unlawful use of legal persons by money launderers. Countries should ensure that there is adequate, accurate and timely information on the beneficial ownership and control of legal persons that can be obtained or accessed in a timely fashion by competent authorities. In particular, countries that have legal persons that are able to issue bearer shares should take appropriate measures to ensure that they are not misused for money laundering and be able to demonstrate the adequacy of those measures. Countries could consider measures to facilitate access to beneficial ownership and control information to financial institutions undertaking the requirements set out in Recommendation 5.

34. Countries should take measures to prevent the unlawful use of legal arrangements by money launderers. In particular, countries should ensure

that there is adequate, accurate and timely information on express trusts, including information on the settlor, trustee and beneficiaries, that can be obtained or accessed in a timely fashion by competent authorities. Countries could consider measures to facilitate access to beneficial ownership and control information to financial institutions undertaking the requirements set out in Recommendation 5.

D. International Co-operation

35. Countries should take immediate steps to become party to and implement fully the *Vienna Convention*, the *Palermo Convention*, and the 1999 United Nations International Convention for the Suppression of the Financing of Terrorism. Countries are also encouraged to ratify and implement other relevant international conventions, such as the 1990 Council of Europe Convention on Laundering, Search, Seizure and Confiscation of the Proceeds from Crime and the 2002 Inter-American Convention against Terrorism.

Mutual legal assistance and extradition

36. Countries should rapidly, constructively and effectively provide the widest possible range of mutual legal assistance in relation to money laundering and terrorist financing investigations, prosecutions, and related proceedings. In particular, countries should:

a) Not prohibit or place unreasonable or unduly restrictive conditions on the provision of mutual legal assistance.
b) Ensure that they have clear and efficient processes for the execution of mutual legal assistance requests.
c) Not refuse to execute a request for mutual legal assistance on the sole ground that the offence is also considered to involve fiscal matters.
d) Not refuse to execute a request for mutual legal assistance on the grounds that laws require financial institutions to maintain secrecy or confidentiality.

Countries should ensure that the powers of their competent authorities required under Recommendation 28 are also available for use in response to requests for mutual legal assistance, and if consistent with their domestic framework, in response to direct requests from foreign judicial or law enforcement authorities to domestic counterparts.

To avoid conflicts of jurisdiction, consideration should be given to devising and applying mechanisms for determining the best venue for prosecution of defendants in the interests of justice in cases that are subject to prosecution in more than one country.

37. Countries should, to the greatest extent possible, render mutual legal assistance notwithstanding the absence of dual criminality.

Where dual criminality is required for mutual legal assistance or extradition, that requirement should be deemed to be satisfied regardless of whether both countries place the offence within the same category of offence or denominate the offence by the same terminology, provided that both countries criminalise the conduct underlying the offence.

38.*There should be authority to take expeditious action in response to requests by foreign countries to identify, freeze, seize and confiscate property laundered, proceeds from money laundering or predicate offences, instrumentalities used in or intended for use in the commission of these offences, or property of corresponding value. There should also be arrangements for co-ordinating seizure and confiscation proceedings, which may include the sharing of confiscated assets.

39. Countries should recognise money laundering as an extraditable offence. Each country should either extradite its own nationals, or where a country does not do so solely on the grounds of nationality, that country should, at the request of the country seeking extradition, submit the case without undue delay to its competent authorities for the purpose of prosecution of the offences set forth in the request. Those authorities should take their decision and conduct their proceedings in the same manner as in the case of any other offence of a serious nature under the domestic law of that country. The countries concerned should cooperate with each other, in particular on procedural and evidentiary aspects, to ensure the efficiency of such prosecutions.

Subject to their legal frameworks, countries may consider simplifying extradition by allowing direct transmission of extradition requests between appropriate ministries, extraditing persons based only on warrants of arrests or judgements, and/or introducing a simplified extradition of consenting persons who waive formal extradition proceedings.

Other forms of co-operation

40.* Countries should ensure that their competent authorities provide the widest possible range of international co-operation to their foreign counterparts. There should be clear and effective gateways to facilitate the prompt and constructive exchange directly between counterparts, either spontaneously or upon request, of information relating to both money laundering and the underlying predicate offences. Exchanges should be permitted without unduly restrictive conditions. In particular:

a) Competent authorities should not refuse a request for assistance on the sole ground that the request is also considered to involve fiscal matters.

b) Countries should not invoke laws that require financial institutions to maintain secrecy or confidentiality as a ground for refusing to provide co-operation.

c) Competent authorities should be able to conduct inquiries; and where possible, investigations; on behalf of foreign counterparts.

Where the ability to obtain information sought by a foreign competent authority is not within the mandate of its counterpart, countries are also encouraged to permit a prompt and constructive exchange of information with non-counterparts. Co-operation with foreign authorities other than counterparts could occur directly or indirectly. When uncertain about the appropriate avenue to follow, competent authorities should first contact their foreign counterparts for assistance.

Countries should establish controls and safeguards to ensure that information exchanged by competent authorities is used only in an authorised manner, consistent with their obligations concerning privacy and data protection.

Glossary

In these Recommendations the following abbreviations and references are used:

"Beneficial owner" refers to the natural person(s) who ultimately owns or controls a customer and/or the person on whose behalf a transaction is being conducted. It also incorporates those persons who exercise ultimate effective control over a legal person or arrangement.

"Core Principles" refers to the Core Principles for Effective Banking Supervision issued by the Basel Committee on Banking Supervision, the Objectives and Principles for Securities Regulation issued by the International Organization of Securities Commissions, and the Insurance Supervisory Principles issued by the International Association of Insurance Supervisors.

"Designated categories of offences" means:

- participation in an organised criminal group and racketeering;
- terrorism, including terrorist financing;
- trafficking in human beings and migrant smuggling;
- sexual exploitation, including sexual exploitation of children;
- illicit trafficking in narcotic drugs and psychotropic substances;
- illicit arms trafficking;
- illicit trafficking in stolen and other goods;
- corruption and bribery;
- fraud;
- counterfeiting currency;
- counterfeiting and piracy of products;
- environmental crime;

- murder, grievous bodily injury;
- kidnapping, illegal restraint and hostage-taking;
- robbery or theft;
- smuggling;
- extortion;
- forgery;
- piracy; and
- insider trading and market manipulation.

When deciding on the range of offences to be covered as predicate offences under each of the categories listed above, each country may decide, in accordance with its domestic law, how it will define those offences and the nature of any particular elements of those offences that make them serious offences.

"Designated non-financial businesses and professions" means:

a) Casinos (which also includes internet casinos).

b) Real estate agents.

c) Dealers in precious metals.

d) Dealers in precious stones.

e) Lawyers, notaries, other independent legal professionals and accountants—this refers to sole practitioners, partners or employed professionals within professional firms. It is not meant to refer to 'internal' professionals that are employees of other types of businesses, nor to professionals working for government agencies, who may already be subject to measures that would combat money laundering.

f) Trust and Company Service Providers refers to all persons or businesses that are not covered elsewhere under these Recommendations, and which as a business, provide any of the following services to third parties:

  – acting as a formation agent of legal persons;

  – acting as (or arranging for another person to act as) a director or secretary of a company, a partner of a partnership, or a similar position in relation to other legal persons;

- providing a registered office; business address or accommodation, correspondence or administrative address for a company, a partnership or any other legal person or arrangement;
- acting as (or arranging for another person to act as) a trustee of an express trust;
- acting as (or arranging for another person to act as) a nominee shareholder for another person.

"**Designated threshold**" refers to the amount set out in the Interpretative Notes.

"**Financial institutions**" means any person or entity who conducts as a business one or more of the following activities or operations for or on behalf of a customer:

1. Acceptance of deposits and other repayable funds from the public.[3]
2. Lending.[4]
3. Financial leasing.[5]
4. The transfer of money or value.[6]
5. Issuing and managing means of payment (e.g. credit and debit cards, cheques, traveller's cheques, money orders and bankers' drafts, electronic money).
6. Financial guarantees and commitments.
7. Trading in:
   a) money market instruments (cheques, bills, CDs, derivatives etc.);
   b) foreign exchange;
   c) exchange, interest rate and index instruments;
   d) transferable securities;
   e) commodity futures trading.

---

3. This also captures private banking.
4. This includes inter alia: consumer credit; mortgage credit; factoring, with or without recourse; and finance of commercial transactions (including forfeiting).
5. This does not extend to financial leasing arrangements in relation to consumer products.
6. This applies to financial activity in both the formal or informal sector e.g. alternative remittance activity. See the Interpretative Note to Special Recommendation VI. It does not apply to any natural or legal person that provides financial institutions solely with message or other support systems for transmitting funds. See the Interpretative Note to Special Recommendation VII.

8. Participation in securities issues and the provision of financial services related to such issues.

9. Individual and collective portfolio management.

10. Safekeeping and administration of cash or liquid securities on behalf of other persons.

11. Otherwise investing, administering or managing funds or money on behalf of other persons.

12. Underwriting and placement of life insurance and other investment related insurance.[7]

13. Money and currency changing.

When a financial activity is carried out by a person or entity on an occasional or very limited basis (having regard to quantitative and absolute criteria) such that there is little risk of money laundering activity occurring, a country may decide that the application of anti-money laundering measures is not necessary, either fully or partially.

In strictly limited and justified circumstances, and based on a proven low risk of money laundering, a country may decide not to apply some or all of the Forty Recommendations to some of the financial activities stated above.

"FIU" means financial intelligence unit.

"Legal arrangements" refers to express trusts or other similar legal arrangements.

"Legal persons" refers to bodies corporate, foundations, anstalt, partnerships, or associations, or any similar bodies that can establish a permanent customer relationship with a financial institution or otherwise own property.

"Payable-through accounts" refers to correspondent accounts that are used directly by third parties to transact business on their own behalf.

----

7. This applies both to insurance undertakings and to insurance intermediaries (agents and brokers).

"Politically Exposed Persons" (PEPs) are individuals who are or have been entrusted with prominent public functions in a foreign country, for example Heads of State or of government, senior politicians, senior government, judicial or military officials, senior executives of state owned corporations, important political party officials. Business relationships with family members or close associates of PEPs involve reputational risks similar to those with PEPs themselves. The definition is not intended to cover middle ranking or more junior individuals in the foregoing categories.

"Shell bank" means a bank incorporated in a jurisdiction in which it has no physical presence and which is unaffiliated with a regulated financial group.

"STR" refers to suspicious transaction reports.

"Supervisors" refers to the designated competent authorities responsible for ensuring compliance by financial institutions with requirements to combat money laundering and terrorist financing.

"the FATF Recommendations" refers to these Recommendations and to the FATF Special Recommendations on Terrorist Financing.

Interpretative Notes to the Forty Recommendations

General

1.   Reference in this document to "countries" should be taken to apply equally to "territories" or "jurisdictions."

2.   Recommendations 5–16 and 21–22 state that financial institutions or designated non-financial businesses and professions should take certain actions. These references require countries to take measures that will oblige financial institutions or designated non-financial businesses and professions to comply with each Recommendation. The basic obligations under Recommendations 5, 10 and 13 should be set out in law or regulation, while more detailed elements in those Recommendations, as well as obligations

under other Recommendations, could be required either by law or regulation or by other enforceable means issued by a competent authority.

3. Where reference is made to a financial institution being satisfied as to a matter, that institution must be able to justify its assessment to competent authorities.

4. To comply with Recommendations 12 and 16, countries do not need to issue laws or regulations that relate exclusively to lawyers, notaries, accountants and the other designated non-financial businesses and professions so long as these businesses or professions are included in laws or regulations covering the underlying activities.

5. The Interpretative Notes that apply to financial institutions are also relevant to designated nonfinancial businesses and professions, where applicable.

Recommendations 5, 12 and 16

The designated thresholds for transactions (under Recommendations 5 and 12) are as follows:

- Financial institutions (for occasional customers under Recommendation 5)—USD/EUR 15,000.
- Casinos, including internet casinos (under Recommendation 12)—USD/EUR 3000
- For dealers in precious metals and dealers in precious stones when engaged in any cash transaction (under Recommendations 12 and 16)—USD/EUR 15,000.

Financial transactions above a designated threshold include situations where the transaction is carried out in a single operation or in several operations that appear to be linked.

Recommendation 5

CUSTOMER DUE DILIGENCE AND TIPPING OFF

1.   If, during the establishment or course of the customer relationship, or when conducting occasional transactions, a financial institution suspects that transactions relate to money laundering or terrorist financing, then the institution should:

  a) Normally seek to identify and verify the identity of the customer and the beneficial owner, whether permanent or occasional, and irrespective of any exemption or any designated threshold that might otherwise apply.

  b) Make a STR to the FIU in accordance with Recommendation 13.

2.   Recommendation 14 prohibits financial institutions, their directors, officers and employees from disclosing the fact that an STR or related information is being reported to the FIU. A risk exists that customers could be unintentionally tipped off when the financial institution is seeking to perform its customer due diligence (CDD) obligations in these circumstances. The customer's awareness of a possible STR or investigation could compromise future efforts to investigate the suspected money laundering or terrorist financing operation.

3.   Therefore, if financial institutions form a suspicion that transactions relate to money laundering or terrorist financing, they should take into account the risk of tipping off when performing the customer due diligence process. If the institution reasonably believes that performing the CDD process will tip-off the customer or potential customer, it may choose not to pursue that process, and should file an STR. Institutions should ensure that their employees are aware of and sensitive to these issues when conducting CDD.

CDD FOR LEGAL PERSONS AND ARRANGEMENTS

4.   When performing elements (a) and (b) of the CDD process in relation to legal persons or arrangements, financial institutions should:

a) Verify that any person purporting to act on behalf of the customer is so authorised, and identify that person.

b) Identify the customer and verify its identity—the types of measures that would be normally needed to satisfactorily perform this function would require obtaining proof of incorporation or similar evidence of the legal status of the legal person or arrangement, as well as information concerning the customer's name, the names of trustees, legal form, address, directors, and provisions regulating the power to bind the legal person or arrangement.

c) Identify the beneficial owners, including forming an understanding of the ownership and control structure, and take reasonable measures to verify the identity of such persons. The types of measures that would be normally needed to satisfactorily perform this function would require identifying the natural persons with a controlling interest and identifying the natural persons who comprise the mind and management of the legal person or arrangement. Where the customer or the owner of the controlling interest is a public company that is subject to regulatory disclosure requirements, it is not necessary to seek to identify and verify the identity of any shareholder of that company.

The relevant information or data may be obtained from a public register, from the customer or from other reliable sources.

RELIANCE ON IDENTIFICATION AND VERIFICATION ALREADY PERFORMED

5. The CDD measures set out in Recommendation 5 do not imply that financial institutions have to repeatedly identify and verify the identity of each customer every time that a customer conducts a transaction. An institution is entitled to rely on the identification and verification steps that it has already undertaken unless it has doubts about the veracity of that information. Examples of situations that might lead an institution to have such doubts could be where there is a suspicion of money laundering in relation to that customer, or where there is a material change in the way that the customer's account is operated which is not consistent with the customer's business profile.

6.   Examples of the types of circumstances where it would be permissible for verification to be completed after the establishment of the business relationship, because it would be essential not to interrupt the normal conduct of business include:

- Non face-to-face business.
- Securities transactions. In the securities industry, companies and intermediaries may be required to perform transactions very rapidly, according to the market conditions at the time the customer is contacting them, and the performance of the transaction may be required before verification of identity is completed.
- Life insurance business. In relation to life insurance business, countries may permit the identification and verification of the beneficiary under the policy to take place after having established the business relationship with the policyholder. However, in all such cases, identification and verification should occur at or before the time of payout or the time where the beneficiary intends to exercise vested rights under the policy.

7.   Financial institutions will also need to adopt risk management procedures with respect to the conditions under which a customer may utilise the business relationship prior to verification.

These procedures should include a set of measures such as a limitation of the number, types and/or amount of transactions that can be performed and the monitoring of large or complex transactions being carried out outside of expected norms for that type of relationship. Financial institutions should refer to the Basel CDD paper[8] (section 2.2.6.) for specific guidance on examples of risk management measures for non-face to face business.

---

8. "Basel CDD paper" refers to the guidance paper on Customer Due Diligence for Banks issued by the Basel Committee on Banking Supervision in October 2001.

REQUIREMENT TO IDENTIFY EXISTING CUSTOMERS

8. The principles set out in the Basel CDD paper concerning the identification of existing customers should serve as guidance when applying customer due diligence processes to institutions engaged in banking activity, and could apply to other financial institutions where relevant.

SIMPLIFIED OR REDUCED CDD MEASURES

9. The general rule is that customers must be subject to the full range of CDD measures, including the requirement to identify the beneficial owner. Nevertheless there are circumstances where the risk of money laundering or terrorist financing is lower, where information on the identity of the customer and the beneficial owner of a customer is publicly available, or where adequate checks and controls exist elsewhere in national systems. In such circumstances it could be reasonable for a country to allow its financial institutions to apply simplified or reduced CDD measures when identifying and verifying the identity of the customer and the beneficial owner.

10. Examples of customers where simplified or reduced CDD measures could apply are:

- Financial institutions—where they are subject to requirements to combat money laundering and terrorist financing consistent with the FATF Recommendations and are supervised for compliance with those controls.
- Public companies that are subject to regulatory disclosure requirements.
- Government administrations or enterprises.

11. Simplified or reduced CDD measures could also apply to the beneficial owners of pooled accounts held by designated non financial businesses or professions provided that those businesses or professions are subject to requirements to combat money laundering and terrorist financing consistent with the FATF Recommendations and are subject to effective systems for monitoring and ensuring their compliance with those requirements. Banks

should also refer to the Basel CDD paper (section 2.2.4.), which provides specific guidance concerning situations where an account holding institution may rely on a customer that is a professional financial intermediary to perform the customer due diligence on his or its own customers (i.e. the beneficial owners of the bank account). Where relevant, the CDD Paper could also provide guidance in relation to similar accounts held by other types of financial institutions.

12. Simplified CDD or reduced measures could also be acceptable for various types of products or transactions such as (examples only):

- Life insurance policies where the annual premium is no more than USD/EUR 1000 or a single premium of no more than USD/EUR 2500.
- Insurance policies for pension schemes if there is no surrender clause and the policy cannot be used as collateral.
- A pension, superannuation or similar scheme that provides retirement benefits to employees, where contributions are made by way of deduction from wages and the scheme rules do not permit the assignment of a member's interest under the scheme.

13. Countries could also decide whether financial institutions could apply these simplified measures only to customers in its own jurisdiction or allow them to do for customers from any other jurisdiction that the original country is satisfied is in compliance with and has effectively implemented the FATF Recommendations.

Simplified CDD measures are not acceptable whenever there is suspicion of money laundering or terrorist financing or specific higher risk scenarios apply.

Recommendation 6

Countries are encouraged to extend the requirements of Recommendation 6 to individuals who hold prominent public functions in their own country.

Recommendation 9

This Recommendation does not apply to outsourcing or agency relationships.

This Recommendation also does not apply to relationships, accounts or transactions between financial institutions for their clients. Those relationships are addressed by Recommendations 5 and 7.

Recommendations 10 and 11

In relation to insurance business, the word "transactions" should be understood to refer to the insurance product itself, the premium payment and the benefits.

Recommendation 13

1. The reference to criminal activity in Recommendation 13 refers to:

    a) all criminal acts that would constitute a predicate offence for money laundering in the jurisdiction; or
    b) at a minimum to those offences that would constitute a predicate offence as required by Recommendation 1.

    Countries are strongly encouraged to adopt alternative (a). All suspicious transactions, including attempted transactions, should be reported regardless of the amount of the transaction.

2. In implementing Recommendation 13, suspicious transactions should be reported by financial institutions regardless of whether they are also thought to involve tax matters. Countries should take into account that, in order to deter financial institutions from reporting a suspicious transaction, money launderers may seek to state inter alia that their transactions relate to tax matters.

Recommendation 14 (tipping off)

Where lawyers, notaries, other independent legal professionals and accountants acting as independent legal professionals seek to dissuade a client from engaging in illegal activity, this does not amount to tipping off.

Recommendation 15

The type and extent of measures to be taken for each of the requirements set out in the Recommendation should be appropriate having regard to the risk of money laundering and terrorist financing and the size of the business.

For financial institutions, compliance management arrangements should include the appointment of a compliance officer at the management level.

Recommendation 16

1.   It is for each jurisdiction to determine the matters that would fall under legal professional privilege or professional secrecy. This would normally cover information lawyers, notaries or other independent legal professionals receive from or obtain through one of their clients: (a) in the course of ascertaining the legal position of their client, or (b) in performing their task of defending or representing that client in, or concerning judicial, administrative, arbitration or mediation proceedings. Where accountants are subject to the same obligations of secrecy or privilege, then they are also not required to report suspicious transactions.

2.   Countries may allow lawyers, notaries, other independent legal professionals and accountants to send their STR to their appropriate self-regulatory organisations, provided that there are appropriate forms of co-operation between these organisations and the FIU.

Recommendation 23

Recommendation 23 should not be read as to require the introduction of a
system of regular review of licensing of controlling interests in financial institutions merely for anti-money laundering purposes, but as to stress the desir-
ability of suitability review for controlling shareholders in financial institutions (banks and non-banks in particular) from a FATF point of view. Hence,
where shareholder suitability (or "fit and proper") tests exist, the attention
of supervisors should be drawn to their relevance for anti-money laundering
purposes.

Recommendation 25

When considering the feedback that should be provided, countries should
have regard to the FATF Best Practice Guidelines on Providing Feedback to
Reporting Financial Institutions and Other Persons.

Recommendation 26

Where a country has created an FIU, it should consider applying for membership in the Egmont Group. Countries should have regard to the Egmont
Group Statement of Purpose, and its Principles for Information Exchange
Between Financial Intelligence Units for Money Laundering Cases. These documents set out important guidance concerning the role and functions of FIUs,
and the mechanisms for exchanging information between FIU.

Recommendation 27

Countries should consider taking measures, including legislative ones, at
the national level, to allow their competent authorities investigating money
laundering cases to postpone or waive the arrest of suspected persons and/
or the seizure of the money for the purpose of identifying persons involved
in such activities or for evidence gathering. Without such measures the use

of procedures such as controlled deliveries and undercover operations are precluded.

Recommendation 38

Countries should consider:

a) Establishing an asset forfeiture fund in its respective country into which all or a portion of confiscated property will be deposited for law enforcement, health, education, or other appropriate purposes.

b) Taking such measures as may be necessary to enable it to share among or between other countries confiscated property, in particular, when confiscation is directly or indirectly a result of co-ordinated law enforcement actions.

Recommendation 40

1. For the purposes of this Recommendation:

- "Counterparts" refers to authorities that exercise similar responsibilities and functions.
- "Competent authority" refers to all administrative and law enforcement authorities concerned with combating money laundering and terrorist financing, including the FIU and supervisors.

2. Depending on the type of competent authority involved and the nature and purpose of the cooperation, different channels can be appropriate for the exchange of information. Examples of mechanisms or channels that are used to exchange information include: bilateral or multilateral agreements or arrangements, memoranda of understanding, exchanges on the basis of reciprocity, or through appropriate international or regional organisations. However, this Recommendation is not intended to cover co-operation in relation to mutual legal assistance or extradition.

3.   The reference to indirect exchange of information with foreign authorities other than counterparts covers the situation where the requested information passes from the foreign authority through one or more domestic or foreign authorities before being received by the requesting authority. The competent authority that requests the information should always make it clear for what purpose and on whose behalf the request is made.

4.   FIUs should be able to make inquiries on behalf of foreign counterparts where this could be relevant to an analysis of financial transactions. At a minimum, inquiries should include:

- Searching its own databases, which would include information related to suspicious transaction reports.
- Searching other databases to which it may have direct or indirect access, including law enforcement databases, public databases, administrative databases and commercially available databases.

Where permitted to do so, FIUs should also contact other competent authorities and financial institutions in order to obtain relevant information.

Annex V

The Financial Action Task Force Special Recommendations on Terrorist Financing

I. Ratification and implementation of UN instruments

Each country should take immediate steps to ratify and to implement fully the 1999 United Nations International Convention for the Suppression of the Financing of Terrorism.

Countries should also immediately implement the United Nations resolutions relating to the prevention and suppression of the financing of terrorist acts, particularly United Nations Security Council Resolution 1373.

II. Criminalising the financing of terrorism and associated money laundering

Each country should criminalise the financing of terrorism, terrorist acts and terrorist organisations. Countries should ensure that such offences are designated as money laundering predicate offences.

III. Freezing and confiscating terrorist assets

Each country should implement measures to freeze without delay funds or other assets of terrorists, those who finance terrorism and terrorist organisations in accordance with the United Nations resolutions relating to the prevention and suppression of the financing of terrorist acts.

Each country should also adopt and implement measures, including legislative ones, which would enable the competent authorities to seize and confiscate property that is the proceeds of, or used in, or intended or allocated for use in, the financing of terrorism, terrorist acts or terrorist organisations.

IV. Reporting suspicious transactions related to terrorism

If financial institutions, or other businesses or entities subject to anti-money laundering obligations, suspect or have reasonable grounds to suspect that funds are linked or related to, or are to be used for terrorism, terrorist acts or by terrorist organisations, they should be required to report promptly their suspicions to the competent authorities.

V. International co-operation

Each country should afford another country, on the basis of a treaty, arrangement or other mechanism for mutual legal assistance or information exchange, the greatest possible measure of assistance in connection with criminal, civil enforcement, and administrative investigations, inquiries and proceedings relating to the financing of terrorism, terrorist acts and terrorist organisations.

Countries should also take all possible measures to ensure that they do not provide safe havens for individuals charged with the financing of terrorism, terrorist acts or terrorist organisations, and should have procedures in place to extradite, where possible, such individuals.

Each country should take measures to ensure that persons or legal entities, including agents, that provide a service for the transmission of money or value, including transmission through an informal money or value transfer system or network, should be licensed or registered and subject to all the FATF Recommendations that apply to banks and non-bank financial institutions. Each country should ensure that persons or legal entities that carry out this service illegally are subject to administrative, civil or criminal sanctions.

VII. Wire transfers

Countries should take measures to require financial institutions, including money remitters, to include accurate and meaningful originator information (name, address and account number) on funds transfers and related messages that are sent, and the information should remain with the transfer or related message through the payment chain.

Countries should take measures to ensure that financial institutions, including money remitters, conduct enhanced scrutiny of and monitor for suspicious activity funds transfers which do not contain complete originator information (name, address and account number).

VIII. Non-profit organisations

Countries should review the adequacy of laws and regulations that relate to entities that can be abused for the financing of terrorism. Non-profit organisations are particularly vulnerable, and countries should ensure that they cannot be misused:

i. by terrorist organisations posing as legitimate entities;
ii. to exploit legitimate entities as conduits for terrorist financing, including for the purpose of escaping asset freezing measures; and
iii.to conceal or obscure the clandestine diversion of funds intended forlegitimate purposes to terrorist organisations.

IX. Cash couriers

Countries should have measures in place to detect the physical cross-border transportation of currency and bearer negotiable instruments, including a declaration system or other disclosure obligation.

Countries should ensure that their competent authorities have the legal authority to stop or restrain currency or bearer negotiable instruments that are suspected to be related to terrorist financing or money laundering, or that are falsely declared or disclosed.

Countries should ensure that effective, proportionate and dissuasive sanctions are available to deal with persons who make false declaration(s) or disclosure(s). In cases where the currency or bearer negotiable instruments are related to terrorist financing or money laundering, countries should also adopt measures, including legislative ones consistent with Recommendation 3 and Special Recommendation III, which would enable the confiscation of such currency or instruments.

Annex VI

The Financial Action Task Force Interpretative Notes and Guidance Notes for the Special Recommendations on Terrorist Financing and the Self-Assessment Questionnaire

Interpretative Notes

Interpretative Note to Special Recommendation II: Criminalising the financing of terrorism and associated money laundering

OBJECTIVE

1. Special Recommendation II (SR II) was developed with the objective of ensuring that countries have the legal capacity to prosecute and apply criminal sanctions to persons that finance terrorism. Given the close connection between international terrorism and *inter alia* money laundering, another objective of SR II is to emphasise this link by obligating countries to include terrorist financing offences as predicate offences for money laundering. The basis for criminalising terrorist financing should be the United Nations

International Convention for the Suppression of the Financing of Terrorism, 1999.[1]

DEFINITIONS

2. For the purposes of SR II and this Interpretative Note, the following definitions apply:

a) The term *funds* refers to assets of every kind, whether tangible or intangible, movable or immovable, however acquired, and legal documents or instruments in any form, including electronic or digital, evidencing title to, or interest in, such assets, including, but not limited to, bank credits, travellers cheques, bank cheques, money orders, shares, securities, bonds, drafts, letters of credit.

b) The term *terrorist* refers to any natural person who: (i) commits, or attempts to commit, terrorist acts by any means, directly or indirectly, unlawfully and wilfully; (ii) participates as an accomplice in terrorist acts; (iii) organises or directs others to commit terrorist acts; or (iv) contributes to the commission of terrorist acts by a group of persons acting with a common purpose where the contribution is made intentionally and with the aim of furthering the terrorist act or with the knowledge of the intention of the group to commit a terrorist act.

c) The term *terrorist act* includes:

   i) An act which constitutes an offence within the scope of, and as defined in one of the following treaties: Convention for the Suppression of Unlawful Seizure of Aircraft (1970), Convention for the Suppression of Unlawful Acts against the Safety of Civil Aviation (1971), Convention on the Prevention and Punishment of Crimes against Internationally Protected Persons, including Diplomatic Agents (1973), International Convention against the Taking of Hostages (1979), Convention on the Physical Protection

---

1. Although the UN Convention had not yet come into force at the time that SR II was originally issued in October 2001—and thus is not cited in the SR itself—the intent of the FATF has been from the issuance of SR II to reiterate and reinforce the criminalisation standard as set forth in the Convention (in particular, Article 2). The Convention came into force in April 2003.

of Nuclear Material (1980), Protocol for the Suppression of Unlawful Acts of Violence at Airports Serving International Civil Aviation, supplementary to the Convention for the Suppression of Unlawful Acts against the Safety of Civil Aviation (1988), Convention for the Suppression of Unlawful Acts against the Safety of Maritime Navigation (1988), Protocol for the Suppression of Unlawful Acts against the Safety of Fixed Platforms located on the Continental Shelf (1988), and the International Convention for the Suppression of Terrorist Bombings (1997); and

ii) Any other act intended to cause death or serious bodily injury to a civilian, or to any other person not taking an active part in the hostilities in a situation of armed conflict, when the purpose of such act, by its nature or context, is to intimidate a population, or to compel a Government or an international organisation to do or to abstain from doing any act.

d) The term *terrorist financing* includes the financing of terrorist acts, and of terrorists and terrorist organisations.

e) The term *terrorist organisation* refers to any group of terrorists that: (i) commits, or attempts to commit, terrorist acts by any means, directly or indirectly, unlawfully and wilfully; (ii) participates as an accomplice in terrorist acts; (iii) organises or directs others to commit terrorist acts; or (iv) contributes to the commission of terrorist acts by a group of persons acting with a common purpose where the contribution is made intentionally and with the aim of furthering the terrorist act or with the knowledge of the intention of the group to commit a terrorist act.

CHARACTERISTICS OF THE TERRORIST FINANCING OFFENCE

3. Terrorist financing offences should extend to any person who wilfully provides or collects funds by any means, directly or indirectly, with the unlawful intention that they should be used or in the knowledge that they are to be used, in full or in part: (a) to carry out a terrorist act(s); (b) by a terrorist organisation; or (c) by an individual terrorist.

4. Criminalising terrorist financing solely on the basis of aiding and abetting, attempt, or conspiracy does not comply with this Recommendation.

5. Terrorist financing offences should extend to any funds whether from a legitimate or illegitimate source.

6. Terrorist financing offences should not require that the funds: (a) were actually used to carry out or attempt a terrorist act(s); or (b) be linked to a specific terrorist act(s).

7. It should also be an offence to attempt to commit the offence of terrorist financing.

8. It should also be an offence to engage in any of the following types of conduct:

   a) Participating as an accomplice in an offence as set forth in paragraphs 3 or 7 of this Interpretative Note;
   b) Organising or directing others to commit an offence as set forth in paragraphs 3 or 7 of this Interpretative Note;
   c) Contributing to the commission of one or more offence(s) as set forth in paragraphs 3 or 7 of this Interpretative Note by a group of persons acting with a common purpose. Such contribution shall be intentional and shall either: (i) be made with the aim of furthering the criminal activity or criminal purpose of the group, where such activity or purpose involves the commission of a terrorist financing offence; or (ii) be made in the knowledge of the intention of the group to commit a terrorist financing offence.

9. Terrorist financing offences should be predicate offences for money laundering.

10. Terrorist financing offences should apply, regardless of whether the person alleged to have committed the offence(s) is in the same country or a different country from the one in which the terrorist(s)/terrorist organisation(s) is located or the terrorist act(s) occurred/will occur.

11. The law should permit the intentional element of the terrorist financing offence to be inferred from objective factual circumstances.

12. Criminal liability for terrorist financing should extend to legal persons. Where that is not possible (i.e. due to fundamental principles of domestic law), civil or administrative liability should apply.

13. Making legal persons subject to criminal liability for terrorist financing should not preclude the possibility of parallel criminal, civil or administrative proceedings in countries in which more than one form of liability is available.

14. Natural and legal persons should be subject to effective, proportionate and dissuasive criminal, civil or administrative sanctions for terrorist financing.

Interpretative Note to Special Recommendation III: Freezing and Confiscating Terrorist Assets Objectives

1. FATF Special Recommendation III consists of two obligations. The first requires jurisdictions to implement measures that will freeze or, if appropriate, seize terrorist-related funds or other assets without delay in accordance with relevant United Nations resolutions. The second obligation of Special Recommendation III is to have measures in place that permit a jurisdiction to seize or confiscate terrorist funds or other assets on the basis of an order or mechanism issued by a competent authority or a court.

2. The objective of the first requirement is to freeze terrorist-related funds or other assets based on reasonable grounds, or a reasonable basis, to suspect or believe that such funds or other assets could be used to finance terrorist activity. The objective of the second requirement is to deprive terrorists of these funds or other assets if and when links have been adequately established between the funds or other assets and terrorists or terrorist activity. The intent of the first objective is preventative, while the intent of the second objective is mainly preventative and punitive. Both requirements are necessary to deprive terrorists and terrorist networks of the means to conduct future terrorist activity and maintain their infrastructure and operations.

SCOPE

3. Special Recommendation III is intended, with regard to its first requirement, to complement the obligations in the context of the United Nations
Security Council (UNSC) resolutions relating to the prevention and suppression of the financing of terrorist acts—S/RES/1267(1999) and its successor
resolutions,[2] S/RES/1373(2001) and any prospective resolutions related to
the freezing, or if appropriate seizure, of terrorist assets. It should be stressed
that none of the obligations in Special Recommendation III is intended to
replace other measures or obligations that may already be in place for dealing with funds or other assets in the context of a criminal, civil or administrative investigation or proceeding.[3] The focus of Special Recommendation
III instead is on the preventative measures that are necessary and unique in
the context of stopping the flow or use of funds or other assets to terrorist
groups.

4. S/RES/1267(1999) and S/RES/1373(2001) differ in the persons and entities
whose funds or other assets are to be frozen, the authorities responsible for
making these designations, and the effect of these designations.

5. S/RES/1267(1999) and its successor resolutions obligate jurisdictions
to freeze without delay the funds or other assets owned or controlled by
Al-Qaida, the Taliban, Usama bin Laden, or persons and entities associated with them as designated by the United Nations Al-Qaida and Taliban
Sanctions Committee established pursuant to United Nations Security
Council Resolution 1267 (the Al-Qaida and Taliban Sanctions Committee),
including funds derived from funds or other assets owned or controlled,

---

2. When issued, S/RES/1267(1999) had a time limit of one year. A series of resolutions have been
   issued by the United Nations Security Council (UNSC) to extend and further refine provisions of
   S/RES/1267(1999). By successor resolutions are meant those resolutions that extend and are directly related to the original resolution S/RES/1267(1999). At the time of issue of this Interpretative Note, these resolutions included S/RES/1333(2000), S/RES/1363(2001), S/RES/1390(2002)
   and S/RES/1455(2003). In this Interpretative Note, the term S/RES/1267(1999) refers to
   S/RES/1267(1999) and its successor resolutions.
3. For instance, both the UN Convention against Illicit Traffic in Narcotic Drugs and Psychotropic
   Substances (1988) and UN Convention against Transnational Organised Crime (2000) contain
   obligations regarding freezing, seizure and confiscation in the context of combating transnational crime. Those obligations exist separately and apart from obligations that are set forth in
   S/RES/1267(1999), S/RES/1373(2001) and SpecialRecommendation III.

directly or indirectly, by them or by persons acting on their behalf or at their direction, and ensure that neither these nor any other funds or other assets are made available, directly or indirectly, for such persons' benefit, by their nationals or by any person within their territory. The Al-Qaida and Taliban Sanctions Committee is the authority responsible for designating the persons and entities that should have their funds or other assets frozen under S/RES/1267(1999). All jurisdictions that are members of the United Nations are obligated by S/RES/1267(1999) to freeze the assets of persons and entities so designated by the Al-Qaida and Taliban Sanctions Committee.[4]

6. S/RES/1373(2001) obligates jurisdictions[5] to freeze without delay the funds or other assets of persons who commit, or attempt to commit, terrorist acts or participate in or facilitate the commission of terrorist acts; of entities owned or controlled directly or indirectly by such persons; and of persons and entities acting on behalf of, or at the direction of such persons and entities, including funds or other assets derived or generated from property owned or controlled, directly or indirectly, by such persons and associated persons and entities. Each individual jurisdiction has the authority to designate the persons and entities that should have their funds or other assets frozen. Additionally, to ensure that effective co-operation is developed among jurisdictions, jurisdictions should examine and give effect to, if appropriate, the actions initiated under the freezing mechanisms of other jurisdictions. When (i) a specific notification or communication is sent and (ii) the jurisdiction receiving the request is satisfied, according to applicable legal principles, that a requested designation is supported by reasonable grounds, or a reasonable basis, to suspect or believe that the proposed designee is a terrorist, one who finances terrorism or a terrorist organisation, the jurisdiction receiving the request must ensure that the funds or other assets of the designated person are frozen without delay.

---

4. When the UNSC acts under Chapter VII of the UN Charter, the resolutions it issues are mandatory for all UN members.
5. The UNSC was acting under Chapter VII of the UN Charter in issuing S/RES/1373(2001) (see previous footnote).

7. For the purposes of Special Recommendation III and this Interpretive Note, the following definitions apply:

a) The term *freeze* means to prohibit the transfer, conversion, disposition or movement of funds or other assets on the basis of, and for the duration of the validity of, an action initiated by a competent authority or a court under a freezing mechanism. The frozen funds or other assets remain the property of the person(s) or entity(ies) that held an interest in the specified funds or other assets at the time of the freezing and may continue to be administered by the financial institution or other arrangements designated by such person(s) or entity(ies) prior to the initiation of an action under a freezing mechanism.

b) The term *seize* means to prohibit the transfer, conversion, disposition or movement of funds or other assets on the basis of an action initiated by a competent authority or a court under a freezing mechanism. However, unlike a freezing action, a seizure is effected by a mechanism that allows the competent authority or court to take control of specified funds or other assets. The seized funds or other assets remain the property of the person(s) or entity(ies) that held an interest in the specified funds or other assets at the time of the seizure, although the competent authority or court will often take over possession, administration or management of the seized funds or other assets.

c) The term *confiscate*, which includes forfeiture where applicable, means the permanent deprivation of funds or other assets by order of a competent authority or a court. Confiscation or forfeiture takes place through a judicial or administrative procedure that transfers the ownership of specified funds or other assets to be transferred to the State. In this case, the person(s) or entity(ies) that held an interest in the specified funds or other assets at the time of the confiscation or forfeiture loses all rights, in principle, to the confiscated or forfeited funds or other assets.[6]

---

6. Confiscation or forfeiture orders are usually linked to a criminal conviction or a court deci-

d) The term *funds* or *other assets* means financial assets, property of every kind, whether tangible or intangible, movable or immovable, however acquired, and legal documents or instruments in any form, including electronic or digital, evidencing title to, or interest in, such funds or other assets, including, but not limited to, bank credits, travellers cheques, bank cheques, money orders, shares, securities, bonds, drafts, or letters of credit, and any interest, dividends or other income on or value accruing from or generated by such funds or other assets.

e) The term *terrorist* refers to any natural person who: (i) commits, or attempts to commit, terrorist acts[7] by any means, directly or indirectly, unlawfully and wilfully; (ii) participates as an accomplice in terrorist acts or terrorist financing; (iii) organises or directs others to commit terrorist acts or terrorist financing; or (iv) contributes to the commission of terrorist acts or terrorist financing by a group of persons acting with a common purpose where the contribution is made intentionally and with the aim of furthering the terrorist act or terrorist financing or with the knowledge of the intention of the group to commit a terrorist act or terrorist financing.

f) The phrase *those who finance terrorism* refers to any person, group, undertaking or other entity that provides or collects, by any means, directly or indirectly, funds or other assets that may be used, in full or in part, to facilitate the commission of terrorist acts, or to any persons or entities acting on behalf of, or at the direction of such persons, groups, undertakings or other entities. This includes those who provide or collect funds or other assets with the intention that they should

---

sion whereby the confiscated or forfeited property is determined to have been derived from or intended for use in a violation of the law.

7. A terrorist act includes an act which constitutes an offence within the scope of, and as defined in one of the following treaties: Convention for the Suppression of Unlawful Seizure of Aircraft, Convention for the Suppression of Unlawful Acts against the Safety of Civil Aviation, Convention on the Prevention and Punishment of Crimes against Internationally Protected Persons, including Diplomatic Agents, International Convention against the Taking of Hostages, Convention on the Physical Protection of Nuclear Material, Protocol for the Suppression of Unlawful Acts of Violence at Airports Serving International Civil Aviation, supplementary to the Convention for the Suppression of Unlawful Acts against the Safety of Civil Aviation, Convention for the Suppression of Unlawful Acts against the Safety of Maritime Navigation, Protocol for the Suppression of Unlawful Acts against the Safety of Fixed Platforms located on the Continental Shelf, International Convention for the Suppression of Terrorist Bombings, and the International Convention for the Suppression of the Financing of Terrorism (1999).

be used or in the knowledge that they are to be used, in full or in part, in order to carry out terrorist acts.

g) The term *terrorist organisation* refers to any legal person, group, undertaking or other entity owned or controlled directly or indirectly by a terrorist(s).

h) The term *designated persons* refers to those persons or entities designated by the Al-Qaida and Taliban Sanctions Committee pursuant to S/RES/1267(1999) or those persons or entities designated and accepted, as appropriate, by jurisdictions pursuant to S/RES/1373(2001).

i) The phrase *without delay*, for the purposes of S/RES/1267(1999), means, ideally, within a matter of hours of a designation by the Al-Qaida and Taliban Sanctions Committee. For the purposes of S/RES/1373(2001), the phrase *without delay* means upon having reasonable grounds, or a reasonable basis, to suspect or believe that a person or entity is a terrorist, one who finances terrorism or a terrorist organisation. The phrase *without delay* should be interpreted in the context of the need to prevent the flight or dissipation of terrorist-linked funds or other assets, and the need for global, concerted action to interdict and disrupt their flow swiftly.

FREEZING WITHOUT DELAY TERRORIST-RELATED FUNDS OR OTHER ASSETS

8. In order to fulfil the preventive intent of Special Recommendation III, jurisdictions should establish the necessary authority and adopt the following standards and procedures to freeze the funds or other assets of terrorists, those who finance terrorism and terrorist organisations in accordance with both S/RES/1267(1999) and S/RES/1373(2001):

a) *Authority to freeze, unfreeze and prohibit dealing in funds or other assets of designated persons.* Jurisdictions should prohibit by enforceable means the transfer, conversion, disposition or movement of funds or other assets. Options for providing the authority to freeze and unfreeze terrorist funds or other assets include:

i) empowering or designating a competent authority or a court to issue, administer and enforce freezing and unfreezing actions under relevant mechanisms, or

ii) enacting legislation that places responsibility for freezing the funds or other assets of designated persons publicly identified by a competent authority or a court on the person or entity holding the funds or other assets and subjecting them to sanctions for non-compliance.

The authority to freeze and unfreeze funds or other assets should also extend to funds or other assets derived or generated from funds or other assets owned or controlled directly or indirectly by such terrorists, those who finance terrorism, or terrorist organisations.

Whatever option is chosen there should be clearly identifiable competent authorities responsible for enforcing the measures. The competent authorities shall ensure that their nationals or any persons and entities within their territories are prohibited from making any funds or other assets, economic resources or financial or other related services available, directly or indirectly, wholly or jointly, for the benefit of: designated persons, terrorists; those who finance terrorism; terrorist organisations; entities owned or controlled, directly or indirectly, by such persons or entities; and persons and entities acting on behalf of or at the direction of such persons or entities.

b) *Freezing procedures.* Jurisdictions should develop and implement procedures to freeze the funds or other assets specified in paragraph (c) below without delay and without giving prior notice to the persons or entities concerned. Persons or entities holding such funds or other assets should be required by law to freeze them and should furthermore be subject to sanctions for non-compliance with this requirement. Any delay between the official receipt of information provided in support of a designation and the actual freezing of the funds or other assets of designated persons undermines the effectiveness of designation by affording designated persons time to remove funds or other assets from identifiable accounts and places. Consequently, these procedures must ensure (i) the prompt determination whether reasonable grounds or a reasonable basis exists to initiate an action under a freezing mechanism and (ii) the subsequent freezing of funds or other assets without delay upon determination that such grounds or basis for freezing exist. Jurisdictions should develop efficient and effective systems for communicating actions taken under their freezing mechanisms to the financial sector immediately upon taking such action. As well, they should provide clear guidance, particularly financial institutions and other persons or entities that may be holding targeted funds or other assets on obligations in taking action under freezing mechanisms.

c) *Funds or other assets to be frozen or, if appropriate, seized.* Under Special Recommendation III, funds or other assets to be frozen include those subject to freezing under S/RES/1267(1999) and S/RES/1373(2001). Such funds or other assets would also include those wholly or jointly owned or controlled, directly or indirectly, by designated persons. In accordance with their obligations under the United Nations International Convention for the Suppression of the Financing of Terrorism (1999) (the Terrorist Financing Convention (1999)), jurisdictions should be able to freeze or, if appropriate, seize any funds or other assets that they identify, detect, and verify, in accordance with applicable legal principles, as being used by, allocated for, or being made available to terrorists, those who finance terrorists or terrorist organisations. Freezing or seizing under the Terrorist Financing Convention (1999) may be conducted by freezing or seizing in the context of a criminal investigation or proceeding. Freezing action taken under Special Recommendation III shall be without prejudice to the rights of third parties acting in good faith.

d) *De-listing and unfreezing procedures.* Jurisdictions should develop and implement publicly known procedures to consider de-listing requests upon satisfaction of certain criteria consistent with international obligations and applicable legal principles, and to unfreeze the funds or other assets of de-listed persons or entities in a timely manner. For persons and entities designated under S/RES/1267(1999), such procedures and criteria should be in accordance with procedures adopted by the Al-Qaida and Taliban Sanctions Committee under S/RES/1267(1999).

e) *Unfreezing upon verification of identity.* For persons or entities with the same or similar name as designated persons, who are inadvertently affected by a freezing mechanism, jurisdictions should develop and implement publicly known procedures to unfreeze the funds or other assets of such persons or entities in a timely manner upon verification that the person or entity involved is not a designated person.

f) *Providing access to frozen funds or other assets in certain circumstances.* Where jurisdictions have determined that funds or other assets, which are otherwise subject to freezing pursuant to the obligations under S/RES/1267(1999), are necessary for basic expenses; for the payment of certain types of fees, expenses and service charges, or for extraordinary expenses,[8] jurisdictions should authorise access to such funds or other assets in accordance with the procedures set out in S/RES/1452(2002) and subject to approval of the Al-Qaida and Taliban Sanctions Committee. On the same grounds, jurisdictions may authorise access to funds or other assets, if freezing measures are applied pursuant to S/RES/1373(2001).

g) *Remedies.* Jurisdictions should provide for a mechanism through which a person or an entity that is the target of a freezing mechanism in the context of terrorist financing can challenge that measure with a view to having it reviewed by a competent authority or a court.

h) *Sanctions.* Jurisdictions should adopt appropriate measures to monitor effectively the compliance with relevant legislation, rules or regulations governing freezing mechanisms by financial institutions and other persons or entities that may be holding funds or other assets as indicated in paragraph 8(c) above. Failure to comply with such legislation, rules or regulations should be subject to civil, administrative or criminal sanctions.

SEIZURE AND CONFISCATION

9. Consistent with FATF Recommendation 3, jurisdictions should adopt measures similar to those set forth in Article V of the United Nations Convention against Illicit Traffic in Narcotic Drugs and Psychotropic Substances (1988), Articles 12 to 14 of the United Nations Convention on Transnational Organised Crime (2000), and Article 8 of the Terrorist Financing Convention

---

8. See Article 1, S/RES/1452(2002) for the specific types of expenses that are covered.

(1999), including legislative measures, to enable their courts or competent authorities to seize and confiscate terrorist funds or other assets.

Interpretative Note to Special Recommendation VI: Alternative Remittance

GENERAL

1. Money or value transfer systems have shown themselves vulnerable to misuse for money laundering and terrorist financing purposes. The objective of Special Recommendation VI is to increase the transparency of payment flows by ensuring that jurisdictions impose consistent anti-money laundering and counter-terrorist financing measures on all forms of money/value transfer systems, particularly those traditionally operating outside the conventional financial sector and not currently subject to the FATF Recommendations. This Recommendation and Interpretative Note underscore the need to bring all money or value transfer services, whether formal or informal, within the ambit of certain minimum legal and regulatory requirements in accordance with the relevant FATF Recommendations.

2. Special Recommendation VI consists of three core elements:

 a) Jurisdictions should require licensing or registration of persons (natural or legal) that provide money/value transfer services, including through informal systems;

 b) Jurisdictions should ensure that money/value transmission services, including informal systems (as described in paragraph 5 below), are subject to applicable FATF Forty Recommendations (2003) (in particular, Recommendations 4–16 and 21–25)[9] and the Eight Special Recommendations (in particular SR VII); and

 c) Jurisdictions should be able to impose sanctions on money/value transfer services, including informal systems, that operate without

---

9. When this Interpretative Note was originally issued, these references were to the 1996 FATF Forty Recommendations. Subsequent to the publication of the revised FATF Forty Recommendations in June 2003, this text was updated accordingly. All references are now to the 2003 FATF Forty Recommendations.

a license or registration and that fail to comply with relevant FATF Recommendations.

Scope and Application

3. For the purposes of this Recommendation, the following definitions are used.

4. *Money or value transfer service* refers to a financial service that accepts cash, cheques, other monetary instruments or other stores of value in one location and pays a corresponding sum in cash or other form to a beneficiary in another location by means of a communication, message, transfer or through a clearing network to which the money/value transfer service belongs. Transactions performed by such services can involve one or more intermediaries and a third party final payment.

5. A money or value transfer service may be provided by persons (natural or legal) formally through the regulated financial system or informally through non-bank financial institutions or other business entities or any other mechanism either through the regulated financial system (for example, use of bank accounts) or through a network or mechanism that operates outside the regulated system. In some jurisdictions, informal systems are frequently referred to as *alternative remittance services* or *underground* (or *parallel*) *banking systems*. Often these systems have ties to particular geographic regions and are therefore described using a variety of specific terms. Some examples of these terms include *hawala*, *hundi*, *fei-chien*, and the *black market peso exchange*.[10]

6. *Licensing* means a requirement to obtain permission from a designated competent authority in order to operate a money/value transfer service legally.

---

10. The inclusion of these examples does not suggest that such systems are legal in any particular jurisdiction.

7. *Registration* in this Recommendation means a requirement to register with or declare to a designated competent authority the existence of a money/value transfer service in order for the business to operate legally.

8. The obligation of licensing or registration applies to *agents*. At a minimum, the principal business must maintain a current list of agents which must be made available to the designated competent authority. An *agent* is any person who provides money or value transfer service under the direction of or by contract with a legally registered or licensed remitter (for example, licensees, franchisees, concessionaires).

APPLICABILITY OF SPECIAL RECOMMENDATION VI

9. Special Recommendation VI should apply to all persons (natural or legal), which conduct for or on behalf of another person (natural or legal) the types of activity described in paragraphs 4 and 5 above as a primary or substantial part of their business or when such activity is undertaken on a regular or recurring basis, including as an ancillary part of a separate business enterprise.

10. Jurisdictions need not impose a separate licensing / registration system or designate another competent authority in respect to persons (natural or legal) already licensed or registered as financial institutions (as defined by the FATF Forty Recommendations [2003]) within a particular jurisdiction, which under such license or registration are permitted to perform activities indicated in paragraphs 4 and 5 above and which are already subject to the full range of applicable obligations under the FATF Forty Recommendations (2003) (in particular, Recommendations 4–16 and 21–25) and the Eight Special Recommendations (in particular SR VII).

LICENSING OR REGISTRATION AND COMPLIANCE

11. Jurisdictions should designate an authority to grant licences and/or carry out registration and ensure that the requirement is observed. There

should be an authority responsible for ensuring compliance by money/value transfer services with the FATF Recommendations (including the Eight Special Recommendations). There should also be effective systems in place for monitoring and ensuring such compliance. This interpretation of Special Recommendation VI (i.e., the need for designation of competent authorities) is consistent with FATF Recommendation 23.

SANCTIONS

12. Persons providing money/value transfer services without a license or registration should be subject to appropriate administrative, civil or criminal sanctions.[11] Licensed or registered money/value transfer services which fail to comply fully with the relevant measures called for in the FATF Forty Recommendations (2003) or the Eight Special Recommendations should also be subject to appropriate sanctions.

Interpretative Note to Special Recommendation VII: Wire Transfers[12]

OBJECTIVE

1. Special Recommendation VII (SR VII) was developed with the objective of preventing terrorists and other criminals from having unfettered access to wire transfers for moving their funds and for detecting such misuse when it occurs. Specifically, it aims to ensure that basic information on the originator of wire transfers is immediately available (1) to appropriate law enforcement and/or prosecutorial authorities to assist them in detecting, investigating, prosecuting terrorists or other criminals and tracing the assets of terrorists or other criminals, (2) to financial intelligence units for analysing suspicious or unusual activity and disseminating it as necessary, and (3) to beneficiary financial institutions to facilitate the identification and reporting of suspicious

---

11. The inclusion of these examples does not suggest that such systems are legal in any particular jurisdiction.
12. It is recognised that jurisdictions will need time to make relevant legislative or regulatory changes and to allow financial institutions to make necessary adaptations to their systems and procedures. This period should not be longer than two years after the adoption of this Interpretative Note.

transactions. It is not the intention of the FATF to impose rigid standards or to mandate a single operating process that would negatively affect the payment system.

DEFINITIONS

2. For the purposes of this interpretative note, the following definitions apply.

   a) The terms *wire transfer* and *funds transfer* refer to any transaction carried out on behalf of an originator person (both natural and legal) through a financial institution by electronic means with a view to making an amount of money available to a beneficiary person at another financial institution. The originator and the beneficiary may be the same person.

   b) *Cross-border transfer* means any wire transfer where the originator and beneficiary institutions are located in different jurisdictions. This term also refers to any chain of wire transfers that has at least one cross-border element.

   c) *Domestic transfer* means any wire transfer where the originator and beneficiary institutions are located in the same jurisdiction. This term therefore refers to any chain of wire transfers that takes place entirely within the borders of a single jurisdiction, even though the system used to effect the wire transfer may be located in another jurisdiction.

   d) The term *financial institution* is as defined by the FATF Forty Recommendations (2003).[13] The term does not apply to any persons or entities that provide financial institutions solely with message or other support systems for transmitting funds.[14]

---

13. When this Interpretative Note was originally issued, these references were to the 1996 FATF Forty Recommendations. Subsequent to the publication of the revised FATF Forty Recommendations in June 2003, this text was updated accordingly. All references are now to the 2003 FATF Forty Recommendations.
14. However, these systems do have a role in providing the necessary means for the financial institutions to fulfil their obligations under SR VII and, in particular, in preserving the integrity of the information transmitted with a wire transfer.

e) The *originator* is the account holder, or where there is no account, the person (natural or legal) that places the order with the financial institution to perform the wire transfer.

SCOPE

3. SR VII applies, under the conditions set out below, to cross-border and domestic transfers between financial institutions.

CROSS-BORDER WIRE TRANSFERS

4. Cross-border wire transfers should be accompanied by accurate and meaningful originator information.[15]

5. Information accompanying cross-border wire transfers must always contain the name of the originator and where an account exists, the number of that account. In the absence of an account, a unique reference number must be included.

6. Information accompanying the wire transfer should also contain the address of the originator. However, jurisdictions may permit financial institutions to substitute the address with a national identity number, customer identification number, or date and place of birth.

7. Cross-border wire transfers that are contained within batch transfers, except for those sent by money remitters, will be treated as domestic wire transfers. In such cases, the ordering institutions must retain the information necessary to identify all originators and make it available on request to the authorities and to the beneficiary financial institution. Financial institutions

---

15. Jurisdictions may have a de minimis threshold (no higher than USD 3,000) for a one-year period from publication of this Interpretative Note. At the end of this period, the FATF will undertake a review of this issue to determine whether the use of a de minimis threshold is acceptable. Notwithstanding any thresholds, accurate and meaningful originator information must be retained and made available by the ordering financing institution as set forth in paragraph 9.

should ensure that non-routine transactions are not batched where this would increase the risk of money laundering or terrorist financing.

DOMESTIC WIRE TRANSFERS

8. Information accompanying domestic wire transfers must also include originator information as indicated for cross-border wire transfers, unless full originator information can be made available to the beneficiary financial institution and appropriate authorities by other means. In this latter case, financial institutions need only include the account number or a unique identifier provided that this number or identifier will permit the transaction to be traced back to the originator.

9. The information must be made available by the ordering financial institution within three business days of receiving the request either from the beneficiary financial institution or from appropriate authorities. Law enforcement authorities should be able to compel immediate production of such information.

EXEMPTIONS FROM SR VII

10. SR VII is not intended to cover the following types of payments:

a) Any transfer that flows from a transaction carried out using a credit or debit card so long as the credit or debit card number accompanies all transfers flowing from the transaction. However, when credit or debit cards are used as a payment system to effect a money transfer, they are covered by SR VII, and the necessary information should be included in the message.

b) Financial institution-to-financial institution transfers and settlements where both the originator person and the beneficiary person are financial institutions acting on their own behalf.

ROLE OF ORDERING, INTERMEDIARY AND BENEFICIARY FINANCIAL INSTITUTIONS

ORDERING FINANCIAL INSTITUTION

11. The ordering financial institution must ensure that qualifying wire transfers contain complete originator information. The ordering financial institution must also verify this information for accuracy and maintain this information in accordance with the standards set out in the FATF Forty Recommendations (2003).[16]

INTERMEDIARY FINANCIAL INSTITUTION

12. For both cross-border and domestic wire transfers, financial institutions processing an intermediary element of such chains of wire transfers must ensure that all originator information that accompanies a wire transfer is retained with the transfer.

13. Where technical limitations prevent the full originator information accompanying a crossborder wire transfer from remaining with a related domestic wire transfer (during the necessary time to adapt payment systems), a record must be kept for five years by the receiving intermediary financial institution of all the information received from the ordering financial institution.

BENEFICIARY FINANCIAL INSTITUTION

14. Beneficiary financial institutions should have effective risk-based procedures in place to identify wire transfers lacking complete originator information. The lack of complete originator information may be considered as a factor in assessing whether a wire transfer or related transactions are suspicious and, as appropriate, whether they are thus required to be reported to the financial intelligence unit or other competent authorities. In some cases, the beneficiary financial institution should consider restricting or even terminat-

---

16. See footnote 2.

ing its business relationship with financial institutions that fail to meet SRVII standards.

ENFORCEMENT MECHANISMS FOR FINANCIAL INSTITUTIONS THAT DO NOT COMPLY WITH WIRE TRANSFER RULES AND REGULATIONS

15. Jurisdictions should adopt appropriate measures to monitor effectively the compliance of financial institutions with rules and regulations governing wire transfers. Financial institutions that fail to comply with such rules and regulations should be subject to civil, administrative or criminal sanctions.

Guidance Notes

1.The Eight Special Recommendations on terrorist financing were adopted by the FATF in October 2001. Immediately following their adoption, the FATF undertook to assess the level of implementation of the Special Recommendations through a self-assessment exercise. A self-assessment questionnaire on terrorist financing (SAQTF) was developed with a series of questions for each Special Recommendation. The questions were designed to elicit details that would help determine whether a particular jurisdiction has in fact implemented a particular Special Recommendation.

2. Since the adoption of the Special Recommendations, the FATF has had little time to develop interpretations based on the experience of implementing these measures. Upon completion of the initial phase of this exercise by FATF members, it was therefore decided that additional guidance would be drafted and published to assist non-FATF members in understanding some of the concepts contained in the Special Recommendations on terrorist financing and to clarify certain parts of the SAQTF. This document therefore contains additional clarification of the Eight Special Recommendations and the SAQTF.

3. It should be emphasised at the start that the information presented here is meant primarily to serve as a guide to jurisdictions attempting to fill in and

submit the SAQTF. For this reason, they should not be considered exhaustive or definitive. Any questions on particular interpretations or implications of the Special Recommendations should be directed to the FATF Secretariat at contact@fatf-gafi.org.

SR I: Ratification and implementation of UN instruments

4. This Recommendation contains six elements:

- Jurisdictions should ratify and fully implement the 1999 United Nations International Convention for the Suppression of the Financing of Terrorism, and
- Jurisdictions should implement five UN Security Council Resolutions: S/RES/1267(1999), S/RES/1269(1999), S/RES/1333(2000), S/RES/1373(2001) and S/RES/1390(2001).

5. For the purposes of this Special Recommendation, *ratification* means having carried out any necessary national legislative or executive procedures to approve the UN Convention and having delivered appropriate ratification instruments to the United Nations. *Implementation* as used here means having put measures in place to bring the requirements indicated in the UN Convention and UNSC Resolutions into effect. *The measures may be established by law, regulation, directive, decree, or any other appropriate legislative or executive act according to national law.*

6. The UN Convention was open for signature from 10 January 2000 to 31 December 2001, and upon signature is subject to ratification, acceptance or approval. Ratification, acceptance or approval instruments must be deposited with the Secretary-General of the United Nations in New York. Those countries that have not signed the Convention may accede to it (see Article 25 of the Convention). The full text of the UN Convention may be consulted at http://untreaty.un.org/English/Terrorism/conv12.pdf. As of 19 March 2002, 132 countries have signed, and 24 have deposited ratification instruments. On 10 March 2002, the UN Convention reached the minimum number of ratifications (22) stipulated as necessary for it to come into effect. The effec-

tive date of the Convention is 10 April 2002. The web page containing information on the status of the Convention is located on the UN website at http://untreaty.un.org/ENGLISH/status/Chapter_xviii/ treaty11.asp. For general information about UN treaties, see http://untreaty. un.org/english/guide. asp and the *Treaty Handbook* of the UN Office of Legal Affairs at http:// untreaty.un.org/English/TreatyHandbook/hbframeset.htm. The texts of the relevant UN Security Council Resolutions may be consulted on the UN website at http://www.un.org/documents/scres.htm.

SR II: Criminalising the financing of terrorism and associated money laundering

7. This Recommendation contains two elements:

- Jurisdictions should criminalise "the financing of terrorism, of terrorist acts and of terrorist organisations"; and
- Jurisdictions should establish terrorist financing offences as predicate offences for money laundering.

8. In implementing SR II, jurisdictions must either establish specific criminal offences for terrorist financing activities, or they must be able to cite existing criminal offences that may be directly applied to such cases. The terms financing of terrorism or financing of terrorist acts refer to the activities described in the UN Convention (Article 2) and S/RES/1373(2001), paragraph 1b (see the UN website at http://www.un.org/documents/scres.htm for text of this Resolution). It should be noted that each jurisdiction should also ensure that terrorist financing offences apply as predicate offences even when carried out in another State. This corollary interpretation of SR II is then consistent with FATF Recommendation 4.

9. FATF Recommendation 4 already calls for jurisdictions to designate "serious offences" as predicates for the offence of money laundering. SR II builds on Recommendation 4 by requiring that,given the gravity of terrorist financing offences, terrorism financing offences should be specifically included among the predicates for money laundering. For the full text of the FATF

Forty Recommendations, along with their Interpretative Notes, see the FATF website at http://www.fatfgafi.org/40Recs_en.htm.

10. Finally, as in general with other predicates for money laundering, jurisdictions should ensure that terrorist financing offences are predicate offences even if they are committed in a jurisdiction different from the one in which the money laundering offence is being applied.

SR III: Freezing and confiscating terrorist assets

11. This Recommendation contains three major elements:

- Jurisdictions should have the authority to *freeze* funds or assets of (a) terrorists and terrorist organisations and (b) those who finance terrorist acts or terrorist organisations;
- They should have the authority to *seize* (a) the proceeds of terrorism or of terrorist acts, (b) the property used in terrorism, in terrorist acts or by terrorist organisations and (c) property intended or allocated for use in terrorism, in terrorist acts or by terrorist organisations; and
- They should have the authority to *confiscate* (a) the proceeds of terrorism or of terrorist acts, (b) the property used in terrorism, in terrorist acts or by terrorist organisations and (c) property intended or allocated for use in terrorism, in terrorist acts or by terrorist organisations.

12. The term *measures*, as used in SR III, refers to explicit (legislative or regulatory) provisions or "executive powers" that permit the three types of action. As with the preceding Recommendation, it is not necessary that the texts authorising these powers mention terrorist financing in particular. However, jurisdictions with already existing laws must be able to cite specific provisions that permit them to freeze, to seize or to confiscate terrorist related funds and assets within the national legal/judicial context.

13. The definitions of the concepts of freezing, seizure and confiscation vary from one jurisdiction to another. For the purposes of general guidance, the following descriptions of these terms are provided:

14. *Freezing*: In the context of this Recommendation, a competent government or judicial authority must be able to freeze, to block or to restrain specific funds or assets and thus prevent them from being moved or disposed of. The assets/funds remain the property of the original owner and may continue to be administered by the financial institution or other management arrangement designated by the owner.

15. *Seizure*: As with freezing, competent government or judicial authorities must be able to take action or to issue an order that allows them to take control of specified funds or assets. The assets/funds remain the property of the original owner, although the competent authority will often take over possession, administration or management of the assets/funds.

16. *Confiscation* (or *forfeiture*): Confiscation or forfeiture takes place when competent government or judicial authorities order that the ownership of specified funds or assets be transferred to the State. In this case, the original owner loses all rights to the property. Confiscation or forfeiture orders are usually linked to a criminal conviction and a court decision whereby the property is determined to have been derived from or intended for use in a violation of the law.

17. With regard to freezing in the context of SR III, the terms *terrorists*, *those who finance terrorism* and *terrorist organisations* refer to individuals and entities identified pursuant to S/RES/1267 (1999) and S/RES/1390 (2002), as well as to any other individuals and entities designated as such by individual national governments.

SR IV: Reporting suspicious transactions related to terrorism

18. This Recommendation contains two major elements:

- Jurisdictions should establish a requirement for making a report to competent authorities when there is a *suspicion* that funds are linked to terrorist financing; or

- Jurisdictions should establish a requirement for making a report to competent authorities when there are *reasonable grounds* to suspect that funds are linked to terrorist financing.

19. For SR IV, the term *financial institutions* refers to both banks and non-bank financial institutions (NBFIs). In the context of assessing implementation of FATF Recommendations, NBFIs include, as a minimum, the following types of financial services: bureaux de change, stockbrokers, insurance companies and money remittance/transfer services. This definition of *financial institutions* is also understood to apply to SR IV in order to be consistent with the interpretation of the FATF Forty Recommendations. With regard specifically to SR IV, if other types of professions, businesses or business activities currently fall under anti-money laundering reporting obligations, jurisdictions should also extend terrorist financing reporting requirements to those entities or activities.

20. The term *competent authority*, for the purposes of SR IV, is understood to be either the jurisdiction's financial intelligence unit (FIU) or another central authority that has been designated by the jurisdiction for receiving disclosures related to money laundering.

21. With regard to the terms *suspect* and *have reasonable grounds to suspect*, the distinction is being made between levels of mental certainty that could form the basis for reporting a transaction. The first term—that is, a requirement to report to competent authorities when a financial institution suspects that funds are derived from or intended for use in terrorist activity—is a subjective standard and transposes the reporting obligation called for in FATF Recommendation 15 to SR IV. The requirement to report transactions when there are reasonable grounds to suspect that the funds are derived from or intended for use in terrorist activity is an objective standard, which is consistent with the intent of Recommendation 15 although somewhat broader. In the context of SR IV, jurisdictions should establish a reporting obligation that may be based either on suspicion or on having reasonable grounds to suspect.

SR V: International Co-operation

22. This Recommendation contains five elements:

- Jurisdictions should permit the exchange of information regarding terrorist financing with other jurisdictions through *mutual legal assistance mechanisms*;
- Jurisdictions should permit the exchange of information regarding terrorist financing with other jurisdictions by means *other than through mutual legal assistance mechanisms*;
- Jurisdictions should have specific measures to permit the denial of "safe haven" to individuals involved in terrorist financing;
- Jurisdictions should have procedures that permit the extradition of individuals involved in terrorist financing; and
- Jurisdictions should have provisions or procedures to ensure that "claims of political motivation are not recognised as a ground for refusing requests to extradite persons alleged to be involved in terrorist financing."

23. To obtain a clear picture of the situation in each jurisdiction through the self-assessment process, an artificial distinction has been made for some questions in the SAQTF between international co-operation through *mutual legal assistance mechanisms* on the one hand and information exchange through means *other than through mutual legal assistance.*

24. For the purposes of SR V, the term *mutual legal assistance* means the power to provide a full range of both non-coercive legal assistance, including the taking of evidence, the production of documents for investigation or as evidence, the search and seizure of documents or things relevant to criminal proceedings or to a criminal investigation, the ability to enforce a foreign restraint, seizure, forfeiture or confiscation order in a criminal matter. In this instance, *mutual legal assistance* would also include information exchange through rogatory commissions (that is, from the judicial authorities in one jurisdiction to those in another).

25. Exchange of information by means *other than through mutual legal assistance* includes any arrangement other than those described in the preceding paragraph. Under this category should be included exchanges that take place between FIUs or other agencies that communicate bilaterally on the basis of memoranda of understanding (MOUs), exchanges of letters, etc.

26. With regard to the last three elements of SR V, these concepts should be understood as referred to in the relevant UN documents. These are S/RES/1373 (2001), paragraph 2c (for denial of safe haven); the UN Convention, Article 11 (for extradition); and the UN Convention, Article 14 (for rejection of claims of political motivation as related to extradition). The text of the UN Convention may be consulted at http://untreaty.un.org/English/Terrorism.asp; the text of S/RES/1373 (2001) may be accessed at http://www.un.org/documents.scres.htm.

27. The term *civil enforcement* as used in SR V is intended to refer only to the type of investigations, inquiries or procedures conducted by regulatory or administrative authorities that have been empowered in certain jurisdictions to carry out such activities in relation to terrorist financing. *Civil enforcement is not meant to include civil procedures and related actions as understood in civil law jurisdictions.*

SR VI: Alternative Remittance

28. This Recommendation consists of three major elements:

- Jurisdictions should require licensing or registration of persons or legal entities providing money/value transmission services, including through informal systems or networks;
- Jurisdictions should ensure that money/value transmission services, including informal systems or networks, are subject to FATF Recommendations 10–12 and 15; and
- Jurisdictions should be able to impose sanctions on money/value transmission services, including informal systems or networks, that fail to

obtain a license/register and that fail to comply with relevant FATF Recommendations.

29. Money or value transfer systems have shown themselves vulnerable to misuse for money laundering or terrorist financing purposes. The intention of SR VI is to ensure that jurisdictions impose anti-money laundering and counter-terrorist financing measures on all forms of money/value transfer systems. To obtain a clear picture of the situation in each jurisdiction through the selfassessment process, an artificial distinction has been made between formal and informal transfer systems in some questions.

30. The term *money remittance* or *transfer service* refers to a financial service—often provided by a distinct category of non-bank financial institutions—whereby funds are moved for individuals or entities through a dedicated network or through the regulated banking system. For the purposes of assessing compliance with the FATF Recommendations, money remitter/transfer services are included as a distinct category of NBFI and are thus considered part of the regulated financial sector. Nevertheless, such services are used in some laundering or terrorist financing operations, often as part of a larger alternate remittance or underground banking scheme.

31. The term *informal money* or *value transfer system* also refers to a financial service whereby funds or value are moved from one geographic location to another. However, in some jurisdictions, these informal systems have traditionally operated outside the regulated financial sector in contrast to the "formal" money remittance/transfer services described in the preceding paragraph. Some examples of informal systems include the parallel banking system found in the Americas (often referred to as the "Black Market Peso Exchange"), the *hawala* or *hundi* system of South Asia, and the Chinese or East Asian systems. For more information on this topic, see the FATF-XI Typologies Report (3 February 2000), available through the FATF website at http://www.fatfgafi.org/FATDocs_en.htm#Trends, or the Asia Pacific Group Report on Underground Banking and Alternate Remittance Systems (18 October 2001), available through the APG website at http://www.apgml.org/.

32. Where *licensing* or *registration* are indicated in the questionnaire, either licensing or registration is considered sufficient to meet the requirements of the Recommendation. *Licensing* in this Recommendation means a requirement to obtain permission from a designated government authority in order to operate a money/value transmission service. *Registration* in this Recommendation means a requirement to register or declare the existence of a money/value transmission service in order for the business to operate. It should be noted that the logical consequence of the requirements of SR VI is that jurisdictions should designate a licensing or registration authority and an authority to ensure compliance with FATF Recommendations for money/value transmission services, including informal systems or networks. This corollary interpretation of SR VI (i.e., the need for designation of competent authorities) is consistent with FATF Recommendation 26. 33. The reference to "all FATF Recommendations that apply to banks and non-bank financial institutions" includes as a minimum Recommendations 10, 11, 12, and 15. Other applicable Recommendations include Recommendations 13, 14, 16–21 and 26–29. The full text of these and all other FATF Recommendations may be consulted on the FATF website http://www.fatfgafi.org/40Recs_en.htm.

SR VII: Wire transfers

34. This Recommendation consists of three elements:

- Jurisdictions should require financial institutions to include originator information on funds transfers sent within or from the jurisdiction;
- Jurisdictions should require financial institutions to retain information on the originator of funds transfers, including at each stage of the transfer process; and
- Jurisdictions should require financial institutions to examine more closely or to monitor funds transfers when complete originator information is not available.

35. For the purpose of SR VII, three categories of financial institution are specifically concerned (banks, bureaux de change, and money remittance/transfer

services), although other financial services (for example, stockbrokers, insurance companies, etc.) may be subject to such requirements in certain jurisdictions.

36. The list of types of *accurate and meaningful* originator information indicated in the Special Recommendation (that is, name, address and account number) is not intended to be exhaustive. In some instances—in the case of an occasional customer, for example—there may not be an account number. In certain jurisdictions, a national identity number or a date and place of birth could also be designated as required originator information.

37. The term *enhanced scrutiny* for the purposes of SR VII means examining the transaction in more detail in order to determine whether certain aspects related to the transaction could make it suspicious (origin in a country known to provide safe haven to terrorists or terrorist organisations, for example) and thus warrant eventual reporting to the competent authority.

SR VIII: Non-profit organisations

38. The intent of SR VIII is to ensure that legal entities (juridical persons), other relevant legal arrangements, and in particular *non-profit organisations* may not be used by terrorists as a cover for or a means of facilitating the financing of their activities. This Recommendation consists of two elements:

- Jurisdictions should review the legal regime of entities, in particular non-profit organisations, to prevent their misuse for terrorist financing purposes; and
- With respect specifically to non-profit organisations, jurisdictions should ensure that such entities may not be used to disguise or facilitate terrorist financing activities, to escape asset freezing measures or to conceal diversions of legitimate funds to terrorist organisations.

39. As stated above, the intent of SR VIII is to ensure that legal entities, other relevant legal arrangements, and *non-profit organisations* may not be misused by terrorists. Legal entities have a variety of forms that differ from one jurisdiction to another. The degree to which a particular type of entity may be vulnerable to misuse in terrorist financing may also vary from one

jurisdiction to another. For this reason, a selection of types of legal entities and other legal arrangements has been presented in the SAQTF in an attempt to obtain a clear picture of the situation in individual jurisdictions. The selection is based on types of entities that have been observed as being involved in money laundering and/or terrorist financing activities in the past. Individual categories may overlap, and in some instances, a jurisdiction may not have all the categories indicated in the SAQTF.

40. Similarly it should be pointed out that non-profit organisations, a particular focus of SR VIII, may exist in legal forms that vary from one jurisdiction to another. Again, the selection of entity types in the SAQTF has been made with the intention of permitting jurisdictions to find entities or arrangements that correspond to their individual situation. The term non-profit organisation can be generally understood to include those types of entities that are organised for charitable, religious, educational, social or fraternal purposes, or for the carrying out of other types of "good works". In addition, the earnings of such entities or activities should normally not benefit any private shareholder or individual, and they may be restricted from direct or substantial involvement in political activities. In many jurisdictions, non-profit organizations are exempt from fiscal obligations.

41. In the SAQTF, the term offshore companies refers to what are usually established as limited liability juridical persons in certain jurisdictions and which often fall under a separate or privileged regulatory regime. Such entities may be used to own and operate businesses (a shell or holding company), issue shares or bonds, or raise capital in other manners. They are generally exempt from local taxes or subject to a preferential rate and may be prohibited from doing business in the jurisdiction in which they are incorporated. The International Business Corporation (IBC) is an example of such an entity. In the SAQTF, jurisdictions should only respond to relevant offshore questions if they have an offshore sector within their jurisdiction.

42. The SAQTF also includes a category "Trusts and/or foundations" under SR VIII. Trusts are legal arrangements available in certain jurisdictions. Although they are not strictly speaking legal entities, they are used as a means for holding or transmitting assets and may, as with certain legal entities, be

misused as a means for hiding or disguising true ownership of an asset. The term foundations refers primarily to "private foundations or establishments" that exist in some civil law jurisdictions and which may engage in commercial and/or non-profit activities. Some examples of these include *Stiftung*, *stichting*, *Anstalt*, etc.

Interpretative Note to Special Recommendation IX: Cash Couriers

Objectives

1. FATF Special Recommendation IX was developed with the objective of ensuring that terrorists and other criminals cannot finance their activities or launder the proceeds of their crimes through the physical cross-border transportation of currency and bearer negotiable instruments. Specifically, it aims to ensure that countries have measures 1) to detect the physical cross-border transportation of currency and bearer negotiable instruments, 2) to stop or restrain currency and bearer negotiable instruments that are suspected to be related to terrorist financing or money laundering, 3) to stop or restrain currency or bearer negotiable instruments that are falsely declared or disclosed, 4) to apply appropriate sanctions for making a false declaration or disclosure, and 5) to enable confiscation of currency or bearer negotiable instruments that are related to terrorist financing or money laundering. Countries should implement Special Recommendation IX subject to strict safeguards to ensure proper use of information and without restricting either: (i) trade payments between countries for goods and services; or (ii) the freedom of capital movements in any way.

Definitions

2. For the purposes of Special Recommendation IX and this Interpretative Note, the following definitions apply.

3. The term *bearer negotiable instrument* includes monetary instruments in bearer form such as: travellers cheques; negotiable instruments (including

cheques, promissory notes and money orders)that are either in bearer form, endorsed without restriction, made out to a fictitious payee, or other wise in such form that title thereto passes upon delivery; incomplete instruments (including cheques, promissory notes and money orders) signed, but with the payee's name omitted.[17]

4. The term *currency* refers to banknotes and coins that are in circulation as a medium of exchange.

5. The term *physical cross-border transportation* refers to any in-bound or out-bound physical transportation of currency or bearer negotiable instruments from one country to another country. The term includes the following modes of transportation: (1) physical transportation by a natural person, or in that person's accompanying luggage or vehicle; (2) shipment of currency through containerized cargo or (3) the mailing of currency or bearer negotiable instruments by a natural or legal person.

6. The term *false declaration* refers to a misrepresentation of the value of currency or bearer negotiable instruments being transported, or a misrepresentation of other relevant data which is asked for in the declaration or otherwise requested by the authorities. This includes failing to make a declaration as required.

7. The term *false disclosure* refers to a misrepresentation of the value of currency or bearer negotiable instruments being transported, or a misrepresentation of other relevant data which is asked

8. When the term *related to terrorist financing or money laundering* is used to describe currency or bearer negotiable instruments, it refers to currency or bearer negotiable instruments that are: (i) the proceeds of, or used in, or

---

17. For the purposes of this Interpretative Note, gold, precious metals and precious stones are not included despite their high liquidity and use in certain situations as a means of exchange or transmitting value. These items may be otherwise covered under customs laws and regulations. If a country discovers an unusual cross-border movement of gold, precious metals or precious stones, it should consider notifying, as appropriate, the Customs Service or other competent authorities of the countries from which these items originated and/or to which they are destined, and should co-operate with a view toward establishing the source, destination, and purpose of the movement of such items and toward the taking of appropriate action.

intended or allocated for use in, the financing of terrorism, terrorist acts or terrorist organisations; or (ii) laundered, proceeds from money laundering or predicate offences, or instrumentalities used in or intended for use in the commission of these offences.

The types of systems that may be implemented to address the issue of cash couriers

9. Countries may meet their obligations under Special Recommendation IX and this Interpretative Note by implementing one of the following types of systems; however, countries do not have to use the same type of system for incoming and outgoing cross-border transportation of currency or bearer negotiable instruments:

    a. **Declaration system:** The key characteristics of a declaration system are as follows. All persons making a physical cross-border transportation of currency or bearer negotiable instruments, which are of a value exceeding a pre-set, maximum threshold of EUR/USD 15,000, are required to submit a truthful declaration to the designated competent authorities. Countries that implement a declaration system should ensure that the pre-set threshold is sufficiently low to meet the objectives of Special Recommendation IX.

    b. **Disclosure system:** The key characteristics of a disclosure system are as follows. All persons making a physical cross-border transportation of currency or bearer negotiable instruments are required to make a truthful disclosure to the designated competent authorities upon request. Countries that implement a disclosure system should ensure that the designated competent authorities can make their inquiries on a targeted basis, based on intelligence or suspicion, or on a random basis.

Additional elements applicable to both systems

10.   Whichever system is implemented, countries should ensure that their system incorporates the following elements:

a. The declaration/disclosure system should apply to both incoming and outgoing transportation of currency and bearer negotiable instruments.

b. Upon discovery of a false declaration/disclosure of currency or bearer negotiable instruments or a failure to declare/disclose them, designated competent authorities should have the authority to request and obtain further information from the carrier with regard to the origin of the currency or bearer negotiable instruments and their intended use.

c. Information obtained through the declaration/disclosure process should be available to the financial intelligence unit (FIU) either through a system whereby the FIU is notified about suspicious cross-border transportation incidents or by making the declaration/disclosure information directly available to the FIU in some other way.

d. At the domestic level, countries should ensure that there is adequate co-ordination among customs, immigration and other related authorities on issues related to the implementation of Special Recommendation IX.

e. In the following two cases, competent authorities should be able to stop or restrain cash or bearer negotiable instruments for a reasonable time in order to ascertain whether evidence of money laundering or terrorist financing may be found: (i) where there is a suspicion of money laundering or terrorist financing; or (ii) where there is a false declaration or false disclosure.

f. The declaration/disclosure system should allow for the greatest possible measure of international co-operation and assistance in accordance with Special Recommendation V and Recommendations 35 to 40. To facilitate such co-operation, in instances when: (i) a declaration or disclosure which exceeds the maximum threshold of EUR/USD 15,000 is made, or (ii) where there is a false declaration or false disclosure, or (iii) where there is a suspicion of money laundering or terrorist financing, this information shall be retained for use by the appropriate authorities. At a minimum, this information will cover: (i) the amount of currency or bearer negotiable instruments declared / disclosed or otherwise detected; and (ii) the identification data of the bearer(s).

Sanctions

11. Persons who make a false declaration or disclosure should be subject to effective, proportionate and dissuasive sanctions, whether criminal civil or administrative. Persons who are carrying out a physical cross-border transportation of currency or bearer negotiable instruments that are related to terrorist financing or money laundering should also be subject to effective, proportionate and dissuasive sanctions, whether criminal, civil or administrative, and should be subject to measures, including legislative ones consistent with Recommendation 3 and Special Recommendation III, which would enable the confiscation of such currency or bearer negotiable instruments.

Annex VII

Cross-Reference of The Forty Recommendations to Reference Guide

Recommendation	Reference Guide
1	Chapter I, footnote 8 Chapter V, footnotes 4, 20–22, 25–27 Chapter VIII, footnote 7
2	Chapter V, footnotes 38, 39
3	Chapter V, footnotes 51, 53, 55, 58–60
4	Chapter V, footnotes 57, 80 Chapter VI, footnotes 75 Chapter VII, footnotes 14–20, 33 Chapter IX, footnote 58

5   Chapter V, footnotes 67–68
          Chapter VI, footnotes 5, 17–19, 21–22, 41
          Chapter IX, footnote 58

6   Chapter V, footnote 67–68
          Chapter VI, footnote 41
          Chapter IX, footnote 58

7   Chapter V, footnotes 67–68
          Chapter VI, footnote 32
          Chapter IX, footnote 58

8   Chapter V, footnotes 67–68
          Chapter VI, footnotes 35, 41
          Chapter IX, footnote 58

9   Chapter V, footnotes 67–68
          Chapter VI, footnotes 36, 41
          Chapter IX, footnote 58

10   Chapter V, footnote 67–68
          Chapter VI, footnotes 41, 46–48, 59
          Chapter VII, footnote 5
          Chapter IX, footnote 58

11   Chapter V, footnotes 67–68
          Chapter VI, footnotes 37, 41, 60
          Chapter VII, footnote 4
          Chapter IX, footnote 58

12   Chapter V, footnotes 67–68
          Chapter VI, footnotes 42–45, 55
          Chapter VII, footnote 4
          Chapter IX, footnote 58

13	Chapter V, footnotes 67–68, 79
	Chapter VI, footnote 56
	Chapter VII, footnotes 4, 12
	Chapter IX, footnotes 39, 58

14	Chapter V, footnotes 67–68
	Chapter VI, footnotes 58, 62
	Chapter VII, footnote 4
	Chapter IX, footnote 58

15	Chapter V, footnotes 67–68
	Chapter VI, footnotes 76, 77, 79
	Chapter VII, footnote 4
	Chapter IX, footnote 58

16	Chapter V, footnotes 67–68
	Chapter VI, footnotes 65, 66, 68, 69
	Chapter VII, footnote 4
	Chapter IX, footnote 58

17	Chapter V, footnotes 67–68
	Chapter VII, footnote 4
	Chapter IX, footnote 58

18	Chapter V, footnotes 67–68
	Chapter VI, footnote 34
	Chapter VII, footnotes 4, 12
	Chapter IX, footnote 58

19	Chapter V, footnotes 67–68
	Chapter VI, footnotes 70, 73
	Chapter VII, footnotes 4, 12
	Chapter IX, footnote 58

20	Chapter V, footnotes 67–68, 74
	Chapter VI, footnote 74
	Chapter VII, footnote 4
	Chapter IX, footnote 58
21	Chapter V, footnotes 67–68
	Chapter VI, footnote 38
	Chapter VII, footnote 4
	Chapter IX, footnote 58
22	Chapter V, footnotes 67–68
	Chapter VI, footnotes 9, 10
	Chapter VII, footnote 4
	Chapter IX, footnote 58
23	Chapter V, footnotes 67–68, 76–78
	Chapter IX, footnotes 58, 59, 60
24	Chapter V, footnotes 67–68
	Chapter IX, footnote 58
25	Chapter V, footnotes 67–68
	Chapter VI, footnote 61
	Chapter VII, footnote 38
	Chapter IX, footnote 58
26	Chapter VII, footnotes 3, 9
27	Chapter V, footnote 82
	Chapter VIII, footnotes 27, 29
28	Chapter VI, footnotes 59, 74, 75
29	Chapter V, footnotes 76, 77
30	Chapter V, footnote 84

Annex VIII

Cross-Reference of the Special Recommendations to Reference Guide

Recommendation	Reference Guide
I	Chapter I, footnote 12
	Chapter VIII, footnote 7
	Chapter IX, footnotes 8, 10, 21
II	Chapter I, footnotes 13, 14, 15
	Chapter V, footnotes 24, 48, 49
	Chapter IX, footnotes 23–26, 35
III	Chapter IX, footnotes 6, 27, 28, 29, 30, 31, 32, 33
IV	Chapter IX, footnote 36
V	Chapter IX, footnotes 41, 42